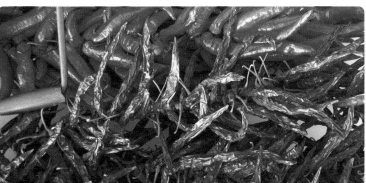

Lidia's Italy

Lidia's Italy

Lidia Matticchio Bastianich

and Tanya Bastianich Manuali

with David Nussbaum

Full-page photographs by Christopher Hirsheimer
Other photographs by Lidia Matticchio Bastianich and Wanda Radetti

Alfred A. Knopf   New York   2007

This Is a Borzoi Book
Published by Alfred A. Knopf

Copyright © 2007 by Tutti a Tavola, LLC

www.aaknopf.com

The photographs on the following pages are by
Christopher Hirsheimer: 15, 23, 26, 44, 53, 74, 89, 104,
112, 123, 136, 147, 168, 177, 189, 196, 227, 251, 258, 271,
283, 295, 299, 303, 309, 316, 317 (bottom), 322, 330.

All other photographs are courtesy of Lidia
Matticchio Bastianich and Wanda Radetti.

Library of Congress Cataloging-in-Publication Data
Bastianich, Lidia.
  Lidia's Italy / by Lidia Matticchio Bastianich
and Tanya Bastianich Manuali ; photographs by
Christopher Hirsheimer.
    p. cm.
  ISBN 978-1-4000-4036-0
  1. Cookery, Italian. 2. Italy—Social life and
customs. I. Manuali, Tanya. II. Title.

TX723.B3224 2007
641.5945—dc22
                                        2006043046

Printed in the United States of America
First Edition

This book is dedicated to Erminia, my mother, the nonna to my children and the bis nonna to my grandchildren. Without your unconditional love, your unwavering guidance and support, all of this could never have happened.

Contents

Acknowledgments

So many individuals in so many far-flung places have generously lent us assistance and support in writing this book. We must turn in many directions to express our appreciation and gratitude.

As Italy is both the subject of our book and its source, we first wish to thank the colleagues, family, and friends all over the country (and in Istria) who guided us to their local culinary and cultural treasures; introduced their favorite restaurants, artisans, and farms; and often opened their kitchens to share their wonderful dishes.

In my native Istria, where we treasure a colony of relatives and friends, special thanks to cousin Sonia Fonio and her husband, Zlatko Perdija; cousins Renato and Mariuccia, who keep a watchful eye on my childhood home; my attorney and dear friend Dobrovko Zic, who keeps me within the law; and his cousin Boris Zic, who takes me scampi fishing. Thank you to Gina Bergiê for the delicious food served at Ristorante Gina in Stoja, Pula. Thank you to the musicians of Istria—the magnificent male chorus Società Artistico Culturale Lino Mariani of Pula and my dear friend Mirko Cetinski, whose melodious voice I have been enjoying for years, and his quartet from Rovingo. Thanks also to Mayor Rino Dunis, who has been keeping the arts alive and well in his picturesque medieval hilltop town of Groznjan. For promoting all these cultural and culinary treasures, our gratitude to Denis Ivosevic, *Assessore* of Tourism in Istria.

In Trieste, where we've forged lasting friendships, we offer many thanks to Bruno Vesnaver and his family for the wonderful food and fun we always have at their Antica Ghiaccetteria and Trattoria da Giovanni. Thanks to the Benvenuti family of the Grand Hotel Duchi D'Aosta, who always have a fresh linen–lined bed for a weary traveler.

In Friuli, where we have a home and winery, we are grateful for the help and friendship of so many: first, of course, our old friend, the winemaker Valter Scarbolo; managing director Dennis Lepore, who makes it all happen; and Emilio del Medico, oenologist with a superb sense of taste. *Grazie* to Gianluigi D'Orlandi, the *commercialista* and mayor of Fagagna, who knows all the artisanal producers of the Consorzio Prosciutto di San Daniele and in particular for bringing me to Prosciuttificio Giobatta Zanin and the Latteria de Fagagna Borgo Pauldo, producers of exceptional Montasio cheese. Thanks to Josko Sirk from La Subdia. Also thanks to Dott. Attilio Vuga, the mayor of Cividale del Friuli, and *Assessore* Enrico Bertossi of the region of Friuli-Venezia Giulia, who both understand the importance of preserving local traditions.

My travels in Friuli have been enriched immeasurably by my dear friend Mario Picozzi of Trieste. Thank you, Mario, for taking me to Le Malghe and the high mountain farm of Maiaso Dienemonzo, where they make extraordinary Montasio by hand; for sharing Sauris di Sopra, your little piece of heaven; for introducing me to the family Wolf-Petris, producers of the renowned speck and prosciutto *di Sauris;* and for the unforgettable visit to the polenta mill, Il Mulino di Godia. (And thank you, Doctor Mario, for fixing my teeth if they chip from all the chewing!)

In the area of Padova and Treviso, thanks to Dott. Walter Brunello and Dott.ssa Sanguin of the Veneto Region, who opened so many doors to memorable experiences, like our tour of the cultivation of *radicchio trevisano* at Azienda Agricola Fratelli. And I am grateful to Celeste Tonon, proprietor of the esteemed Ristorante Celeste in Venegazzu (near Treviso), both for his wonderful company and sharing his privileged knowledge of the original *tiramisù.*

In Piemonte, a cherished region, first and special thanks to my dear friend Gianandrea Noseda, principal conductor of the BBC Philharmonic and principal conductor of Teatro Regio di Torino. Thanks also to Raffaela Bologna of Braida, Luca Vietti of the Vietti winery, and Lidia Alcianti from Guido da Costigliole at Relais San Maurizio, a very special chef and friend. Thanks as well to the Slow Food Movement in Bra, an organization that has awakened us to the need to preserve our culinary traditions.

In Maremma, thanks first to Maurizio Castelli, *grande*-over-all enologist, and his son, winemaker Simone Castelli, who direct La Mozza, our winery. To the attentive and caring staff at the Azienda Alberese, thanks for revealing the wild beauty of Maremma. Thanks to Alma Amaddii, whose wonderful recipe for *acqua cotta* enriches this book, and to Lucia Simoni for those luscious ravioli.

As we journey south, a warm and affectionate hug to old friend Paola di Mauro, the matron of Roman cuisine and a producer of great wines from her Azienda Colle Picchioni in the Lazio region.

And another hug to a great friend, Campanian wine guru, and true *Napoletano,* Bruno de Rosa, for guiding us to the heart of Naples. Thanks to Alfonso Matozzi, the fourth-generation proprietor of L'Europeo restaurant, for memorable dining and talk of food. Thanks to my cousin Clara and her husband, Francesco Pacelli; and to Sig.ra Mirella Capaldo of Feudi di San Gregorio winery and her husband, Dott. Enzo Ercolino.

One more hug—a big one—to Nonna Lisa Porcella (maternal grandmother of Tanya's husband, Corrado) for her great *tiella*, first enjoyed in Gaeta and now shared in these pages.

In Sicily, great thanks to dear friend Manfredi Barbera and family, merchants of wonderful Sicilian olive oil; to Santi Palazzolo, master *pasticciere;* and to Anna Santoro, the mistress of couscous making in Custonaci, and her husband, Giuseppe, and their family.

In Puglia, warm thanks to two restaurateur colleagues in Montegrosso: Pietro Petroni, who runs the wonderful Masseria Lama di Luna, and Pietro Zito, who expertly cooks the bounty of the region at Antichi Sapori. Thanks also to Domenico Asseliti and his family in Andria for making the most spectacular burrata, and to Eliah Pellegrino, producer of great Pugliese olive oil, and his mother, Signora Titina Pellegrino, who showed me how to make orecchiette. In Altamura I had some of the best bread, made by the Carlucci family.

Finally, thanks to New York City pal Francesco Luisi, who returned to his native Basilicata (just over the border of Puglia) and shared the wonderful products of the region as well as the wonderful folk songs and dances from the talented teenagers of Gruppo Musicisti e Ballerini-Folk-Art Stigliano.

To all of the above (and others too numerous to name) we say, *"Siamo riconoscenti del vostro contributo che arrichisce questo libro . . . Mille grazie."*

And how could we have completed *Lidia's Italy*—this book and its companion PBS television series—without the support and encouragement of our sponsors? You have made it possible! So thank you—to Cuisinart for a long-lasting friendship and support; to the premier pasta company, De Cecco; to Palm Bay Imports and their wonderful portfolio of Italian wine producers; and to the Consorzio per la Tutela del Formaggio Grana Padano, whose exceptional product I have been grating over my pasta and using in my recipes for years.

We would also like to thank the businesses who support us through their generous product donations for the filming of the TV show: www.freshdirect.com; Jones New York; Arte Italica; American Pearl; Borghese; Keil Brothers; ceramicadirect.com; Omnipak; www.sambonetusa.com; Le Creuset; Villeroy & Boch Hotel and Restaurant Division; Tutto Mio; the Perrier Group; and Alitalia and Visit Italy Tours, who have facilitated many a research trip to Italy.

As always, the dedication and talents of everyone at my restaurants made it possible for us to devote ourselves to this book. Special thanks to Felidia's chef, Fortunato Nicotra, managers Genji Ridley and Mario Pincic, and the entire

Felidia staff; Shelly Burgess and the Felidia office staff; the staff of Becco; the staff of Lidia's KC; and the staff of Lidia's Pittsburgh.

We are grateful to all in the publishing community who helped us take our idea for a joint exploration of Italy and make it into a beautiful book, beginning with our agent, Jane Dystel, as well as Miriam Goderich and the staff of Dystel and Goderich Literary Management. At Alfred A. Knopf, our publisher, we thank Ken Schneider for always being on the other end of the phone; Carol Carson for a great cover; Carole Goodman for a flowing interior; and Paul Bogaards and Sheila O'Shea, a promotional team with no equals.

A special thanks to Christopher Hirsheimer for zooming in on those dishes and to David Nussbaum for inserting, cutting, and pasting thoughts, ideas, words, and passion and making this book into a whole.

Most of all a big hug and thank-you to Judith Jones, our editor, for her guiding wisdom and contributions—always given with tenderness, patience, and love. Thank you for this book.

Finally, we send our love and appreciation to Giovanni Bencina, a member of our family and a stalwart kitchen helper during the recipe testing of this book, as he was on earlier ones. Gianni passed away before the work was finished—there's never been such a good garlic peeler before or since—and we miss him in many ways. *Grazie*, Giovanni.

Lidia Matticchio Bastianich

Tanya Bastianich Manuali

Recipe Finder by Course

In this special index, I have grouped the recipes according to course to give you ideas when you are planning a meal.

Pastas and Risottos

Desserts

Introduction

You have been inviting me regularly into your homes, getting to know me through my books, my television show, my magazine, and I am grateful. Thank you for having me. Some of you have met me and tasted my food at my restaurants, and with each encounter, I was able to share with you further my passion for Italian food and my love of Italy.

Now I ask you to come with me to some of my favorite places in Italy. I want to introduce you to my friends and to some of the very fine food artisans who are keeping the Italian culinary tradition alive. I want you to meet some of the special people who make up the heartbeat of the cities in Italy, to experience the way they enjoy life, to see how they shop, and how they cook with these traditional products. And I want you to meet my family and friends who live in the places that are so dear to me.

I will take you to cities where you will immediately feel that you belong. We will go to sleepy towns that will mesmerize you with their beauty and tantalize you with their traditions. I will introduce you to whole regions that have nourished my ever-curious palate over the years. And I will send you off with a bundle of recipes to make your own, so that you will be able to capture the flavors of the places we visit. I will send you off with the flavors of Italy.

This journey will take you first to Istria, my place of birth, where my childhood years were spent, which is now part of Croatia. Next we will go to Trieste and visit friends and have some of my favorite soup, *jota* (sauerkraut-and-bean soup). To the north, in the Collio area of Friuli, where some of the best Italian white wines are being produced, our winery is nestled. Padova and Treviso are jewels, two cities that I particularly love for their food treasures—perfectly ripe and full-of-flavor fruits, rice, *radicchio trevisano*—as well as their magnificent art treasures.

When I have the chance to abandon myself to decadence, I treat myself to some fall days in Piemonte. There I can revel in mounds of the local fresh pasta *tajarin* topped with cascades of white-truffle shavings, washed down by a glorious Barbaresco and finished with a *bicerin* (a Torinese chocolate espresso).

When I feel Diana the huntress at my back, then Maremma beckons me with the aroma of musty porcini mushrooms, with wonderfully complex boar and other game sauces, with meaty chestnuts that I wash down with a good fruity and friendly Morellino di Scansano. So much do we love the ruggedness of this part of Tuscany that we bought another winery in La Mozza, and the Morellino now flows liberally at our table.

For me, Rome is like an old lover; there are always good memories, and one always feels comfortable in Rome. I have relatives and in-laws there, and I love the opportunity to cook for them. Shopping for food in Italy is always rewarding, but I particularly love shopping at Campo dei Fiori in Rome, where every stand seems to be set up so artfully that the fruits and vegetables look as though they were posing for a still life.

Speaking of markets, in Palermo's Ballerò and Vuccheria, and Naples's Porta Nolana, these markets make you feel as though you were in the theater, where colorful real-life episodes are being enacted before your eyes. But in the midst of the chaos of this drama, you soon realize that this is life, and that there is a true harmony—the harmony of joyful inter-play and coexistence between Italians.

When my senses beckon me toward fields of golden grain, silvery olive leaves shimmer-ing in the breeze, and a mouthful of scrumptious burrata cheese with a piece of some of the best bread ever, then I head for the heel of Italy. I go to Puglia.

I have visited these places many times, and traveling is always better when you share it with somebody. I especially love traveling through Italy with my daughter Tanya Bastianich Manuali. While I am finding food in the most unexpected and secluded corners of Italy, she finds art, masterpieces that have somehow evaded the guidebooks. As a child, she would visit family in Italy every summer, but her love for Italy and its art became a profession; after her first semester in business management at Georgetown, her interest turned to art history, and she went on to further studies, receiving her Ph.D. in Renaissance art history from Oxford. So I asked her if she would guide us to some of the cultural treasures and out-of-the-way sights she has discovered that are close by the places in this book that I explore for food, and you will find at the end of each chapter the additional reward of Tanya's Tour.

Recipes are as much a part of the cultural heritage of a people as art and music are. Through travel, you come to recognize the similarities and differences between various places and regions of Italy. Tasting and cooking the food of a place enlarges the understand-ing of the territory and its people. Where certain foods are found or cultivated, how and when the indigenous culture enjoys them, all provide stories that are an entrée to a place. So I hope this is a journey that you will want to take with me and with Tanya.

Some of the recipes I've gathered here are more strictly traditional and demanding. But you take liberties, as you wish. Add something of your own to a dish, or simplify it, or pre-pare only the part of it that interests you. Never feel that you must do all or nothing.

I know this journey will give you much satisfaction and bring to your family and to your table new glorious and splendid flavors of Italy.

Tutti a tavola a mangiare.

Lidia Matticchio Bastianich

Lidia's Italy

ISTRIA

Chapter 1

Soup with Chickpeas and Smoked Pork
MINESTRA DI CECI

Poultry Broth
BRODO DI POLLO

Asparagus and Rice Soup
MINESTRA DI ASPARAGI E RISO

Frittata with Asparagus and Scallions
FRITTATA CON ASPARAGI E SCALOGNO

Makaruni with Chanterelle Mushrooms
MAKARUNI CON FUNGHI GALLINACCI

Fresh Pasta Quills with Chicken Sauce
FUZI CON SUGO DI POLLO

Pasutice with Seafood Sauce
PASUTICE ALL'ISTRIANA

Fresh Pastas: Fuzi, Mlinzi, and Pasutice

Jumbo Shrimp Buzara Style
BUZARA DI SCAMPI

Istrian Mixed Seafood Stew
BRODETTO ALL'ISTRIANA

Sauerkraut with Pork
CAPPUCCI GUARNITI

Roast Goose with Mlinzi
ARROSTO D'OCA CON MLINZI

Crêpes with Chocolate and Walnuts
PALACINKE

Quince Soup
ZUPPA ISTRIANA ALLE MELE COTOGNE

I was born in Pula, Istria. It was there that I took my first steps, and it is where my palate was awakened. I cherish many food memories from this area that have formed me as a cook, and I want to share some of them with you. Sometime, I plan to write a memoir that will concentrate on this area, so rich and varied in its food culture and yet relatively unknown, but for now I will give you just some of the tantalizing highlights along with some of my favorite recipes.

The cuisine of Istria is quite diversified because of its topography and its strategic geographical location. Istria lies on the northeastern coast of the Adriatic Sea, now Croatia, with a population of two hundred thousand. Geographically, it is a combination of bare rocky terrain and green fertile land, lush with pinewood forests. It has a gentle Mediterranean climate, with temperate, rainy winters and dry, hot summers.

The inland cuisine of Istria is rich in game and wild edibles; sheep and goat are herded, and animals are raised in almost every courtyard. Mediterranean crops flourish here—olives, grapes, figs, corn, wheat—and small family vegetable gardens abound. Curing pork meats and making pasta are part of every Istrian household.

The sea nearby is rich with bluefish, sardines, mackerel, and whitefish such as skate and monkfish. Just east of the Istrian shores is a patch of sea called the Kvarner, where one is bound to find the best scampi in the world; powdery-pink, sweet, and succulent, they make the best *buzara,* an old mariners' preparation. On any given day, countless *brodetti* will be perking away in seaside homes in Istria, made with an assortment of the above fishes.

Istria, such a small piece of land, is diversified not only because of its topography but because, through the centuries, it has been occupied by many different cultures and regimes. The original Illyrian settlers were conquered by the Romans in 177 B.C.; thus began nearly eight hundred years of Roman rule and cultural influence. Then such early European powers as the Goths, Longobards, Franks, Carinthians, and Bavarians ruled the peninsula for short periods. More lasting was the absorption of Istria into the Serenissima—the Republic of Venice—between the thirteenth and eighteenth centuries, during which time Italian culture and language took root in the region.

In more modern times, Istria was part of the Austro-Hungarian Empire; then, between the World Wars (in the youth of my parents), it was a province of

Italy in Friuli-Venezia Giulia. When Yugoslavia was created after World War II, Italy ceded Istria, and when Yugoslavia broke up in 1991, the territory was divided between Croatia (which now contains the main part of the peninsula) and Slovenia.

In its diversity today, Istria reflects this turbulent history, and the blended heritage of the Slavic and Italian cultures is vibrant. In the markets of Pula, one can speak either language and be understood. And the foods and cooking reflect the varied influences, too. The use of spices such as cloves, black pepper, and cinnamon in Istria is a mark of the Serenissima, while sauerkrauts, palacinke, goulash, and strudel are sure evidence of the Middle European influence.

My fondest memories are of the time spent with my grandmother Rosa in the courtyard in Busoler, a little town outside of Pula. It was a large courtyard full of chickens, ducks, geese, and other "courtyard animals," as we called them. I fed them, chased them, and gathered their warm eggs to make some of the best pasta and frittatas of my life. The courtyard looks rather small to me today, and the stone cottages that surround it are not as vibrant with life as I remember them from my childhood. Money was not plentiful then, but life was rich and flavorful. My maternal grandparents were self-reliant and produced most of the things we ate. They made wine, distilled grappa, and cured prosciutto and pancetta from the pigs. They milled their wheat at the communal mill, and in the cold of November harvested the olives to make olive oil.

I also fed and played with Nonna Rosa's goats and pigs; watching them grow from squealing, soft pink piglets to massive animals, until the dark November ritual of the slaughter, followed by the making of prosciutto, pancetta, sausage, *testina,* and blood sausage. The vegetable patch behind the courtyard produced all the vegetables and salads needed to feed us, and the surplus was jarred, dried, cured, and saved for winter use. We put up tomatoes, pickled cabbage and turnips, and dried shell beans, chickpeas, corn, figs, grapes, and all kinds of herbs. Braided shallots, garlic, and onions would hang in the *cantina,* the cellar, along with the prosciutto and slabs of pork-belly bacon. Apples were lined like soldiers on a wooden plank, and Seckel pears and quince would be tucked into the wheat berries to ripen. Those different, intense, yet pristine flavors are my reference library when I cook today.

Soup with Chickpeas and Smoked Pork

MINESTRA DI CECI

This is a hearty soup that my grandmother made—though never the same way twice. Sometimes she would add some pasta near the end of cooking, in the style of *pasta e fagioli*, or add another kind of bean, since legumes were so important. In season she would toss in a cup or two of fresh corn kernels.

This is really a one-pot meal, in two courses. First you have the velvety, rich soup, then sliced sausage and ribs as a second course. With a piece of country bread and a small salad, who could ask for more?

Makes 5 to 6 quarts of soup and meat, serving 12 or more

1 pound dried chickpeas

8 quarts water

2 bay leaves, preferably fresh

1½ pounds potatoes, peeled and quartered

2 medium-large onions, peeled and cut in large chunks (about 4 cups)

6 to 8 celery ribs, cut in large chunks (about 4 cups)

4 large carrots, peeled and cut in large chunks (about 4 cups)

6 plump garlic cloves, peeled

½ cup extra-virgin olive oil, plus more for finishing

2 cups canned Italian plum tomatoes, preferably San Marzano, crushed by hand

2 tablespoons coarse sea salt or kosher salt, or to taste

1-pound slab smoked pork ribs

Rinse the chickpeas and put them in the soup pot with enough cold water to cover them by at least 4 inches. Let them soak for 12 to 24 hours in a cool place.

Drain and rinse the chickpeas; put them in the soup pot with 8 quarts of fresh cold water, the bay leaves, and potatoes. Over high heat, bring the water to a boil, stirring often, and then keep it gently bubbling.

Meanwhile, prepare the *pestata*, the paste that is the seasoning base. Put about half of the onion, celery, and carrot chunks and half the garlic cloves in the food processor. Process into a finely minced paste, scraping down the bowl a few times. Empty the paste into a mixing bowl, process the remaining vegetables the same way, and mix the *pestata* batches together. (If your food processor is small, make the *pestata* in three batches.)

Pour the olive oil into the big skillet, and set over medium-high heat. Stir in all of the *pestata*—now it becomes a *soffritto*—and cook until the moisture has largely evaporated, about 10 minutes, stirring frequently. Pour in the crushed tomatoes, stir well, bring to a boil, and cook for a few minutes, until slightly reduced.

Scrape the *soffritto* into the pot of beans and potatoes, and stir to disperse it completely. Cover the pot partially, and bring the broth to a gentle bubbling boil. When the chickpeas have been cooking for about 1 hour total, stir in the 2 tablespoons salt and drop in the slab of pork ribs. Bring to a gentle boil, and cook for another ½ hour, partially covered, allowing the volume to reduce slowly and steadily.

1 pound smoked pork sausage
(such as kielbasa)

½ teaspoon coarsely ground
black pepper

½ cup freshly grated pecorino

Recommended Equipment
A large soup- or stockpot,
10-quart capacity or larger

A food processor

A heavy skillet or sauté pan,
12 inches or wider

After cooking for 1½ hours, by which time the beans should be nearly tender, drop in the smoked sausage and bring the soup to the boil again. Cook uncovered until the beans are completely soft and the soup has a nice density, 30 minutes or longer, then turn off the heat.

Remove the meats to a platter. To create a thickening, scoop out half of the chickpeas (about 3 cups) and as many chunks of potato as you can find, and drop them in the food-processor bowl. Add a cup or two of broth, process to a thick purée, and scrape it back into the soup. Stir well, and simmer for 5 minutes or longer if the soup needs more reduction. Season to taste with freshly ground black pepper and salt if needed.

Serve the soup first—with a drizzle of olive oil and a sprinkling of grated cheese over each portion—then the sliced meats as a second course. Or put a rib and a few slices of sausage in every soup bowl, and enjoy them together.

Poultry Broth

BRODO DI POLLO

With hens, ducks, and geese in the courtyard, my grandmother never worried about making a particular kind of broth. When she needed broth for a soup or a sauce, she might dispatch a skinny old rooster or an old fowl whose useful days were done. If she had a pile of bones and trimmings saved from a big meal with several roasts—chicken, ducks, or a goose—she'd make broth. If the bones were from different kinds of birds, it made no difference: they would go into the pot together.

That's the way I encourage you to think about making broth with this recipe (or even without a recipe). You may not have a skinny old rooster running around, but you can certainly search the supermarket meat case for packages of bony poultry parts, such as drumsticks, wings, and backs, or ask the butcher for backs and ribs. Gizzards are good, too. And you should save and freeze the neck and gizzards that you'll usually find in a package tucked into a roasting chicken (they'll all be good in your broth except for the liver). Also, use trimmings and the remnants of your holiday roast. If there's not enough of one kind of poultry, buy two kinds and cook them together. If you should come across a nice beef or veal bone that you've frozen and forgotten, could you use it? Though my recipe does not call for it, here's what my grandmother would tell you: "So the broth has stronger flavor? That's good. Throw it in."

Makes 5 quarts

3 pounds chicken, turkey, or other poultry parts (see above suggestions), fat removed

2 medium-large onions (1 pound)

4 large carrots, peeled and cut in 2-inch chunks

4 big celery stalks with leaves, peeled and cut in 4-inch chunks

6 garlic cloves, peeled

3 or 4 plum tomatoes (about ¾ pound), fresh or canned

Wash the poultry pieces, and put them in the stockpot. Peel and cut the onions in half. Place them, cut sides down, directly over an open flame, resting on a stove burner grate. Cook until the surface is well browned, about 3 minutes, shifting them with tongs so they're evenly seared. Drop them in the pot with all the other vegetables and seasonings and pour in 6 quarts of water.

Cover the pot, and bring the water to a boil over high heat, then cook uncovered for 15 minutes or so, skimming off any foam or residue that rises to the top. Set the cover ajar, and adjust heat to keep the broth boiling gently and reducing slowly.

Cook for about 2 hours, stirring occasionally, and taste for flavor and consistency. If it has a good brothy taste, stop cooking, or, if you want a stronger flavor, continue boiling, uncovered.

A handful of fresh Italian parsley, about a dozen long stems with lots of leaves, left whole

2 teaspoons whole black peppercorns

1 tablespoon coarse sea salt or kosher salt

6 quarts water

Recommended Equipment
An 8- or (preferably) 10-quart stockpot with a cover

Turn off the heat, and lift the cooked poultry and vegetables from the broth with a spider or a slotted spatula, into a colander set in a big bowl. Press down to squeeze out all the broth. Strain the broth through a wire-mesh sieve to remove any small bits, then skim the fat off the surface. Or chill overnight, and then remove the layer of solidified fat. Pour into containers, seal, and refrigerate or freeze until needed.

Foraging for Wild Asparagus

As well as cultivating our own vegetables, we loved to go foraging. In the springtime, we'd look for wild asparagus, *bruscandoli* (butcher's broom shoots), dandelion greens, nettles, chamomile, violets, wild leeks, chives, and all kinds of mints. Plus there were all the mushrooms in the springtime—*ovoli* (egglike mushrooms), chanterelles, *gallinelle,* morels, *prataioli* (portobellolike), and *chiodini* ("little nails"—honey fungus)—and in the fall, porcini, *griffola* (hen of the woods), and others. And most of these were turned into a frittata or a soup or a sauce for pasta.

I liked best of all foraging for wild asparagus—and I still love it. Wild asparagus—or *asparagina,* as we call it—depending on the spring rain, begin to sprout in mid-March and continue well into April. They flourish in rather arid and rocky terrain, where the mature plants spread their prickly fernlike branches over the ground. Each subsequent year, the new shoots mature from soft green ferns to prickly branches. The treat is those young shoots, the skinny spears poking through the ground every spring, and the challenge is to pick them when they are close to the earth and still tender.

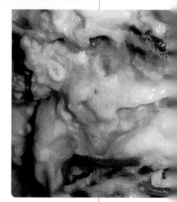

I always carried a stick to push away the older, prickly branches, but the markings of a good asparagus-forager are wounded hands that look as if they have been scratched by a cat. Today when I go foraging, I bring my gloves. We each had our special places where we knew exactly where the asparagus plants would be, and we would walk for miles, gathering as one gathers a bouquet of flowers. When our hands could not hold any more, we would tie the asparagus in bunches, then shove them in under our arms. When we had an armful, the foraging was successful, and we would return home.

I can still savor the frittata of wild asparagus made with Nonna Rosa's virgin olive oil, still-warm goose eggs, and a slab of homemade bread to mop it all up. Gnocchi with asparagus, olive oil, garlic, and pecorino cheese were a Sunday treat. Salads of cooked asparagus with boiled eggs and soups of asparagus and spring peas and fava are still vivid in my taste memory.

Asparagus and Rice Soup

MINESTRA DI ASPARAGI E RISO

This simple soup can be made anytime, but it is best with locally grown asparagus (if you can possibly get it) with the sweetness of springtime. It's also important to cook this soup sufficiently to develop the full flavor and silkiness from the base of leek and potatoes.

Makes about 3 quarts, serving 8

1½ pounds fresh asparagus spears

½ cup extra-virgin olive oil, plus more for serving

4 plump garlic cloves, crushed and peeled

2 cups potatoes peeled and cut in ½-inch cubes

3 cups chopped leek, ¼-inch pieces, white and green

5 quarts water

2 bay leaves

1 tablespoon coarse sea salt or kosher salt, plus more to taste

1 cup Arborio rice

Freshly ground black pepper to taste

1 cup freshly grated Grana Padano or Parmigiano-Reggiano

Recommended Equipment
A heavy-bottomed 6-quart saucepan or soup pot, with a cover

Rinse the asparagus, and snap off the tough bottom stubs. Slice the spears crosswise into ⅓-inch chunks, including tips.

Pour ⅓ cup of the olive oil into the pot, drop in the crushed garlic, and set over a medium-high flame. Golden the garlic for a minute or two, just until fragrant and lightly colored, and stir the potato cubes into the hot oil. Cook, stirring now and then, until the potatoes are crusty and starting to stick to the bottom but not browned—lower the heat if necessary—4 or 5 minutes. Stir in the chopped leeks, and cook until softened and sizzling, 3 or 4 minutes more.

Pour 5 quarts of water into the pot, drop in the bay leaves and tablespoon of salt, and stir well, scraping up any crusty potatoes on the bottom. Cover, and bring to the boil over high heat. Stir in all the cut asparagus, return to the boil, and adjust heat to keep the broth bubbling steadily and slowly reducing.

Cook uncovered for about 1½ hours, stirring occasionally, until the soup volume is reduced by almost a third and the broth is full of flavor—tasting is the way to test for doneness. Stir in the rice, return to the boil, and cook for 10 minutes, until the grains are *al dente*, then turn off the heat.

Season with freshly ground black pepper, and more salt to taste. Stir in 2 tablespoons fresh olive oil and ½ cup grated cheese. Serve immediately in warm bowls, with more cheese and oil at the table.

Frittata with Asparagus and Scallions

FRITTATA CON ASPARAGI E SCALOGNO

This is a different sort of frittata, not the neat golden round of well-set eggs that's probably most familiar. Here the eggs are in the skillet for barely a minute, just long enough to gather in soft, loose folds, filled with morsels of asparagus and shreds of prosciutto. In fact, when I make this frittata or the "dragged" eggs—*uova strapazzate*, page 143—I leave my eggs still wet and glistening so I can mop up the plate with a crust of country bread. That's the best part of all.

Serves 4 as a light meal or 6 as an appetizer

1 pound fresh, thin asparagus spears

4 ounces prosciutto or bacon, thick slices with ample fat (about 4 slices)

½ pound scallions

3 tablespoons extra-virgin olive oil

½ teaspoon coarse sea salt or kosher salt, or more to taste

8 large eggs

Freshly ground black pepper to taste

Recommended Equipment
A sturdy 12-inch nonstick skillet with a cover

A heat-proof rubber spatula

Snap off the tough bottom stubs of the asparagus, peel the bottom few inches of each spear, and cut them crosswise in 1½-inch pieces. Slice prosciutto or bacon into strips, or lardoons, about 1 inch long and ⅓ inch wide. Trim the scallions, and cut crosswise into 1-inch pieces.

Pour the olive oil into the skillet, scatter in the lardoons, and set over medium heat. When the strips are sizzling and rendering fat, toss in the cut asparagus, and roll and toss them over a few times. Cover the skillet, and cook, still over moderate heat, shaking the pan occasionally, until the asparagus is slightly softened, 5 minutes or so.

Scatter the scallion pieces in the pan, season with a couple pinches of salt, and toss the vegetables and lardoons together. Cover the skillet, and cook, shaking the pan and stirring occasionally, until the scallions and asparagus are soft and moist, 7 or 8 minutes more. Meanwhile, beat the eggs thoroughly with the remaining salt and generous grinds of black pepper.

When the vegetables are steaming in their moisture, uncover the skillet, raise the heat, and cook, tossing, for a minute or so, until the water has evaporated and the asparagus and scallions seem about to color.

Quickly spread them out in the pan, and pour the eggs over at once. Immediately begin folding the eggs over with the spatula, clearing the sides and skillet bottom continuously, so the eggs flow and coagulate around the vegetables and lardoons.

When all the eggs are cooked in big soft curds—in barely a minute—take the skillet off the heat. Tumble the frittata over a few more times to keep it loose and moist. Spoon portions onto warm plates, and serve hot and steaming.

Makaruni with Chanterelle Mushrooms

MAKARUNI CON FUNGHI GALLINACCI

Makaruni are traditional in Istria, a kind of pasta made when there was no time to roll, cut, and shape it. Rolling little pieces of dough between the palms of one's hands was quick and effective.

My grandmother and other women of her generation were expert *makaruni*-makers. In no time, they would take a big batch of pasta dough and turn it into slim little noodles. Instead of rolling the bits of dough back and forth for a second or two, my grandmother could compress and stretch a piece of dough into a perfect *makaruni* with one swipe of her hands—and flick it right onto her floured tray in the same movement.

Forming *makaruni* is truly simple, and once you start rolling, you'll quickly become proficient. Today, as when I was a child, the whole process is fun, so get the family to help and the *makaruni* will be done fast. And in a few minutes you'll enjoy the great taste and texture of your handiwork.

This delicious sauce is traditionally made with *gallinacci*, or chanterelles, though other mushrooms can be used. *Makaruni* are also wonderful with the *amatriciana* sauce of tomato and bacon on page 228.

Serves 6 as a first course or 4 as a main course

For the pasta
2 cups all-purpose flour, plus more for working

½ teaspoon salt

2 large eggs

⅓ cup very cold water, or as needed

For the sauce
½ cup extra-virgin olive oil

2 garlic cloves, crushed and peeled

1 cup thinly sliced onion

1 tablespoon shredded fresh sage leaves, packed to measure (4 to 6 leaves)

To mix the *makaruni* dough, put the flour and salt in the food processor and blend for a few seconds. Beat the eggs with a fork, then mix with the water in a spouted measuring cup. Start the food processor running, and pour in the liquids through the feed tube. Process for 30 to 40 seconds, until a soft dough forms and gathers on the blade. If it doesn't and is wet and sticky, process in more flour in small additions. If it is dry and stiff, process in more cold water, by spoonfuls. Turn out the dough and knead it briefly, until smooth and stretchy. Form into a round, cover it in plastic wrap, and let rest at room temperature for 30 minutes.

To make *makaruni*, cut off a lemon-sized lump of dough; wrap the rest in plastic. Lightly flour the work surface, and have a floured tray close by. Pinch off six or so marble-sized bits of dough. Roll each between your palms, back and forth, into a strand about 2 inches long, and drop it on the floured tray.

The *makaruni* won't be uniform, so don't worry if some are fatter and shorter or skinnier and longer. Cut more small bits for rolling,

2 teaspoons coarse sea salt or kosher salt, plus more to cook the *makaruni*

2 pounds fresh chanterelles and/or mixed fresh mushrooms, such as porcini, shiitake, cremini, and common white, cleaned and sliced

4 tablespoons tomato paste

2 cups hot light stock (chicken, turkey, or vegetable broth), or more as needed

Freshly ground black pepper to taste

2 tablespoons chopped fresh Italian parsley

½ cup freshly grated Grana Padano or Parmigiano-Reggiano

Recommended Equipment
A food processor fitted with metal blade

A dough cutter and trays for the *makaruni*

A heavy-bottomed sauté- or saucepan, 13-inch diameter, with a cover

A large pot for cooking the *makaruni*

as needed, keeping most of the dough wrapped. Occasionally flour and toss the rolled strands and separate them on the tray, spaced apart in one layer so they don't stick together.

To make the mushroom sauce, pour the olive oil into the large sauté pan, and set over medium-high heat. Toss in the garlic, cook until sizzling, then scatter in the sliced onion and shredded sage leaves. Stir well, season with ½ teaspoon salt, and cook until the onion is softened and sizzling. Add the sliced mushrooms, sprinkle on 1 teaspoon salt, and tumble the mushrooms over and over with a big spoon, mixing them with the onion and oil.

Cover the pan, and cook over medium heat, stirring occasionally, until the mushrooms are wilted and bubbling in their own juices. Uncover, raise the heat, and cook, tossing and stirring, to evaporate almost all the liquid. Clear a spot on the pan bottom, drop in the tomato paste, and stir it in the spot for a minute or so, until toasted and fragrant, then stir it all around the pan, to blend with the mushrooms and onions as they caramelize.

Pour in 1 cup of the hot broth, salt again, stir well, and bring to a boil. Lower the heat, and cook at a bubbling simmer, stirring now and then, until the liquid has cooked down and the sauce is very thick. Stir in another ½ cup broth, and cook again until quite concentrated. Stir in the remaining ½ cup broth, and cook now to a nice saucy consistency, dense but flowing. The addition of and cooking in broth should take about 15 minutes total. If the mushrooms are not tender, stir in more broth and cook them longer. Adjust the sauce seasonings, adding more salt and freshly ground black pepper to taste, and stir in the chopped parsley.

Meanwhile, heat 6 quarts of salted water to a rolling boil in the large pot. Shake the *makaruni* in a colander to remove excess flour, and dump them into the pot. Stir well, and return to the boil. At first the *makaruni* will drop to the bottom of the pot, then rise to the surface of the water. Check for doneness by tasting and cook until just *al dente*, about 3 minutes or more at the boil.

Bring the mushroom sauce back to a simmer—if it has thickened, loosen it with pasta-cooking water. Lift out the *makaruni* with a spider, drain briefly, and drop them onto the sauce. Over low heat, toss together until the pasta is fully dressed and cooked. Turn off the heat, and toss in the grated cheese. Serve immediately in warm pasta bowls.

Fresh Pasta Quills with Chicken Sauce

FUZI CON SUGO DI POLLO

This is a thoroughly traditional Istria-style pasta, the very best of its kind. The sauce, or *sugo*, is the kind of long-cooking sauce my grandmother made, patiently, from a tough courtyard hen, rooster, or rabbit. It would perk on the stove forever, or so it seemed: whenever I thought it was done, she would pour in a little more broth and let it cook longer. Finally, though, the *sugo* would be finished—velvety in texture, dense with meat, and rich with flavor. Then Nonna Rosa would use it to dress her handmade *fuzi*—little quill-like cylinders of fresh pasta. Though the *sugo* and *fuzi* would be delicious in other pairings, to me they are meant to go together, and that's how I give them to you here.

Today's *sugo* will not take forever. With a smallish hen—organically raised and free-ranging, for the best flavor and nutrition—it takes only a couple of hours to make a thick, brothy sauce with concentrated flavor.

For taste, texture, and convenience too, I recommend that you make the *sugo* the day before serving, so the flavor permeates the meat. The *fuzi* can be made a few hours ahead and kept at room temperature (or frozen long in advance, as detailed on page 20). If you want to make and serve everything in one day, mix the dough, start the *sugo*, then form the *fuzi* while the sauce is cooking.

Serves 6

For the sugo

½ cup dried porcini slices (about ½ ounce)

1 free-range chicken (or rooster), about 3 pounds

1 teaspoon coarse sea salt or kosher salt, or to taste

¼ cup extra-virgin olive oil

2 medium onions, finely chopped (about 2 cups)

2 bay leaves, preferably fresh

4 whole cloves

Soak the dried porcini slices in 2 cups hot water for 30 minutes or longer. When rehydrated, lift them out of the container; squeeze out (and save) the soaking liquid. Chop the porcini into fine pieces.

Cut the chicken into six or more pieces—divide the legs and breast pieces if the bird is big. Rinse the pieces well, pat dry, and season lightly with salt.

Pour the olive oil into the saucepan and set over medium-high heat. Stir in the onions, ¼ teaspoon salt, bay leaves, cloves, and rosemary. Cook, stirring, until the onions are wilted and lightly colored, then push them to the side of the pan, clearing the bottom, and lay in the chicken pieces. Fry, turning frequently, until golden brown on all sides. Clear a small space on the pan bottom, drop in the chopped mushrooms and chicken livers, stir them around until brown and caramelized, then mix them into the onions. Finally, clear another hot spot on the bottom, drop in the tomato paste, and stir it in place for a couple of minutes, until toasted and fragrant. Toss everything together, coating the chicken with paste and other seasonings.

1 small branch fresh rosemary with lots of needles

2 ounces chicken livers, trimmed of membranes and finely chopped (¼ cup)

¼ cup tomato paste

3 to 6 cups hot Poultry Broth, page 8, or other light stock, as needed

Freshly ground black pepper to taste

For cooking and dressing the fuzi and serving
1 batch (1½ pounds) fresh *fuzi*, page 20

1½ tablespoons coarse sea salt or kosher salt

Extra-virgin olive oil for finishing

2 cups freshly grated Grana Padano or Parmigiano-Reggiano

Recommended Equipment
A heavy 12-inch saucepan with 4-to-5-inch sides, with a cover

A pasta machine for rolling the dough

A big pot for cooking the pasta

A heavy 14-inch skillet or sauté pan for dressing the pasta

Pour in the reserved mushroom-soaking liquid, carefully leaving behind the sediment in the bottom. Turn up the heat and bring to a boil, stirring the meat and vegetables and scraping up the caramelization on the bottom and sides of the pan. Cook for a few minutes, until slightly reduced, then ladle in a cup or more of hot stock, enough almost to submerge the chicken pieces. Season with another ¼ teaspoon salt, cover the pan, and set the heat so the broth is bubbling gently all over the surface.

Cook, covered, reducing the broth steadily and slowly. Check and replenish the liquid every 15 minutes or so to keep the meat about three-quarters covered, and turn the pieces over occasionally, adjusting the heat if necessary. After 1½ hours or so, when the meat is falling off the bones, turn off the heat. Taste the sauce, and add freshly ground black pepper and more salt if needed. Let the chicken and sauce cool completely in the pan.

To finish the *sugo*, remove the chicken pieces, then pick out and discard the bay leaves, cloves, and rosemary. Strip all the edible meat from the chicken bones, and shred into bite-sized pieces; discard bones, skin, and cartilage. Fold the shredded chicken into the sauce. (You should have roughly equal amounts of meat and sauce—if there's lots more meat, use it in other dishes.) Use the *sugo* within an hour or so, or refrigerate.

To cook the *fuzi*, fill the big pot with 7 quarts of water, add 1½ tablespoons salt, and bring to a rolling boil. Shake excess flour off the *fuzi*, and drop them into the pot. Stir briskly, cover the pot, and bring the water back to the boil rapidly. The *fuzi* will rise to the surface as they cook; stir them and boil until *al dente*, anywhere from 2 to 5 minutes, depending on how thick and dry they are.

Meanwhile, heat the *sugo* to simmering in the large sauté pan or skillet. If the sauce is very dense, loosen it with more broth (or hot pasta-cooking water). If soupy, cook uncovered to evaporate moisture. Lift the *fuzi* from the pot with a spider, drain for a moment, and spill them on top of the simmering sauce. Toss together for a minute or two over medium-low heat, until all the *fuzi* are coated with sauce.

Turn off the heat, drizzle 2 or 3 tablespoons olive oil over, add a cup of the grated cheese, and toss to incorporate. Serve immediately, passing more cheese at the table.

Pasutice with Seafood Sauce

PASUTICE ALL'ISTRIANA

This is typical of Istrian preparations for the abundance of fresh seafood that blesses the region—fast, simple, and full of flavor. The longest step is cutting the pasta dough into diamond-shaped *pasutice*, which can be done hours ahead or frozen way in advance. (And though *pasutice* is the optimal and traditional pasta, linguine would be a fine substitute.)

For the sauce itself, the cooking takes just minutes. Use your widest skillet, so the shellfish sauté and caramelize quickly in the dry pan, then cook them only briefly in the liquid, or they will become rubbery.

Serves 6

1 batch (1½ pounds) fresh *pasutice*, page 20

18 littleneck clams (1½ pounds or so in the shell), scrubbed

½ pound small raw shrimp in the shell (about 20 shrimp, U-40 size)

½ pound sea scallops, preferably "dry" (not soaked in preservative)

½ teaspoon or more coarse sea salt or kosher salt, plus more for the pasta

10 tablespoons extra-virgin olive oil

6 plump garlic cloves, crushed and peeled

½ teaspoon peperoncino flakes, or to taste

1 cup canned Italian plum tomatoes, preferably San Marzano, crushed by hand

The *pasutice* can be made a few hours ahead and kept at room temperature until you cook them (or frozen long in advance, as detailed on page 20).

To prepare the shellfish, put the clams in a single layer on a tray or platter and freeze them for about ½ hour. Open the shells with a shucking knife, cut out the clams, and slice each one into quarters. Collect the clam liquor in a bowl as you shuck, let the sediment settle, and pour off the clean liquor on top, saving it for the sauce.

Remove the shells, tails, and small digestive vein from the shrimp, then rinse and pat them dry.

Pull off and discard the little muscle on the side of each scallop, and slice them in half horizontally, into thin disks.

Meanwhile, bring 7 quarts water and 1½ tablespoons salt to the boil in the big pot. Keep it covered and simmering, so you can cook the *pasutice* quickly when the seafood sauce is ready.

Pour 4 tablespoons of the olive oil into the big skillet, toss in the crushed garlic and the peperoncino, and cook over medium-high heat until the garlic is fragrant and lightly colored. Turn up the heat, scatter the shrimp and scallop slices around the pan, spread out so they start sizzling and caramelizing. Cook for just a minute, toss and turn the shellfish, then scatter the clam chunks in the hot pan and get them sizzling.

Pour in the cup of crushed tomatoes, the clam liquor, and ½ teaspoon salt, and bring to a bubbling boil, then adjust the heat to keep the juices bubbling steadily. Pour another ¼ cup of olive oil into the sauce, and stir in well. Cook for about 2 minutes, slightly

2 tablespoons or so chopped fresh Italian parsley

Recommended Equipment
A pasta machine for rolling the dough

A shucking knife or other knife with sturdy blade

A big pot for cooking the pasta

A heavy 14-inch skillet or sauté pan, or the widest pan you have

reducing, then toss in half of the chopped parsley, and turn off the heat—temporarily.

Meanwhile, bring the pasta water to a rolling boil and drop in the *pasutice* quickly by handfuls, shaking off excess flour, and stirring to keep the pieces from sticking. Cover the pot, and return to the boil rapidly. Cook only until the *pasutice* have risen to the surface and are just *al dente*, a minute or two or maybe more, depending on how dry and thick they are.

When the *pasutice* are almost done, return the shellfish sauce to a bubbling simmer. Lift out the diamonds with a spider, drain briefly, and drop them into the skillet. Toss the *pasutice* and shellfish together for a couple of minutes, until the pasta is perfectly cooked and coated with the dressing. Cook rapidly over high heat if the sauce is soupy, or ladle in a bit of water from the pasta-cooking pot to thin it.

Turn off the heat, and dress the *pasutice* with a final flourish of olive oil, 2 tablespoons or so, and sprinkle the rest of the parsley over. Serve immediately in warm pasta bowls.

The Food from the Sea

Istria is a peninsula, and Pula is on the tip, and the sea surrounding it is rich with life. We used to go swimming on the pebbled beaches and rocky shores and collect periwinkles, sea urchins, *datteri* (sea dates), rock crabs, and mussels, which we proudly brought home and enjoyed with our family. But in our family, Uncle Emilio was the fisherman. An electrician by profession, he was a fisherman by passion, and a good one at that.

On his fishing trips, he would catch enough fish for the family plus some for sale. *Branzini* (sea bass), *orate* (gilded bass), calamari, *scarpene* (rockfish), sardines, *granchi* (crabs), *polipo* (octopus)—whatever was in season—he would bring home, and it would be cooked within a few hours with the brine of the sea still in every bite.

Fresh Pastas: Fuzi, Mlinzi, and Pasutice

Make a whole batch of this pasta dough for Fresh Pasta Quills with Chicken Sauce, page 16; Roast Goose with Mlinzi, page 28; or Pasutice with Seafood Sauce, page 18. Roll, cut, and shape the pasta as detailed below, and use in whichever dish you are preparing.

Makes 1½ pounds

3 cups all-purpose flour, plus more as needed

3 large eggs, lightly beaten

¼ cup extra-virgin olive oil

⅓ cup very cold water, plus more as needed

Put the flour in the bowl of a food processor and process for a few seconds to aerate. Mix the eggs, olive oil, and the water in a measuring cup or other spouted container. Start the food processor running, and pour in the liquids through the feed tube. Process for 30 to 40 seconds, until a soft dough forms and gathers on the blade. If the dough does not gather and is wet and sticky, process in more flour, in small additions. If it is dry and stiff, process in more water, by spoonfuls.

Turn the dough out on a lightly floured surface and knead by hand for a minute, until it's smooth, soft, and stretchy. Press it into a disk, wrap it in plastic wrap, and let it rest at room temperature for 30 minutes before using. To use later, refrigerate for up to a day, or freeze it for a month or more. Defrost frozen dough in the refrigerator; return it to room temperature before rolling.

Rolling and shaping *pasutice* and *fuzi*: To roll the dough in a standard home pasta-roller, cut it into six pieces. Keeping the dough lightly floured, roll the pieces at progressively narrower settings, gradually stretching them into strips about 2 feet long and as wide as your machine allows, usually about 5 inches. Cut each strip in half crosswise, so you have twelve strips about a foot in length. Lay them flat on a lightly floured surface, and keep covered with towels.

One at a time, slice the strips lengthwise into long ribbons, about 1½ inches wide, using a sharp knife or a rotary pasta-cutter and a ruler to guide the blade. You should get three such ribbons from a 5-inch-wide strip.

To make *pasutice*: Cut across the ribbons with parallel diagonal slices, spaced 2 inches apart, forming diamond-shaped *pasutice* (also called *maltagliati*).

Lay them flat on a lightly floured tray or sheet pan, spaced apart

in a single layer. When the tray is filled, cover the *pasutice* with a lightly floured towel, and lay another layer of diamonds on top. Leave the *pasutice* at room temperature on the tray for a few hours. For longer storage, freeze on the tray until solid, then pack in ziplock plastic bags until you are ready to cook them.

To make *fuzi*: First cut a pasta strip into ribbons, and then into diamond-shaped *pasutice*, as described above.

Roll each diamond around a lightly floured chopstick or similar-sized thin rod to form a hollow tube, resembling a quill. Press on the overlapping pasta to seal the cylinder and slide it off the stick. Roll all the pasta diamonds into *fuzi,* using up all the remaining dough.

Place the *fuzi*, spaced apart, on a lightly floured tray, and cover with a floured towel. Fill another tray if needed (do not put one layer on top of another, like *pasutice*). Leave at room temperature for a few hours, or freeze on the tray, then pack in plastic bags until you cook them.

To make *mlinzi*: For *mlinzi,* you'll need a rolling pin or a pasta machine to roll the dough, and several half–sheet pans (12 by 18 inches) or other large baking sheets. Arrange your oven racks to hold as many baking sheets as fit comfortably inside, and preheat to 300˚.

To roll *mlinzi* by hand, cut the dough into four pieces. On a lightly floured board, roll each piece to a rectangle about 11 by 17 inches (to fit in a half-sheet). To roll out in a pasta machine, cut the dough in six pieces and roll each piece at progressively narrower settings, into strips about 2 feet long and as wide as your machine allows. Always keep the dough lightly floured and roll until very thin, as for any fresh pasta.

Lay the rolled pasta out flat on the sheet pans, cutting it as needed to fit. Arrange as many pans as you can in your oven, rotating them and shaking so they don't stick. When they appear dry, flip the *mlinzi* over. Bake a total of 18 to 20 minutes, until the *mlinzi* are completely crisp and crack apart when bent. They should be pale gold all over, or even darker, for a nuttier taste.

Let the *mlinzi* cool on the sheet pans, or move to wire racks. When all the *mlinzi* sheets are baked and cool, stack them up on a tray and leave them uncovered, in a dry place, so the air circulates between the sheets and they remain crisp.

Jumbo Shrimp Buzara Style

BUZARA DI SCAMPI

Shrimp *alla buzara* is common all around the northern Adriatic coast. When I make this quick and delicious dish at our house, I give everyone an empty bowl for the shells. I bring the pan to the table; we roll up our sleeves and dig in, savoring the sweet meat, then sucking and licking every drop of sauce from the shells. All that's needed is some grilled bread.

If you wish, use smaller, inexpensive shrimp (shelled and cleaned) in the recipe to make a terrific dressing for spaghetti or linguine. And leftovers make a great risotto.

Serves 6

24 large raw shrimp, 1 ounce apiece (U-16 size)

8 tablespoons extra-virgin olive oil, or more to taste

3 plump garlic cloves, finely chopped

½ cup finely chopped shallots

1 teaspoon coarse sea salt or kosher salt

1 cup white wine

1 tablespoon tomato paste

1 cup of water

Freshly ground black pepper to taste

1 tablespoon bread crumbs, or more if needed

2 tablespoons chopped fresh Italian parsley

Recommended Equipment
A heavy-bottomed sauté pan, 10-to-12-inch diameter, for the sauce

A heavy-bottomed 13-to-14-inch skillet for searing the shrimp

Without removing any of the shell, remove the vein (digestive tract) that runs inside the curving back of each shrimp: slice open the back with a sturdy sharp paring knife, cutting through the shell, and scrape out the vein. Rinse the shrimp and pat dry.

Pour ¼ cup of the olive oil into the sauté pan, and set over medium-high heat. Scatter in the garlic, cook until sizzling, then stir in the shallots. When they're sizzling, stir in ¼ teaspoon of the salt and ¼ cup of the wine. Cook, stirring frequently, until the wine is nearly completely evaporated and the shallots have softened. Drop in the tomato paste and stir it around the pan for a minute, coating the shallots and caramelizing.

Pour in the rest of the wine, bring to the boil quickly, then add the water and ¼ teaspoon salt, stirring. Bring to a boil, then reduce the heat and let the sauce bubble gently and reduce for about 5 minutes while you sear the shrimp.

Pour 2 tablespoons olive oil into the wide skillet, and set over high heat until very hot. Scatter the shrimp in the pan, toss them in the oil, and season with the remaining ½ teaspoon salt. Cook for just a minute or slightly longer, until the shells are lightly colored and the flesh underneath is opaque, then turn off the heat.

With the sauce still bubbling, slide in the seared shrimp and tumble to coat them all with sauce. Stir in the coarsely ground pepper, then the tablespoon of bread crumbs—use more crumbs if the sauce is thin. Cook for another 2 minutes, then turn off the heat.

Drizzle over the remaining 2 tablespoons olive oil—or more to taste—and incorporate it well, tumbling the shrimp in the pan. Sprinkle the parsley on top, and serve immediately.

Istrian Mixed Seafood Stew

BRODETTO ALL'ISTRIANA

Brodetto means cooked in a soupy medium, and so it is in this recipe: different fish cooked together with aromatics to form a unified, delicious dish. The more varieties of fish in the *brodetto*, the more complex the flavor will be.

Traditionally in Istria, *brodetto* was made with the pick of the catch. But in many a fisherman's household, such fish was sold, and his family ate what he didn't sell, a mix of the smaller fish, which were all harmonized by the *brodetto* cooking method. I remember many *brodetti* of my childhood in which there were only small fish. I wasn't even ten years old, but already my mouth was well attuned, and I would screen with efficiency all the small fish bones— a skill that is still with me.

This dish can be made several hours in advance and reheated, very gently. Set the meaty fish on a platter and keep warm, and use the sauce and remaining bits of fish to dress the pasta (or polenta). I like to let everyone help themselves to fish from the platter. And since the crab should be eaten with the hands, provide an empty bowl for the shells and bones—and plenty of towels!

Serves 6

6 live blue-claw crabs, or 1 pound Alaskan crab (king or snow crab) legs

1-pound whole black sea bass, cleaned and scaled

2 or 3 slices bone-in monkfish, ½ pound total

½ pound conger eel, 3-inch center-cut pieces, cleaned

Flour for dredging

⅓ cup extra-virgin olive oil

1½ teaspoons coarse sea salt or kosher salt

1 cup chopped onion

⅓ cup chopped shallots

Break apart the blue crabs one at a time. Grasping them one by one in a cloth towel, pull off the claws and the tail. Pry up and separate the hard top shell from the bottom body, then remove the gills (or lungs) and cut off the head section (eyes and mouth). Rinse well under cold running water. Cut the body in half (leave roe attached if you have she-crabs), and drain in a colander.

Cut the sea bass crosswise into roughly equal-size head and tail sections. Dredge the bass, monkfish, and eel pieces in flour, shaking off the excess. Heat the oil in the big saucepan over medium-high heat. Put in all the floured fish in a single layer, fry until crisp on the underside, then flip the pieces over. Season with ½ teaspoon salt, and fry until crisp all over, about 4 minutes in all, and remove to a platter.

Dump in the onion, shallots, and garlic, and cook until sizzling and wilted, stirring all around and scraping up the caramelized bits in the pan. Drop in all the blue-crab pieces (but not Alaskan crab legs, if using), then toss and stir over high heat.

Add the bay leaves, and season lightly with salt. When the moisture from the crabs has evaporated, push the pieces aside and drop

2 plump garlic cloves, crushed
and peeled

2 bay leaves, preferably fresh

5 tablespoons tomato paste

¼ cup red wine vinegar

3 cups hot water

1 teaspoon freshly ground black
pepper, or to taste

½ pound calamari, cleaned and
cut in 1-inch pieces

2 tablespoons chopped fresh
Italian parsley

Recommended Equipment
A very wide heavy-bottomed
saucepan or deep sauté pan

the tomato paste in the clear hot spot. Stir it in place for a minute, then stir the crabs and onion and paste together, all around the pan, as they sizzle and caramelize.

Pour the red wine vinegar into 3 cups hot water, stir to mix, then pour all the liquid into the hot pan. Stir well, scraping and melting all the glazed bits in the pan and creating a broth. Bring to a steady boil, season with ½ teaspoon salt and the teaspoon freshly ground pepper, and cook the crab for a couple of minutes by itself.

Add the eel pieces to the broth, bring it back to the boil, and cook for 10 minutes—or more if the eel is very thick—before reintroducing the monkfish and sea bass. Clear space for the fish pieces, and nestle them in gently, so they don't break up; pour in any juices that accumulated on the platter. Scatter the calamari all over, and shake the pan gently, nestling the calamari between the fish and sloshing the sauce over all the seafood. (If using crab legs instead of fresh blue crabs, add them to the saucepan after the fish are in, just before the calamari.)

When everything is in the pan and the broth is perking, cook for 5 minutes or more, shaking the pan now and then. When the firm-fleshed fish are cooked through and tender—in particular the eel and monkfish—turn off the heat.

Scatter the parsley all over, and serve hot, Istrian style. Heap all the meaty fish with a bit of sauce on a big platter, from which people can choose the pieces they want. Dress pasta or polenta with remaining sauce. Provide empty bowls for bones, and plenty of towels for wiping hands.

Sauerkraut with Pork

CAPPUCCI GUARNITI

At every major holiday or event in Istria—no matter what else—there must be a pot of sauerkraut with big cuts of cured and fresh pork buried inside. This dish belongs in the category of treasured one-pot meals, filled with flavor, that can feed a crowd yet require little attention from the cook. It is enjoyed for days—even better reheated—and if there are any leftovers, they are turned into *jota*, page 42.

It is essential that cured meats be of the best quality, so visit a real Eastern European–style butcher if you can. Good sauerkraut is also essential. If you can't find genuine fresh sauerkraut, sold in bulk, I recommend buying bagged sauerkraut, in the refrigerator cases of most supermarkets, rather than canned.

Serves 8 to 10

4 pounds sauerkraut

4 cups fresh cold water

⅓ cup extra-virgin olive oil

5 fresh bay leaves

3 fat garlic cloves, thinly sliced

1 tablespoon black peppercorns

1½ teaspoons coarse sea salt or kosher salt, or more as needed

1-pound solid chunk fresh pork shoulder (butt)

½-pound solid chunk smoked pork loin or Canadian bacon

½-pound slab bacon

1 pound smoked pork sausages

Freshly ground black pepper

Recommended Equipment
A heavy-bottomed, 8-quart, 12-inch saucepan

Drain the sauerkraut in a colander—set in the sink for convenience. Dump the sauerkraut into a big pot or bowl, cover it with fresh water, stir to rinse well, then drain again through the colander. Repeat the rinsing and draining. Taste the sauerkraut, and if it is still very salty or acidic, rinse and drain it a third time.

Put the sauerkraut in the big saucepan, and pour in the 4 cups water. Drizzle the olive oil over the top; drop in the bay leaves, garlic, peppercorns, and salt. Toss the sauerkraut with the seasonings. Rinse the chunks of pork butt and smoked pork loin and the bacon slab, and nestle them into the sauerkraut.

Cover the saucepan, and set it over medium-high heat. Bring to a boil, then reduce the heat and let it simmer, covered, for about 1½ hours. Occasionally, stir up all the sauerkraut and turn the meat over. The liquid should gradually reduce, but don't let the pan get dry.

Rinse the sausages, stir up the sauerkraut, then tuck the sausages in with the pork chunks. Simmer for another 30 minutes, or until the meats are all tender and the liquid is almost completely absorbed. Cook uncovered to evaporate the liquid if necessary.

Turn off the heat, and season with freshly ground black pepper to taste and more salt if needed. Let the sauerkraut sit for 15 minutes. Slice the meats and arrange on a platter, surrounding the sauerkraut, and serve.

Roast Goose with Mlinzi

ARROSTO D'OCA CON MLINZI

Roast goose is a festive dish throughout all of northern Italy, but the Istrian tradition of serving goose with *mlinzi* reflects the culinary customs of Zagreb, the capital of Croatia. And though roast goose by itself is utterly delicious, to have a forkful of *mlinzi* at the same time, drenched with sauce, is absolute bliss.

Mlinzi are a simple form of homemade pasta, with an unusual distinction. After the fresh dough is rolled into thin sheets, it is baked in a low oven until crisp and toasted gold. The stiff sheets are later cracked into jagged shards and cooked like ordinary pasta. As a result, *mlinzi* are more porous and seem to drink up their dressing—in this dish, the richly flavored sauce made from the goose's roasting juices. The baking also imparts a lovely nutty flavor to the pasta, which complements the dark meat deliciously. That's why roast goose and *mlinzi* are a match made in heaven.

This is a large, festive meal and does require considerable time and attention. It is best done in stages, the *mlinzi* prepared and baked a couple of days in advance (see page 20) so you can focus on roasting the goose and making the sauce.

Serves 8 to 10

1 recipe fresh pasta dough, page 20, plus flour for handling

For the goose and pan sauce
10-to-12-pound goose, fresh, or fully defrosted if frozen

3 tablespoons coarse sea salt or kosher salt, or more to taste

2 bay leaves, preferably fresh

2 branches fresh rosemary

2 tablespoons extra-virgin olive oil

1 pound onions, peeled and quartered

½ pound carrots, cut in 2-inch chunks

Roll and bake *mlinzi*, page 20, a day or two in advance, and store in a dry place to keep them crisp.

The night before roasting, open up the goose, remove the giblets and neck if packed inside, and remove the lumps of fat from the main and neck cavities (save the fat for rendering, or discard). Rinse the bird thoroughly in cool running water, washing any residue from the cavity. Rinse the giblets as well, and pat everything dry with paper towels. Rub salt all over the goose, and sprinkle some in the cavity, using about 2 tablespoons in all. Set the goose on the wire rack in the roasting pan, breast up, and put it uncovered in the refrigerator to dry overnight. Wrap and refrigerate the neck and giblets.

The next day, remove the goose from the refrigerator an hour or two before roasting and let it come to room temperature. Arrange a rack in the lower part of the oven, and heat to 425°.

Put the bay leaves and rosemary branches in the cavity of the bird. With the breast up, twist and fold the long wing tips under

½ pound celery stalks with leaves, cut in 2-inch chunks

½ ounce dried porcini slices, chopped into small pieces (about ¼ cup)

6 juniper berries

5 cups Poultry Broth, page 8, or other light stock, or more if needed

Freshly ground black pepper

For cooking and finishing the mlinzi
1½ tablespoons coarse sea salt or kosher salt, for cooking

¼ cup extra-virgin olive oil

1 cup freshly grated Grana Padano or Parmigiano-Reggiano

Recommended Equipment
A heavy-duty roasting pan, 12 by 18 inches or larger, with flat wire roasting rack inside, big enough to hold the goose and vegetables

A thin skewer, kitchen twine, heavy-duty aluminum foil, a fat-and-gravy separator, a large sieve, and a potato masher

A 3- or 4-quart saucepan, for finishing the sauce

1 heavy, wide skillet or sauté pan for dressing the *mlinzi*

the wing joints, so they're wedged tightly against the back. Bring the legs together, crossing the ends of the drumsticks, and wrap with kitchen twine. Loop the twine under the goose tail and tighten to close the cavity, then knot securely. Drizzle the olive oil over the breast and sides of the bird. Prick the skin of the goose all over with the point of a trussing needle or skewer, to speed draining of fat.

Roast the goose for 30 minutes to melt and drain body fat, then remove the pan carefully and lower the oven to 350°. Lift out the wire rack with the goose, and set it on a carving platter or baking sheet. Pour the hot fat from the roasting pan into a large can or milk carton (you'll collect nearly a quart of fat by the end of roasting).

Put the rack with the bird back in the pan, and spread the vegetable chunks and chopped porcini around it. Nestle the goose neck and giblets, including the liver, in with the chunks, scatter in the juniper berries, and sprinkle another tablespoon salt over the vegetables. Pour 3 cups of the broth into the side of the pan, partly submerging the vegetables and giblets. Cover the goose with a tent of heavy aluminum foil, arched so it doesn't touch the skin, and crimp the foil tight against the sides of the roasting pan. Return the pan to the oven.

Roast the covered bird for an hour, then remove the foil tent. If the vegetables are still only partly submerged in liquid, continue roasting uncovered. If more accumulated fat has completely covered the vegetables, carefully pull out the oven rack and spoon off as much fat as you can, removing it to a fat separator, if you have one, or a heat-proof cup. Return the goose to the oven, and continue to roast uncovered. (When the liquid you just removed has settled, discard the fat and pour the recovered broth back into the roasting pan.) After another hour, when the breast is nicely caramelized, dark, and crisp, check for doneness with a meat thermometer inserted in the thickest part of the thigh (without touching a bone). When it reads 170° or above, you can safely take the goose from the oven (it will continue to cook as it rests). If the goose needs more roasting and the breast is already quite dark, cover it loosely with foil. If the opposite is true—that the meat is done but the breast is not caramelized—turn up the heat to darken it quickly.

Meanwhile, bring a large pot of water with 1½ tablespoons salt to a boil for the pasta.

When the goose is perfectly roasted, remove it, still on the rack, to the carving platter. Cover it loosely with the foil tent, and keep in a warm spot.

To make the sauce, transfer the neck and giblets (but not the liver) from the roasting pan to a medium saucepan. Hold back the vegetable chunks and goose liver in the roasting pan as you empty all the liquid through a sieve set over a large measuring container or bowl (a 1-quart fat separator is ideal). Put the liver and vegetables (including any caught in the sieve) in a potato masher, and crush them directly into the saucepan.

When the strained roasting-liquid fat has separated, discard the fat, and pour the juices into the saucepan. Add enough fresh hot broth to make a total of at least 6 cups of liquid. Use some of the additional broth to deglaze any caramelization left in the roasting pan, and add that to the saucepan, as well as the juices the resting goose will release.

Bring the sauce liquid to a boil and cook, partly covered, for 20 minutes or so, to extract flavor and concentrate the broth. When reduced to about 5 cups and slightly thickened, turn off the heat. Taste, and season with more salt and freshly ground black pepper as needed. Pour 3 cups of the sauce into a big skillet to dress the *mlinzi*, and keep the rest to pass later at the table.

Meanwhile, for the *mlinzi:* Break all the baked pasta sheets into irregular shards, 2 to 3 inches wide, and pile them in a large bowl or tray. (If you have youngsters around, they will be happy to assist with the snapping and cracking.)

When the goose has rested at least 20 minutes and the sauce is almost ready, drop the *mlinzi* into the pot of boiling water. Stir well, cover, and cook about 3 minutes, until soft and floppy but still *al dente*. Lift the *mlinzi* out with a spider, drain, and spill on top of the sauce in the big skillet. Toss and tumble the pasta for a couple of minutes over medium heat, until cooked through and saturated with sauce. Turn off the heat, drizzle the ¼ cup olive oil over all, scatter on the grated cheese, then toss. Keep warm while you carve the goose.

Carve the goose at the table (or, if you have a good carver among your guests, call on him or her). Goose joints are tricky to find, lower down than on other birds, and notoriously tight, but just pry the limbs open. Otherwise, carve as you would a chicken. Serve with the dressed *mlinzi*, steaming hot, and pass the extra sauce around.

Crêpes with Chocolate and Walnuts

PALACINKE

Every culture has its pancakes, and Istria has *palacinke*. Though they are no different from *crespelle* or crêpes, *palacinke* is the name I first learned for the delicious thin pancakes my mother would whip up for us for dinner.

As a child, I loved them any way she served them, often with only a sprinkle of sugar or a bit of home-preserved fruits, like rose-hip jam, apricot marmalade, or prune butter. Sometimes *palacinke* were more elaborate: filled with ricotta and baked or layered like a cake with different fillings in between. But the most luxurious—and always our favorite—were *palacinke* spread with melted chocolate.

That's the version I share with you here, but I also encourage you to enjoy these homey treats any way you like. Today my mother still makes *palacinke*, but now it is her great-grandchildren who wait in line for the next one to come out of the pan so they can spread jam on top, roll them up, and devour them, still warm.

Makes a dozen *palacinke,* serving 6 or more

For the palacinke
2 eggs

1 tablespoon dark rum

1 teaspoon vanilla extract

2 tablespoons sugar

⅓ teaspoon salt

2 cups all-purpose flour

8 tablespoons melted butter, or more if needed

Finely grated zest of 2 lemons

For serving
10 ounces excellent bittersweet or semisweet chocolate
(12 ounces, or more, for extreme chocolate lovers)

To make the *palacinke* batter, whisk together the eggs, 2 cups water, the rum, vanilla, sugar, and salt in a large bowl, until well blended. Sift the flour on top, a bit at a time, whisking each addition in until smooth. Drizzle in 4 tablespoons of the melted butter, whisking until the batter has slightly thickened, with the consistency of melted ice cream. Finally, whisk in the lemon zest. Put the remaining 4 tablespoons of melted butter in a small cup and keep it warm.

Break or chop the chocolate into small pieces, and put them in a bowl set in a pan of hot (not boiling) water. When the chocolate begins to melt, stir until completely smooth, and keep it warm, in the water, off the heat.

Set the crêpe pan or skillet over medium-high heat until quite hot. Pour in a couple tablespoons of the reserved melted butter, quickly swirl it all over the pan bottom, then pour excess butter back into the cup, leaving the bottom lightly coated with sizzling butter. (If the butter doesn't sizzle, heat the pan longer before adding the batter.) Immediately ladle in a scant ⅓ cup of batter, tilt and swirl so it coats the bottom, and set the pan on the burner.

Lower the heat to medium, and cook the *palacinka* for a little less than a minute, until the underside is lightly browned in a lacy

1½ cups walnuts, toasted and coarsely chopped

1 cup heavy cream, chilled (plus sugar to taste)

Recommended Equipment
A small ladle (⅓-cup volume or slightly larger)

A 7-inch crêpe pan or a nonstick skillet (7 inches wide on the bottom)

pattern. Flip it over with a spatula, and fry for ½ minute or longer, until the second side is lightly browned, then remove it to a warm platter. Heat the empty pan briefly, then rapidly coat it with butter, fill it with batter, and cook another *palacinka*. Repeat the sequence, stacking up the finished *palacinke* on the platter, until all the batter is used up.

Fill and serve the *palacinke* as soon as possible, while fresh and warm. Keep the platter in a warm spot, and cover the stack with a tent of foil or a large bowl turned upside down. Whip the heavy cream, unsweetened or with sugar to taste, to soft peaks. Stir the melted chocolate, and reheat it if necessary so it is smooth and warm.

Take one *palacinka* off the stack, and place it with its lacy-patterned side down. Spoon a generous tablespoon (or more) warm chocolate in the center of the pancake, and spread it over the *palacinka*, leaving an inch-wide border uncoated. Scatter a spoonful of chopped walnuts on the chocolate layer, then fold the round in half, hiding the fillings, and fold again into a plump quarter-round.

Fill and fold all the *palacinke* the same way. For each serving, place two quarter-rounds, overlapping, on a dessert plate, heap some cream on top, scatter some nuts on top of the cream, and drizzle warm chocolate in streaks and squiggles over the *palacinke* and the plate.

Quince Soup

ZUPPA ISTRIANA ALLE MELE COTOGNE

A cold-weather tradition I remember fondly took place around the *fogoler*, or open hearth, of my maternal grandparents' home. When neighbors would stop by to visit, everybody would gather around the crackling fire and talk. My grandparents would serve *zuppa istriana*, hearty spiced wine, to satisfy and warm their guests. My grandmother would roast some quince in the hearth, and have a pan of wine nestled in the coals, perking away. Then she would combine the two and pour the soup into a *boccaletta*, a ceramic pitcher. The pitcher was then passed around the hearth, and everybody would fish out a piece of quince with a fork (or sometimes with a thin sharp twig), take a good sip from the pitcher, and pass it on. The ceramic *boccaletta* was always considered a hospitable vessel, since no one could see how much one drank from it.

Today I prepare *zuppa istriana* when the snow begins to pile up outside and I want to have something warm and comforting to welcome my friends and family in from the cold.

Serves 6

3 ripe medium-sized quince

1 bottle good red wine (Merlot, Chianti, or Refosco will do)

½ cup sugar

Peel of 1 orange

3-inch piece stick cinnamon

First wipe all the fuzz from the quince, then core and cut each into eight segments. Set the segments on a parchment-paper-lined baking sheet, and bake in a 375° oven for 30 minutes, or until the quince are soft enough for a fork to penetrate easily.

In the meantime, put the wine, sugar, orange peel, and cinnamon in a pot over medium-high heat and boil for 15 minutes. Then strain the hot wine through a sieve into a ceramic bowl or pitcher. Add the roasted quince, and let steep for 20 minutes. Serve warm.

Tanya's Tour

ISTRIA

PULA: Lidia's Coliseum Kitchen
Location: On the southern tip of Istria

My mother has told you how much she loved to cook with Nonna Rosa (my *great-*grandmother) in the farmhouse kitchen in Busoler, where she spent many weekends and holidays. But in Pula, Lidia's birthplace and hometown in Istria, you can see where she and her little girlfriends played house and cooked in a make-believe kitchen. In fact, you can't miss it, since it is the most famous landmark in the region, and one of the most important antiquities in the world: the Roman Arena, an enclosed stone amphitheater built in the same style and at the exact same time (circa 80 A.D.) as the great Colosseum in Rome.

When I was a child and we toured the Arena during visits to Pula, my mother would show me the stone surface where she had set up her play kitchen, and the stone beds where the girls laid their dollies down to sleep. Now, as an art historian, I realize that growing up in Pula was extraordinary. And playing house on stones that were carved and set in place two thousand years ago, has imbued Lidia with a love of history and art, and a fascination with the roots of modern culture, that she has always shared with me and my brother.

The town is in fact filled with marvelous antiquities, and you'll pass them, as Lidia did, just walking through the cobblestone streets. After Julius Caesar established Pula as a Roman colony, it experienced a building boom. The Triumphal Arch of Sergius (built around 29 B.C.), and the Temple of Augustus (completed A.D. 14) are, along with the Arena, the most outstanding of many Roman monuments. Along the way, you'll find Byzantine churches, Renaissance artwork, and Austro-Hungarian palaces too.

The most majestic structure, though, is the Arena (a name bestowed by the Venetians). Smaller than the Roman Colosseum, it ranks as the sixth largest of the seventy-five amphitheaters built by the Roman Empire, and could seat twenty-five thousand spectators. More significant, it is considered today the most intact of all the classical amphitheaters, with its three ranks of wall arches and four side towers largely preserved.

And I can't imagine a more beautiful setting for an amphitheater, right on the edge of the sea, so you can glimpse the blue waves of the Adriatic through the arches. Lidia always talks about the concerts and operas she attended in the Arena when she was young. Such events are still being held today—along with annual summer rock festivals.

ROVINJ: Coastline and Cobblestones
Location: On the western coast of Istria, 36 kilometers north of Pula

Rovinj is a lovely resort town set on a peninsula in a twenty-five-mile stretch of protected coastline. The tall bell tower of the Baroque Church of St. Euphemia dominates the clustered white stone buildings of the town center, and you can spend the days meandering the narrow cobblestone lanes. At the church, visit the namesake saint's sarcophagus, which, according to legend, floated to Rovinj in the eighth century from some distant shore. The Baroque town hall, now a museum, has a collection of classical and contemporary art from the artists who have been drawn to Rovinj. Come nighttime, sit at the small waterfront bar where the tables and seats are carved entirely from stone. This city twinkles, and the streets are alive with people.

POREČ: Istria's Best Mosaics
Location: Up the western coast, north of Rovinj

The art and monuments of the Istrian Peninsula have been touched by the Roman, Byzantine, Venetian, Austro-Hungarian, Italian, Yugoslav, and now Croatian occupations. In the Basilica of Euphrasius (recognized by UNESCO), the early Christian mosaics immediately remind the viewer of Ravenna and highlight the talent of Venetian master mosaic artisans. Venice again comes to mind when one is viewing the slender bell towers or the Lion of St. Mark on the pentagonal tower in town. The Romanesque, Gothic, and early-Renaissance palaces, with biforium windows and sculptural decorations, concentrated around Marafor Square (the old Roman forum), bestow an elegance upon Poreč and allow the visitor to see such structures in a more undisturbed environment with respect to some Italian counterparts. The museum in town has many artifacts recovered from the Roman period, and one of the most spectacular low (*schiacciato*) reliefs from the first century, showing an olive harvest.

BERAM: Medieval Frescoes
Location: In central Istria, 5 kilometers northwest of Pazin, near the Pazin–Poreč main road

Beram is a small town with wonderful medieval frescoes in the Church of St. Martin and in the small Church of St. Mary of the Slate Floor. Occasional tours are offered, but you can get the keys to the church at house no. 33 or 22 (the Gortan family). Having the key and opening the church by yourself is part of the thrill. And then you will be all alone to enjoy the unique nature, high quality, and great preservation of the frescoes, which depict a wonderfully lively macabre dance of death, stories from the life of St. Martin, and the Passion of Christ.

NOVIGRAD: Romanesque Remains, Renaissance Towers, and Relaxation
Location: On the western coast of Istria, 15 kilometers southwest of Buje

A friendly town situated on a small point of land that juts out into the Gulf of Venice, Novigrad has a serenity that is quickly absorbed by its many visitors. In Roman times, the settlement was called Emonia, later Neapolis and Civitas Nova. Novigrad has the usual Roman and Romanesque remains that sprinkle the Istrian countryside and towns. In the Romanesque crypt of the church dedicated to St. Mary, St. Maximillian, and St. Pelagius (the patron saint), you can see the sarcophagus that holds Pelagius' bones. The fortified walls that surround the city are punctuated with two Renaissance towers, and the town hall overlooks the water. The Baroque Rigo Palace has a gallery on the ground floor with stone remains from around town (various periods), as well as contemporary art shows. The tradition of the *passeggiata* is alive and well in Novigrad, and this is the place to join in, walking and dining, both at a leisurely pace, along the water.

RABAC
Location: On the southeastern coast of Istria, 5 kilometers southeast of Labin

Rabac is a resort town where most public attention is paid to the great beaches, and to food and music until dawn. But two historic sites are worth a few hours away from the water. The Baroque palace, now a museum, was once home to the Battiala-Lazzarini family, who left everything behind after World War II, as so many did from Istria, one of the largest mass exoduses in history. The Church of the Blessed Mary's Birth is a two-nave church that has been beautifully maintained, dating from 1336. On the façade there is a representation of the Lion of St. Mark with a sphere in its mouth, and a beautifully executed portrait bust, from the late seventeenth century, of Antonio Bollani, a senator who fought against the Turks. Inside the church there are six marble altars, one of which holds the relics of St. Justin, brought here from Rome in the seventeenth century. There is also a painting on one altar believed to be done by the famous artist Palma Giovane (Palma the Younger), depicting a Madonna.

TRIESTE

Chapter 2

Pork, Sauerkraut, and Bean Soup
JOTA

Steamed Mussels Trieste Style
COZZE ALLA TRIESTINA

Sardines in Onion-Wine Marinade
SARDE IN SAOR

Basic Potato Gnocchi

Gnocchi Ravioli with Sausage-Spinach Filling
OFFELLE TRIESTINE

Potato Gnocchi Stuffed with Prunes
GNOCCHI DOLCI CON LE PRUGNE

Nonna Erminia's Farina Gnocchi
GNOCCHI DI GRIES

Home Fries Trieste Style
PATATE IN TECIA

Beef Goulash
GOULASH TRIESTINO

Breaded Veal Cutlets with Olive-Caper Relish
COTOLETTA ALLA VIENNESE

Sacher Torte
TORTA SACHER

Apple Strudel with Caramelized Walnuts
STRUDEL DI MELE CON NOCI

Trieste is a beautiful city at the apex of the Adriatic Sea, just ten miles from the border of Slovenia (formerly Yugoslavia). With a deep port and strategic location, the city has been fought over and dominated by the great powers of Europe for all of its history. For more than five hundred years, until the end of World War I, Trieste was considered part of the Austrian empire and officially ruled by the Hapsburg and Austro-Hungarian monarchs. Through the centuries, though, this gallant city struggled to keep its autonomy as a free port and trading center, and to preserve its Italian identity in language and culture.

Trieste's spirit of independence and openness to people of all religions and nationalities has long made it a destination of emigrants and fugitives from neighboring countries escaping persecution. My own family is part of this history. We were living in Istria when it became a part of Yugoslavia after World War II and could not accept living under communism. In 1956, we escaped to Trieste, where we had family. But life was hard for everybody in the aftermath of the war, and we ended up in San Sabba, a political-refugee camp on the outskirts of Trieste, where we stayed awaiting our chance to immigrate to the United States, which came at last in 1958.

Now I visit Trieste several times a year, usually my first stop on the way to our winery in Friuli or to my family's home in Istria. I always stay at least a couple of days, to visit with friends and relatives and enjoy the cultural delights of the city. I browse the bookshops and the art galleries, which display this small city's big influence on contemporary literature and modern Italian art. Concerts and operas at the marvelous Teatro Verdi are usually filled to capacity, yet I've been lucky and managed to catch such fine musicians as Placido Domingo and Riccardo Muti on my visits.

Of course, I need a few days to enjoy the food as well. When we fled to Trieste, we stayed first with Zia Nina, my maternal grandfather's sister. A professional cook and private chef for a wealthy family, she took me under her wing. I accompanied her on trips to the markets and specialty shops and assisted her in the kitchen. It was Zia Nina who showed me what the work of a chef entailed. And it was through her that I discovered the wonderful diversity of Triestine cuisine, reflecting the many cultures that have passed through the city or set down stakes there. Along with the distinctly Italian flavors and cookery, there's an enormous culinary influence from Middle Europe—Austria, Hungary, and the various Slavic cultures.

The unique location and landscape of Trieste also shape its cuisine. Since it is nestled in a large bay facing the Adriatic, with a fishing fleet docked along the port and a big fish market in the middle, seafood is very much part of the city's menu. All the restaurants lining the shore boast the catch of the day. On the inland side of Trieste, though, the land rises sharply to the Carso, a rugged and immense highland plateau. As the colorful red-tiled houses climb up the hills, and as the passage becomes steeper, so the cuisine becomes more rustic. Veal and pork shank, gnocchi, and hearty beef goulash are the food of the hill, so different from the food of the port.

For me, Trieste's richness lies in the micro-cuisines you can discover within the confines of the city, as you find microclimates in a vineyard. The diverse flavors and dishes make it an endlessly intriguing place to explore— and in which to eat.

Pork, Sauerkraut, and Bean Soup

JOTA

In Trieste, every home and every trattoria has a pot of this hearty soup perking on the stove, especially during the winter months, when the *bora*, a cold northeasterly wind, blows down from the Carso mountains above the city. Bean soups with pasta (*pasta e fagioli*) or rice are popular here too, as in other parts of Italy, but the combination of beans and sauerkraut is the favorite by far—a perfect example of the Slavic influence on the culinary culture of Trieste.

Serves 8 or more

1½ cups dried red kidney beans

5 quarts water

1-pound chunk fresh pork butt, rinsed before cooking

3 bay leaves

2 tablespoons chopped garlic

2 pounds russet (baking) potatoes, peeled and cut in 3-inch chunks

2 pounds sauerkraut (preferably the bagged, refrigerated variety)

1 tablespoon coarse sea salt or kosher salt, plus more to taste

½ pound smoked pork sausage (such as kielbasa)

½ pound fresh pork sausage (Eastern European–style or sweet Italian)

Freshly ground black pepper to taste

Extra-virgin olive oil for serving

Recommended Equipment
An 8-quart stockpot with a cover

Rinse the beans, and soak in 5 cups cold water for 8 hours or overnight. Drain, and put them in the stockpot with 5 quarts fresh cold water, the chunk of pork butt, bay leaves, chopped garlic, and potato chunks. Cover the pot and bring to a boil, set the cover slightly ajar, and adjust the heat to maintain a steady, gentle perk; cook for about 1½ hours.

Meanwhile, drain the liquid from the packaged sauerkraut, rinse it in a big bowl filled with fresh water, and drain through a colander. Repeat the rinsing and draining.

After 1½ hours, when the beans, pork, and potatoes are soft, add 1 tablespoon salt to the broth. Push the pork butt aside, and roughly mash the potato chunks in the bottom of the pot. Dump in the rinsed sauerkraut, stir well, cover the pot, and return to a moderate boil. Uncover, and cook for about 30 minutes, stirring occasionally, gradually reducing the soup.

Rinse the sausages, drop them into the pot, and cook for another 30 minutes. If the soup seems thin, boil it uncovered and mash the potatoes more, if they're still chunky, to provide thickening. If the soup is already reduced and dense, cook the sausages at a simmer, covered. When the sausages are cooked and the soup has the consistency you like, turn off the heat. Remove the bay leaves, and season generously with black pepper and salt to taste.

Serve the soup right away, or for best flavor, let it cool, refrigerate overnight, and serve the next day. Reheat slowly, stirring frequently. When very hot, remove the sausages and the remainder of the pork butt (most of it will have broken up) to serve later as a separate course. Drizzle extra-virgin olive oil over the *jota* and stir in; serve broth with beans and sauerkraut in warm soup bowls.

Steamed Mussels Trieste Style

COZZE ALLA TRIESTINA

This is one of those recipes that I am sure you will cook again and again. It takes just minutes, and when you set the mussels on the table, steaming and aromatic, they beckon the whole brood. Give everyone a warm soup bowl, put a ladle in the pan to scoop out the shellfish and luscious sauce, and set a basket of grilled country bread in the middle. Nothing could be better.

Serves 6

6 tablespoons extra-virgin olive oil, plus 2 tablespoons for finishing

4 garlic cloves, crushed and peeled

1 or 2 onions, cut into ¼-inch slices (2 cups sliced)

4 bay leaves, preferably fresh

½ teaspoon coarse sea salt or kosher salt

½ teaspoon peperoncino flakes, or to taste

½ cup white wine

3 pounds mussels, scrubbed, rinsed, and drained

¼ to ½ cup dry bread crumbs, or as needed

3 tablespoons chopped fresh Italian parsley

Recommended Equipment
A heavy saucepan, 12 inches or wider and about 5 inches deep, with a tight-fitting cover

Pour the olive oil into the saucepan, drop in the crushed garlic, and set over medium heat. When the garlic is fragrant and sizzling, stir in the onion slices, bay leaves, salt, and peperoncino.

Cook for a couple of minutes, tossing and stirring, just until the onions begin to wilt but still have some crunch. Pour in the wine, and bring to a boil. Immediately dump all the mussels into the pan, tumble them over quickly, cover tightly, and turn the heat up to high. Steam the mussels for 3 minutes, frequently shaking the covered pan, then toss them over, with a wire spider or wide slotted spoon. If the mussel shells have already opened (or almost all are open), leave the pan uncovered—otherwise, replace the cover and steam a bit longer.

As soon as the mussels have steamed open, sprinkle ¼ cup bread crumbs all over the pan. Quickly tumble the mussels over and over, still on high heat, so their liquor and the crumbs fall into the bubbling pan juices and create a sauce. (If the pan sauce is still thin after a minute of bubbling, sprinkle in more bread crumbs.)

Finally, drizzle 2 more tablespoons olive oil and sprinkle the chopped parsley on top, and toss briefly to distribute the seasonings. Turn off the heat, set the pan in the center of the table, and let people scoop mussels and sauce into their own warm soup bowls. (And remember to put out extra bowls for the shells.)

Sardines in Onion-Wine Marinade

SARDE IN SAOR

Fried fish steeped *in saor*, a tangy marinade of onions and vinegar, is enjoyed in all the regions around the northern Adriatic, in the Veneto, Friuli, and Istria. Many fish are suitable for this preparation, including mackerel, monkfish, young trout, even fillet of sole, but I especially love fresh sardines. When I was young and we had fried sardines for dinner, the leftover fried fish went into a crock of *saor*. It would keep for days and become even more delicious. With this recipe, you can assemble the dish and serve the sardines a few hours later. But if you let them marinate (in the refrigerator) for 1, 2, or even 3 days, the results will be worth the wait.

Serves 6 or more as an appetizer or a light dish

3 pounds fresh whole sardines

About 2 teaspoons coarse sea salt or kosher salt, or to taste

Flour for dredging

1½ cups vegetable oil, or as needed

½ cup extra-virgin olive oil, plus more for finishing

2 medium onions, peeled and sliced in ⅓-inch-thick half-moons (about 4 cups)

2 short branches fresh rosemary

4 bay leaves, preferably fresh

2 teaspoons red wine vinegar

½ cup water

1½ cups dry white wine

½ teaspoon coarsely ground black pepper, or to taste

To clean the sardines, first scrape and rub off the scales. To remove the head and innards, slice just behind the gills, severing the head from the back (dorsal side) of the fish, leaving it attached at the belly. Pull the head away from the body, drawing the attached innards from the fish. Slice the belly to open the cavity, and scrape out any remaining guts. Rinse the sardines well, washing away the scales, and pat dry with paper towels.

Salt the sardines lightly all over, and dredge well in flour. Pour vegetable oil into the skillet to a depth of ⅛ inch or so, and set over medium-high heat until it sizzles on contact with fish. Shake excess flour off the sardines, and lay in as many as will fit in the pan with a bit of space between them. Fry on the first side for several minutes, until the skin is crisp and golden and the flesh is cooked, then carefully flip them over and fry on the second side until evenly browned and just cooked through.

Lift the fish from the oil with a slotted spatula and set on paper towels. Salt the fish again, lightly. Fry, drain, and season the remaining sardines in the same way, adding more oil as needed.

When the fish are all cooked, pour out and discard the vegetable oil and wipe out the pan (or use another large skillet, if you have one). Pour in the ½ cup olive oil and set over medium heat. Stir in the sliced onions, rosemary, and bay leaves, and season with 1 teaspoon salt. Cook slowly, stirring occasionally, until the onions are soft and translucent, 5 minutes or so.

Recommended Equipment
A heavy-bottomed skillet or sauté pan, 12-inch diameter or larger

A gratin or casserole dish, about 6-cup capacity, sides at least 2 inches high, to marinate the fish in layers

Stir together the red-wine vinegar and water, and pour into the pan. Raise the heat, and cook the onions in the boiling liquid, stirring now and then, until it is reduced by half. Pour in the wine, bring to a boil, then adjust the heat to maintain steady bubbling. Stir in the coarsely ground black pepper, and cook until half of the wine has been absorbed or evaporated. Stir the onions so they cook evenly and just begin to color, but don't let them overcook or caramelize, as they should still have some texture to the bite.

Remove the skillet from the heat, and assemble the dish while the *saor* is hot. Spread a spoonful of onions in the bottom of the casserole dish, and lay half the sardines on top in a single layer. Cover with a denser layer of onions, then with another layer of sardines. Spread the rest of the onions on top—reserve enough to make this a generous layer—then scrape in all the juices from the skillet. Drop the rosemary and bay leaves on top.

Let the dish cool to room temperature and marinate for at least 2 hours before serving. For the best flavor, cover the dish with plastic wrap and marinate for 1 to 3 days in the refrigerator. Turn the layers occasionally to distribute the *saor*; always leave a layer of onions on top. Remove the dish—or a portion of sardines and *saor*—from the refrigerator several hours ahead, to warm to room temperature. Discard the herbs before serving.

Basic Potato Gnocchi

Use this versatile dough to make small gnocchi with the familiar ridged shape, or in the following recipes for stuffed *offelle* and prune gnocchi. This same dough can also be formed into long gnocchi, page 80, cooked and dressed Friuli style with brown butter, smoked ricotta, cinnamon, and sugar.

With all dishes using potato dough, keep several time factors in mind to get the best results. First, allow the cooked potatoes to air-dry thoroughly before you mix the dough—2 hours or even longer if possible. The drier the potatoes, the lighter the dough will be when cooked. Second, because potato dough is best when freshly mixed and cannot sit around, plan to shape the dough into gnocchi and cook them right away (or freeze them). If you are making stuffed gnocchi or *offelle*, have your filling ingredients ready when you mix the dough.

Makes about 1½ pounds of dough, enough for 6 servings of gnocchi in different shapes

1½ pounds baking potatoes (all about the same size)

¾ teaspoon salt

2 large eggs, beaten well

1½ cups all-purpose flour, plus more for working with the dough

Recommended Equipment
A potato ricer or vegetable mill with medium disk

Put the potatoes, whole and unpeeled, in a large pot with cold water covering them by at least 2 inches. Bring to a steady boil, and cook just until they are easily pierced with a fork or a sharp knife blade—don't overcook or let the skins burst.

Lift potatoes from the water, and let them drain briefly. Peel and press through the ricer or food mill as soon as you can, while they're still very hot, so their moisture will evaporate. Spread the riced potatoes in a thin layer on a baking sheet or tray, sprinkle the salt all over, and let them cool and dry for at least 20 minutes, preferably 2 to 3 hours.

To mix the dough, pile the dried potatoes in a large, loose mound on a board or a marble work surface. Pour the beaten eggs over them, then sprinkle 1 cup of the flour on top. Using your hands, work in the eggs, mixing and moistening the flour and potatoes. Gather into a single mass, and knead for several minutes, scraping in sticky bits from the board and your hands. Incorporate additional flour in small amounts, only as needed, until the dough is smooth, soft, and only slightly sticky. Avoid adding too much flour, which will make the gnocchi heavy and dry. Cover the dough with a towel, and form into gnocchi or *offelle* as soon as possible.

To shape traditional gnocchi, cut the finished dough into three or four pieces. Dust the work surface and your hands with flour. Roll one piece under your hands into a thick cylinder, and gradually stretch it to a long rope, about ⅔ inch thick. With a sharp knife or dough cutter, slice the rope crosswise into ½-inch lengths; sprinkle pieces with flour.

Hold a dinner fork, tines downward, at an angle to your work surface. Place one of the cut sides of a piece of dough against the tines. With your lightly floured thumb, press into the dough, and at the same time push it off the end of the fork onto a floured board. It will be hollow and curved where you pressed it, and ridged on the side that rolled off the fork. Press and roll the other cut pieces into gnocchi, dust them with flour, and set in a single layer on a floured tray, not touching.

Small gnocchi should be cooked (or frozen) as soon as they are all shaped. Follow the instructions for cooking and dressing *offelle* with sage butter and grated cheese, page 49.

Gnocchi—a Tradition in Trieste

Potato dough is used a lot in the *cucina triestina,* whether to make the traditional little dumplings dressed in a sauce or to envelop different fillings. There are the savory stuffed versions called *offelle,* and sweet kinds stuffed with fresh or dried prunes or different marmalades, then rolled in bread crumbs, sugar, and cinnamon.

Gnocchi Ravioli with Sausage-Spinach Filling

OFFELLE TRIESTINE

Offelle are just like ravioli, but what encloses the filling is potato dough rather than pasta dough, which lends a special soft texture. Here's how I coordinate the elements of this recipe so everything comes together perfectly. First I cook and rice the potatoes for the dough (as in the preceding recipe). While they're cooling, I make the sausage-spinach filling and let it cool. Then I mix the dough, roll it out, and stuff it to form plump *offelle*.

Makes about 3 dozen ravioli, serving 6

1 batch Basic Potato Gnocchi (preceding recipe)

For the filling
3 tablespoons butter

1 onion, chopped (about 1 cup)

1 teaspoon coarse sea salt or kosher salt

5 ounces sweet Italian sausage, removed from casing and crumbled

4 ounces ground veal

1 pound tender fresh spinach leaves, rinsed well and drained

For cooking and dressing the offelle with sage butter
2 tablespoons coarse sea salt or kosher salt for the pasta pot

12 tablespoons butter

8 large fresh sage leaves (or more smaller leaves)

Freshly ground black pepper to taste

Cook and rice the potatoes following the preceding dough recipe. While they are cooling, make the *offelle* filling.

Melt the butter in the skillet over medium heat, and stir in the chopped onion. Season with ¼ teaspoon salt, and cook until the onion wilts. Crumble in the sausage and ground veal. Salt again lightly, and fry the meats for a couple of minutes, stirring and breaking up any lumps, until browned. Heap the spinach in the pan, raise the heat, sprinkle the remaining salt over, and toss well. Drizzle a few tablespoons of water into the pan, and stir steadily as the leaves soften and release their liquid. Cook over moderate heat, stirring frequently (and scraping up any caramelization in the skillet), until the spinach is fully cooked and all of its moisture has evaporated. Remove from the heat and let cool (to cool rapidly, spread the filling on a plate).

While the filling cools, mix the potato dough. To form the *offelle*, cut the dough in four pieces; work with one and keep the others covered. Dust the work surface and rolling pin liberally with flour, and roll out the dough to a 12-inch round or slightly larger. Keep the dough from sticking by sliding a spatula or dough scraper under it and flouring the surface frequently. Cut 4-inch circles in the dough, using a round pastry cutter or the rim of a container or jar, dipped in flour. Remove the scraps of dough between the circles and loosen circles with the spatula.

Drop 2 teaspoons of filling on each circle, and fold the dough over, into a half-moon, with the filling enclosed. One at a time, pick up the *offelle* and pinch the edges of dough together with floured fingers. Turn the edges inward, in small overlapping folds,

1 cup freshly grated
Grana Padano or
Parmigiano-Reggiano

Recommended Equipment
A large heavy skillet or sauté
pan for the filling

A rolling pin and a 4-inch
round cutter

A 10-quart pot, with a cover,
for cooking the *offelle*

A 14-inch-wide sauté pan or deep
skillet, for dressing the *offelle*

and crimp to seal. Place completed *offelle* on a floured tray in a single layer, spaced apart. Press the scraps into another piece of dough, and form *offelle* the same way.

Meanwhile, bring 8 quarts of water with 2 tablespoons salt to a rolling boil, as you want to cook *offelle* right away. (Otherwise, freeze them solid on the tray, then pack in airtight containers.)

To make the sage butter for the *offelle*, put the butter in the big sauté pan or skillet, set it over low heat to melt, toss in the sage leaves, and grind in a generous amount of black pepper. Keep the sauce warm—but not cooking—so the sage leaves infuse the melted butter.

When the water is at a rolling boil, quickly brush off excess flour and drop half the *offelle* into the pot. Stir, cover the pot, and return to the boil over high heat. As the *offelle* rise to the surface, turn and stir them occasionally so they cook evenly and don't stick to each other. Boil for about 6 minutes, until cooked through— check for doneness by biting into one on the edge where the dough is thickest.

Lift out the *offelle* with a spider, drain briefly, and spill them into the warm butter in the pan. Tumble them in the pan, and shake it so the butter flows all around them. Return the water to the rolling boil, and cook the remaining *offelle*. Drain and drop them in the pan, on top of the first batch. Raise the heat slightly, turn and tumble the *offelle*, and shake the pan, until all are hot and coated with sage butter.

Turn off the heat, and sprinkle half of the grated cheese on top. Spoon portions of *offelle* onto warm plates, drizzle any hot sage butter left in the pan over each portion, and serve right away. Pass more cheese at the table.

Potato Gnocchi Stuffed with Prunes

GNOCCHI DOLCI CON LE PRUGNE

Sweet gnocchi are among my favorite childhood food memories. These were never dessert but a main course for the children: if the adults were to have gnocchi with venison *guazzetto* or other game sauce, some of the dough would be specially prepared just for us kids, stuffed with prunes or marmalade (or both) in winter, or with fresh ripe plums in late summer. I loved them all and remember that if we had three or four we were full until the next meal.

I make these prune and plum-jam gnocchi for my grandchildren today, but now the adults want them too. And though I still consider them a main dish, on occasion I do serve them for dessert. They also make a wonderful accompaniment to roast duck or goose—and a lovely breakfast!

To make sure these have a sweet, crunchy crumb coating, drop the cooked gnocchi into the bread-crumb mixture while they are still wet from the cooking pot. If you let them dry, the crumb topping will have difficulty adhering.

Makes about 18 gnocchi, serving 4 to 6

1 batch Basic Potato Gnocchi, page 47 (see below for timing of procedure)

4 tablespoons butter

2 cups fine dry bread crumbs

1 cup sugar, plus more for finishing

3 teaspoons cinnamon

½ cup chunky plum jam

18 plump, moist pitted prunes (about 5 ounces)

1 tablespoon coarse sea salt or kosher salt for boiling

Recommended Equipment
A large, heavy skillet for the bread-crumb coating

Make the potato dough, and keep it covered with a towel. Be prepared to cut, shape, and cook the gnocchi without delay.

To make the bread-crumb coating, melt the butter in the skillet over medium heat, stir in the bread crumbs, and toast them until golden. Let cool, then stir in the cup of sugar and the cinnamon. (I suggest you toast and cool the bread crumbs while the riced potatoes are cooling and drying, before mixing the gnocchi dough.)

Cut the potato dough into eighteen equal pieces. Flatten each piece into a disk on a lightly floured surface, and drop a generous teaspoon of jam in the center. Press a prune on the jam, and wrap the dough to enclose it. Pinch all around the edges to seal the gnoccho, roll it gently into a ball, and put it on a floured tray.

Meanwhile, bring 7 quarts of water with a tablespoon of salt to a rolling boil in the big pot. Shake excess flour off the gnocchi, and drop them into the water, stir, cover the pot, and return to the boil rapidly. As the gnocchi rise to the surface, turn and tumble them occasionally so they cook evenly and don't stick to each other. Boil for 20 minutes, until cooked through.

A wide 8-to-10-quart pot, with a cover, for cooking the stuffed gnocchi

Lift out the cooked gnocchi with a spider, drain only for a moment, and immediately spill them into the skillet of sugared bread crumbs. Roll the gnocchi around and around, until they're coated with crumbs on all surfaces.

Arrange the gnocchi on a platter, and dust the tops with more sugar. Serve warm or at room temperature.

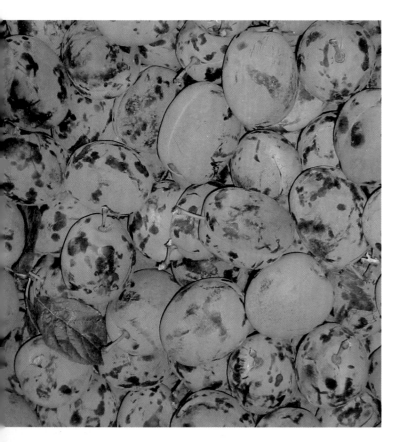

Nonna Erminia's Farina Gnocchi

GNOCCHI DI GRIES

Gnocchi made with *gries* (farina) were a favorite of mine as a child—perhaps because they were often cooked for holiday dinners. And I have especially fond memories of the *gnocchi di gries* made by my great-aunt Nina while we lived with her in Trieste, before we left for the United States. And though Zia Nina is gone, here is the way my mother, Erminia Matticchio, prepares them for our family today.

The little gnocchetti are delicious and simple to make. Because they cook in broth, and take on the flavor, homemade broth is always best, and together they make a festive and satisfying soup course. The gnocchi are a favorite soup garnish for children, and a good dish for infants starting to eat solid food.

To make a larger amount of gnocchetti, simply multiply the recipe. They keep well, so you can make a big batch, drain them after cooking, and pack in ziplock freezer bags; refrigerate or freeze. Reheat in boiling broth (if frozen, defrost them first).

Makes about 2 dozen small gnocchi, enough for 6 servings of broth

12 cups chicken or other poultry broth, preferably homemade

1 large egg

2 tablespoons very soft butter

¼ teaspoon salt, or as needed

½ cup farina (cream-of-wheat cereal—*not* instant), or more as needed

Freshly grated Grana Padano or Parmigiano-Reggiano, for serving

Recommended Equipment
A wide 4-quart saucepan for cooking the gnocchi

Another saucepan, 4-to-5-quart capacity, for the finished soup

Pour 6 cups of the broth into the wide saucepan, cover, and bring to a boil, then lower heat to keep broth at a gentle simmer.

Crack the egg into a small mixing bowl, and beat with a fork just to break it up. Drop in the butter and salt, and mix and mash together until completely blended, with no lumps of butter. Beat in the ½ cup farina—or more if needed—stirring vigorously, to make a stiff, moist dough.

Uncover the simmering broth and dip a teaspoon in, to moisten it. Scoop up a rounded teaspoonful of gnocchi dough, and drop it into the broth. Scoop up and shape all the dough into gnocchi; keep the broth simmering as you drop in the gnocchi (and dip in the spoon now and then, if the dough sticks). The gnocchi will sink at first, then rise to the surface after a few minutes. Stir gently so they don't stick to each other or the bottom of the pot.

When all the gnocchi are in the pan, set the cover ajar and adjust heat to maintain the gentle simmer. Cook for 30 minutes, until the gnocchi have expanded and are soft and cooked through, stirring occasionally. Turn off the heat, and let the gnocchi rest in the broth for at least 15 minutes, or until you are ready to serve.

Heat the remaining 6 cups of broth in another saucepan. Scoop the gnocchi out of their cooking broth and into the fresh, hot broth. If you wish, skim the surface of the cooking broth to remove some or all of the fat released by the gnocchi (it does have good flavor, though). Pour the cooking broth through a fine sieve—to remove any bits of dough—into the pan with the gnocchi and fresh broth, and heat to a simmer.

Serve hot in warm soup bowls, with four or more gnocchi per portion. Pass grated cheese for sprinkling on the soup.

Home Fries Trieste Style

PATATE IN TECIA

Crusty fried potatoes are as popular in northeastern Italy as they are in the United States. This Trieste version is as delicious as any I have ever tasted. You will get best results using a nonstick or cast-iron pan, browning and turning the potatoes over and over, so the caramelization is dispersed throughout. Use the timing here as a guideline, but follow your own tastes to create just the degree of crustiness you love.

Serves 4 or more

2 pounds russet (baking) potatoes

4 tablespoons extra-virgin olive oil

1 small onion, finely chopped (about 1 cup)

4 ounces bacon (about 4 thick-cut strips), cut in 1-inch pieces

½ teaspoon coarse sea salt or kosher salt, or to taste

¼ teaspoon freshly ground black pepper, or to taste

Recommended Equipment
A heavy 10-inch skillet, preferably nonstick or well-seasoned cast iron

Put the potatoes, whole and unpeeled, in a large pot, with cold water covering them by a few inches. Bring to a steady boil, and cook just until they are easily pierced with a fork or a sharp knife blade—don't let them get mushy or fall apart. Drain, cool, and peel the potatoes. Break them up into irregular chunks, roughly 1 inch or larger, with a sharp utensil. I use a large serving spoon with a thin edge, so the pieces have curved surfaces; avoid forking them apart, as the potatoes tend to crumble.

Meanwhile, heat 2 tablespoons of the olive oil in the skillet over moderate heat. Stir in the onion and heat until sizzling gently. Gather it on one side of the pan to cook and soften in a small area, and spread the cut bacon in the rest of the skillet. Fry the bacon, tossing and spreading it out, until the fat is rendered and the pieces are getting crisp, while the onion wilts and starts to color, 5 minutes or more.

Stir onion and bacon together, spill the potato chunks in the pan, and toss to mix everything. Raise the heat slightly, season with the salt and freshly ground pepper, and drizzle the remaining 2 tablespoons olive oil all over. Keep tumbling and tossing until the potatoes are hot and sizzling, spread them to fill the pan in an even layer, and press the top flat with a spatula.

Lower the heat, and cook without disturbing until the underside of the potato disk is caramelized and crispy, 5 minutes or longer. With the spatula, lift and turn the potatoes, breaking up the disk and bringing the crusty bits to the top. Stir and spread the potato chunks, and press flat, as before, and cook until the bottom is golden.

Repeat the sequence of turning the potatoes, pressing them into a flat disk or cake, caramelizing the bottom for a few minutes, then tumbling it over, about a half-dozen times.

After 40 minutes, or longer, when the potatoes have been crusted all over—and there are browned bits in every bite—season with salt and pepper to taste, press flat, and crisp the bottom well for a couple of minutes over medium heat. Place a large plate on top of the skillet and invert, dropping the cake out of the pan, then slide it back into the skillet for a final crusting.

Slide or invert onto the plate, and serve right away.

From the Garden and the Gulf

Garden vegetables are very important in Trieste, especially salads. *Radicchio zuccherino,* a small, green, leafy cluster from the chicory family, might as well be on the local flag, it is so popular; it is enjoyed with just some wine vinegar and olive oil tossed in a bowl that has been rubbed with garlic. The first cut, or *primo taglio,* is the most prized, each leaf being no bigger than a thumbnail. As the season progresses, the radicchio grows dense like grass and is recut at the root four or five times, each time becoming a little tougher and a little more complex and bitter. I love it at that stage, but I also love when it gets older and is mixed with hard-boiled eggs and cooked cannellini beans to soften it.

Radicchio goes well with fish preparations such as grilled *branzino* (Mediterranean sea bass) or grilled *orata* (gilded bass) as well as grilled or fried calamari or *seppia* (cuttlefish) braised in a sauce and served with polenta. So try some of these dishes at the local eating places when you are in Trieste.

You'll also find mussels doused with white wine and finished with some bread crumbs (Steamed Mussels Trieste Style, page 43) in bowls on trattoria tables. And in season there are mackerel and sardines *in saor* (Sardines in Onion-Wine Marinade, page 45), an onion-and-wine-vinegar marinade. It is all good, straightforward eating that you'll get in Trieste.

Beef Goulash

GOULASH TRIESTINO

Paprika is found nowhere in Italian cuisine except in the cooking of Trieste and its surroundings. Though the years of domination by the Austro-Hungarian monarchs were resented by the Italian-speaking Triestines, their descendants have not given up the city's traditional adaptations of Hungarian dishes like this goulash. Serve Middle European style with potatoes (boiled or mashed); Italian style with polenta or fettuccine; or with steamed rice.

Serves 6 to 10

⅓ cup extra-virgin olive oil

2 or 3 large onions (1½ pounds), peeled and cut in thick wedges

2 teaspoons coarse sea salt or kosher salt, or to taste

2½ pounds trimmed boneless beef chuck or round, cut for stewing (1½-inch chunks)

2 teaspoons Hungarian paprika, sweet or hot to taste

1 teaspoon dried oregano

1 branch fresh rosemary with lots of needles

3 cups cold water

1 tablespoon all-purpose flour

4 tablespoons tomato paste

Pour the olive oil into the saucepan, set over medium-low heat, and drop in the onion wedges. Toss to coat in oil, season with ½ teaspoon salt, and cook gently for 3 or 4 minutes, until sizzling and softening.

Spread the onions out on the pan bottom, and drop the beef cubes on top of the wedges, filling the pan in one layer. Sprinkle another ½ teaspoon of the salt, all the paprika, and the oregano over the meat, and drop in the rosemary. Without stirring or turning the meat pieces, cover the pan tightly. Heat the meat—with the seasonings on top and the onions below—so it starts to release its juices and stew. Check once or twice to see that the pan liquid is bubbling and that the onions are melting (not burning), but don't stir.

After 30 minutes or so, set the cover ajar a couple of inches and adjust the heat to keep the juices bubbling and slowly reducing. As they thicken, stir up the onions so they don't burn, and tumble the meat in the pan.

Continue cooking, partially covered, for another ½ hour or so. When the juices are concentrated and thick in the pan bottom, prepare the goulash sauce: Pour 3 cups of cold water in the small pan, and whisk in the flour. Set over low heat, and continue whisking until the flour is dispersed with no lumps, then whisk in the tomato paste. Heat gradually, whisking often, until the tomato-flour water just comes to a bubbling boil. Pour it into the big saucepan and stir well, turning the meat chunks over—they should be nearly covered in sauce.

Bring the sauce to a gentle simmer, put on the cover slightly ajar, and cook 45 minutes to an hour, until the meat is quite tender

Recommended Equipment

A heavy-bottomed 9- or 10-inch saucepan, such as an enameled cast-iron French oven, with a tight-fitting cover

A small saucepan, about 6-cup capacity

and the sauce somewhat reduced. Season with more salt to taste. Turn off the heat, and let the goulash cool in the pan for several hours before serving, or refrigerate overnight.

Reheat slowly, stirring now and then, until the meat is thoroughly heated; thin the sauce with water if it has thickened too much. Serve hot.

Favorite Meats

Meat dishes exemplify the range of influences and flavors that have established themselves in the kitchens of Trieste. Breaded veal cutlets—*Cotoletta alla Viennese*, page 60—and a paprika-laced goulash, *Goulash Triestino,* are clear markers of the Austro-Hungarian domination of the city. And the Slavic influence from the East is evident in dishes like *porcina,* boiled pork with sauerkraut and gratings of fresh horseradish, and *Jota,* the ubiquitous Pork, Sauerkraut, and Bean Soup, page 42.

Breaded Veal Cutlets with Olive-Caper Relish

COTOLETTA ALLA VIENNESE

This quick rendition of breaded cutlets with a lively relish will be a favorite at your house, I am sure. For a special brunch, top a cutlet with a fried or poached egg.

Serves 6

¾ cup large green olives, pitted (10 or more olives)

3 tablespoons small capers, drained

4 small anchovy fillets, finely chopped (1 tablespoon)

Juice of 1 lemon, freshly squeezed and strained

12 veal scallops, 3 ounces each

1½ cups flour, or as needed

2 cups bread crumbs, or as needed

3 large eggs, lightly beaten

½ teaspoon coarse sea salt or kosher salt

Freshly ground black pepper

½ cup vegetable oil, or as needed

5 tablespoons butter, or as needed

Recommended Equipment
A meat mallet

A large sieve or colander

A wide, heavy skillet or sauté pan, preferably 14-inch diameter

For the savory relish, chop the olives and the capers into small bits and stir together in a small bowl with the chopped anchovies and lemon juice.

Pound the veal scallops, one at a time, with the toothed side of the meat mallet, tenderizing and flattening them into very thin ovals.

Spread the flour in one large plate, and the bread crumbs in another. Pour the eggs into a wide, shallow bowl, and beat in the salt and freshly ground pepper to taste. Set the colander or sieve in a bowl. Cover a tray or large platter with several layers of paper towel.

Dredge each cutlet in flour, coat well with egg, and lay it in the sieve to drain (return collected drippings to the egg bowl if needed). When all are in the sieve, coated with egg, start heating the ½ cup of oil and the butter together in the skillet over medium heat.

Bread four cutlets—or as many as will fit in the skillet in an uncrowded layer—pressing both sides in the platter of bread crumbs, so the crumbs adhere and cover the meat. When the butter is melted and bubbling, lay the cutlets in the pan, and fry until nicely colored on the underside, about 2 minutes, then flip and fry the second side another 2 minutes or so, until the veal is cooked and the coating is golden and crisp. Adjust the heat so the crumbs color gradually but don't burn.

Meanwhile, bread another batch of cutlets. Move the fried ones to the paper towels to drain, and clear stray bits of breading from the pan before laying in the next batch. Fry all the cutlets, clearing the skillet between batches and adding oil or butter if needed. Layer cutlets on the platter with paper towels in between to absorb oil, and keep them warm near the stove or in a low oven.

When all the cutlets are cooked and drained, lay two on a warm dinner plate for each portion. Scatter a generous tablespoon of the olive-caper-anchovy relish over the cutlets, and serve right away.

Sacher Torte

TORTA SACHER

Sacher torte is known around the world as a specialty of Vienna (at the Hotel Sacher) but is commonly found in pastry shops and in home kitchens of Trieste. It is sure to delight the chocolate lovers in your household. It will keep well for a few days in a cookie tin without refrigeration, but for longer storing time do refrigerate. You can also bake and freeze the cake layers in advance. Defrost and assemble and glaze the torte before serving.

Serves 10 or more

For the torte
6 ounces (1½ sticks) butter, plus 1 tablespoon for the cake pan

¾ cup sugar

5 large eggs, separated

5 ounces semisweet chocolate, melted and lukewarm

1 cup all-purpose flour, plus more for the cake pan

For filling and glazing the torte
2 cups apricot preserves

⅔ cup light corn syrup

2 tablespoons dark rum

6 tablespoons water

Pinch of salt

10 ounces semisweet chocolate, chopped in small chunks

Whipped cream for serving

Recommended Equipment
A 9-inch springform pan and a 9-inch parchment circle

Butter the bottom of the cake pan, cover it with the parchment, then butter the top of the paper and the sides of the pan. Heat the oven to 375°.

Cream the butter and sugar in the bowl of the electric mixer, using the whisk attachment, until light and smooth. Incorporate the egg yolks, one at a time, and then pour in the chocolate gradually, mixing it in thoroughly and scraping the sides of the bowl as needed. On low speed, incorporate the flour. Whip the egg whites by hand (or by machine, in a clean bowl with a clean whisk) to stiff peaks. Fold the egg whites into the batter with a rubber spatula. Scrape the batter into the prepared cake pan, and spread in an even layer.

Bake until a cake tester comes out clean—or until the top springs back when lightly pressed—35 minutes or longer. Put the pan on the wire rack, cool briefly, then remove the side ring of the springform and let the cake cool completely.

Lift the cake off the metal pan bottom, and peel off the parchment. Slice the cake horizontally in thirds, making three thin layers. Return the top layer of the cake to the metal pan bottom, upside down, so the crusty baked top is against the pan. This will be the base of the *torta*. To prepare for glazing, set the wire rack inside a rimmed baking sheet, and place the base layer, on the metal pan bottom, on the rack.

Put ⅓ cup of the apricot preserves in a small saucepan with ¼ cup of water, and heat, stirring, until the preserves dissolve

An electric mixer

A wire rack and icing spatulas
for glazing the *torta*

into a loose syrup. Brush this syrup on all the cut surfaces of
the layers, including the base, to moisten the cake.

To fill the layers, put 1 cup of thick apricot preserves in a bowl,
and stir just to loosen. Spread ½ cup of the filling over the base
layer. Now place the center layer of the cake (the layer with two
cut surfaces) on top of the base, and spread the remaining apricot
filling over the top. Finally, place the bottom layer of cake over the
filling, upside down, so the flat, smooth surface that was originally
the very bottom of the cake is now the top. Center the three layers
so the sides of the *torta* are straight, and scrape off any drippings of
apricot that oozed out.

To make a thick, smooth apricot glaze to seal the cake, put
the remaining ⅔ cup of apricot preserves in the small saucepan with
4 tablespoons of water, and heat to a simmer, stirring. Pour the
preserves through a small strainer set in a cup, to remove any
solid bits of apricot, and immediately pour the hot strained glaze
from the cup over the *torta*. (If you feel confident, hold the
strainer over the center of the *torta*, and pour the glaze directly out
of the pan.)

Spread the glaze rapidly with an icing spatula, before it cools,
coating the top completely, then spilling glaze over the edge and
down the sides. Smooth the glaze against the sides to seal them.
Let the apricot glaze set, and scrape up any glaze that dripped on
the rack or into the pan underneath.

Meanwhile, prepare the chocolate glaze. Pour the corn syrup,
rum, and 2 tablespoons water into a small heavy saucepan, add the
pinch of salt, and bring to a boil, stirring. Put the chopped
chocolate in a large heat-proof bowl. Boil the syrup for a couple
of minutes, until slightly thickened, then pour it over the chocolate, and stir until all the chunks have melted and the glaze is
smooth and shiny. Let it cool, stirring occasionally, until barely
warm to the touch and just starting to thicken.

Pour the chocolate glaze over the top of the *torta*, spreading
it with a spatula so it coats the top evenly and flows over the edge
and down the sides. Smooth the sides so they are evenly coated,
with no bare spots. Let the glaze solidify at room temperature.

Lift the *torta* off the rack onto a cake plate, still on the metal
disk. If you prefer, slide a broad spatula (or two) under the cake

to separate it from the metal disk, then lift and move. Collect any chocolate glaze that's dripped into the pan, to use again in the future. (If you want, warm up the excess glaze and spoon it into a paper piping cone. Write the name "Sacher" across the top—the traditional inscription on Viennese *Sachertorte*—or pipe other decorative flourishes.)

Cut in wedges to serve, with mounds of whipped cream.

Caffès and Sweets

The evening stroll, the *passeggiata,* with stops at the local *caffè*s and pastry shops, is very much a part of life in Trieste. The strollers often end up at the expansive Piazza Unità, which faces the sea. Here the desserts have a very strong Middle European influence. You can find some of the best strudels made anywhere in Europe, and Sacher and Dobos *torte* that are equal to any Viennese version. Of course, *un caffè* must follow any dessert, and Trieste is the coffee city of Italy. It is through Trieste's duty-free port that most coffee comes into Italy, and Trieste is the home of the renowned Illy Coffee.

Apple Strudel with Caramelized Walnuts

STRUDEL DI MELE CON NOCI

Strudel seems like a complex dessert, but once you have a feeling for the dough and its elasticity, all else is elementary. I recall my grandma saying that for the strudel to be good you need to be able to read the newspaper through the stretched dough, so rolling and stretching it as thin as you can is the key to a special strudel.

Keep one idea in mind: do not be afraid to handle the dough, lift it up on the back of your hands, curl your fingers into a fist, and stretch the dough with your knuckles. It will yield and stretch without tearing. Or grasp one edge and lift the sheet above the work surface and let it hang free—just the force of gravity will make it stretch. Or, if you have someone to help you, pull the dough from opposite sides—it will stretch that way too. Don't worry if the edges remain a bit thicker: you can cut those off with a pizza cutter before filling the strudel.

This is a large strudel; it can be served for a couple of days. Baked strudel freezes well, so leftover pieces can be wrapped securely and frozen for a couple of months. Defrost when needed, and reheat before serving.

Makes 1 large strudel, serving 10 or more

For the strudel dough
1¼ cups all-purpose flour, plus more for working with the dough

⅓ teaspoon salt

1 tablespoon plus 2 teaspoons extra-virgin olive oil

5 tablespoons water or as needed

For the filling
1 cup golden raisins

4 tablespoons dark rum

1 cup fine dry bread crumbs

1 teaspoon cinnamon

1½ cups sugar

Mix the strudel dough several hours or the day before baking. In a large bowl, toss together the 1¼ cups flour and the salt with a fork. Drizzle the oil all over, and toss with the flour. Sprinkle the water over, tossing it in a tablespoon at a time, then mix vigorously to bring the dough together. Incorporate more water in small amounts if the dough seems dry or won't stay together.

Turn the dough out on a work surface, and knead with your hands until the clumps have disappeared and the dough is smooth and elastic, about 3 minutes. Add flour only if the dough remains sticky after you've been kneading for a minute or more.

Flatten the dough into a disk, wrap well in plastic wrap, and let it rest for at least 2 hours at room temperature, or refrigerate for a day. (Let chilled dough sit at room temperature briefly before rolling.)

Plump the raisins with the rum in a small bowl, until all the liquor is absorbed.

Spread the bread crumbs in a large, heavy skillet, and set it over medium heat. Stir and toss the crumbs until they begin to color.

1 cup walnuts, chopped into
¼-inch bits

2 small lemons

3 pounds tart green apples,
such as Granny Smith

10 tablespoons very soft butter,
or more if needed

2 tablespoons cane-sugar crystals

Powdered sugar, whipped cream,
or ice cream for garnish (optional)

Recommended Equipment

A rolling pin or heavy wooden
dowel

A linen tablecloth or sheet,
or other smooth cloth (a yard
square or larger)

A half–sheet pan (12 by 18 inches)
or a similar large, rimmed baking
sheet, lined with baking parchment

A pastry brush

Lower the heat a bit, and keep stirring until they're deep golden brown, then quickly spill the crumbs into a bowl, before they burn. Sprinkle ½ teaspoon cinnamon over the hot crumbs, and toss in. When the crumbs cool completely, stir in 10 tablespoons sugar.

In the same skillet, again over medium heat, stir together the chopped walnuts and 2 tablespoons sugar, until the sugar caramelizes and coats the nuts. Immediately spill onto a sheet pan to cool.

Rinse and dry the lemons, remove their zest with a fine grater, and squeeze out and strain their juice. Peel, core, and cut the apples in thin slices, and toss in a large bowl with the lemon zest and juice, the remaining ¾ cup sugar, and the remaining ½ teaspoon cinnamon. Toss in the plumped raisins, mix well, and let the apples steep in the sweetened fruit juices.

Arrange a rack in the center of the oven, and heat it to 425°. With a pastry brush, lightly coat the parchment in the sheet pan with a tablespoon or two of soft butter.

On a large, lightly floured work surface, start rolling the strudel dough into a rectangular shape, turning it over frequently and dusting the surface with flour as needed. When it becomes a thin sheet, stretch it with your hands, both on the table and as you lift and turn it over. Gradually roll and stretch the rectangle until it's about 30 inches on the long sides and 20 inches on the shorter sides. Trim thick edges with a knife or a pizza cutter.

Now arrange the linen cloth on the table—under the dough sheet—to roll up the strudel. If someone can assist you, hold the dough sheet in the air while the cloth is placed flat and smooth on the work surface. Line up a long edge of cloth with the edge of your counter. Lay the dough, long side facing you, on top of the cloth, setting it a few inches in from the edge of the cloth. (If you *don't* have a helper, lay out the cloth on another surface, and move the dough rectangle over to it.)

When the cloth and the dough are in place, brush the entire surface of the dough with 4 tablespoons or so of soft butter. Sprinkle the bread-crumb mixture evenly all over the dough, then scatter the caramelized walnut pieces on top.

Next, lift the apple slices from the bowl, letting excess juices drain off, and heap them in a narrow row, running left to right, set in about 3 inches from the long edge of dough near you. Make the row straight and compact and slightly shorter than the dough sheet, so there are several inches of bare dough on the left and right sides of the apple row.

To roll the strudel, grasp the edge of the cloth and lift it, bringing the uncovered margin of dough against the apples. Hold the cloth close to the filling, so you have good control, then lift and push it forward, rolling the entire row of apples over and wrapping it snugly in dough. Keep rolling to wrap all the dough around the strudel, forming a long, neat log. Twist the unfilled flaps of dough on the ends of the log, so they're snug against the filling, then trim and tuck them under the strudel.

Position the long side of the parchment-lined baking sheet against the strudel—get a helper again if you can—and use the cloth to roll the long log over the rim, onto the pan (the ends will extend out of the pan). Roll again, if necessary, so the seam of dough is on the bottom. Slide the cloth out from under the dough. Gently curve the ends of the log, bringing them onto the sheet, to give the strudel a crescent or horseshoe shape.

Brush the pastry all over with the remaining butter. With a sharp thin knife, slice several short slits in the top, as steam vents, cutting through the top dough layers. Sprinkle the cane-sugar crystals over the top.

Put the strudel into the oven, and lower the thermostat to 375°. After 30 minutes, rotate the baking sheet back to front. The pastry should be lightly colored—if it's already getting dark, lower the temperature to 350°. Bake another 20 to 30 minutes, until the filling is cooked (the juices may bubble through the slits) and the pastry is deep golden brown and crisp.

Let the strudel cool in the pan for 30 minutes or so, then lift it with two long spatulas to a wire rack or board. Serve slices of the strudel warm or at room temperature, with powdered sugar, whipped cream, or ice cream.

Tanya's Tour

TRIESTE

TEATRO ROMANO AND SAN GIUSTO: A Surprise on the Way Up San Giusto
Location: Uphill from the city center, along the Via del Teatro Romano

Unfortunately, if you read this suggestion, you can't have the experience I had as a youngster. Walking up the hill of San Giusto toward the cathedral and castle that overlook the city, I stumbled one day on a hidden treasure: a small amphitheater, built into the hillside, a relic from the ancient Roman town Tergeste (founded in the first century B.C.), which became the city of Trieste. It was a thrilling surprise.

Even though you now know what lies ahead, you can enjoy the sense of discovery by making a leisurely excursion from the sea side of the city—the Piazza dell'Unità d'Italia is a good starting point—and heading uphill, along the winding Via del Teatro Romano. You will be amazed, I am sure, to see the theater spring up before you, a powerful expression of the past in the midst of modern life. And you might find, as I did, the theater's charming residents—the carefree cats of Trieste—basking in the sun on the seats, and partaking of the offerings from adoring local "cat ladies." A cat fancier myself, I loved the sight and always imagine that the Roman cats of Tergeste must have found these sun-warmed stones equally to their liking.

After visiting the theater—fully excavated and restored, by the way—continue your stroll up the hill, to reach the Castello and Cattedrale di San Giusto. From here, enjoy wonderful views of the city and coast and marvelous glimpses into the past, including mosaic pavements from a temple long gone, and mosaic wall decorations by Venetian masters that will remind you of St. Mark's in Venice and mosaics in Ravenna.

CASTELLO DI MIRAMARE: A Palace by the Sea
Location: About 10 kilometers northeast of Trieste

When you drive to Trieste from Venice, along the cliff-hugging coast road, as you approach the city you'll see a stunning white castle, rising in solitary splendor on a point of land, surrounded by the glistening blue Adriatic. This is the Castello Miramare, built in 1856 for the Austrian Archduke Maximilian and his wife, Carlota, daughter of the King of Belgium; it became their home for several years, and is now open to visitors. A tour of the palace reveals the original luxurious furnishings and royal chambers, including a fantastic music room where Carlota played the piano, and a true throne room. Even more spectacular are the formal gardens studded with botanical rarities. A stroll around the grounds with its sweeping views is a rare delight.

GROTTA GIGANTE: Giant Cave
Location: About 10 miles north of Trieste, in Sgonico

One of the most spectacular geological sites in the rugged Carso plateau is the Grotta Gigante, or "Giant Cave," a famed tourist attraction listed in the *Guinness Book of World Records* as the largest visitable cave in the world. I have always found, both as a child and as a parent, that it is a great place to visit. I think that, no matter what your age, you too will be fascinated by the rock formations, the mysterious atmosphere, and the immensity of the cave. The common wisdom of cave lore is that the whole of St. Peter's Basilica could fit in the main chamber of the cave—easy to believe when you are there. And while you are up in the Carso, be sure to enjoy the rustic "food of the hill," which my mother mentions in her introduction to this chapter.

RISIERA DI SAN SABBA: A Museum of Wartime Memories
Location: About 6 kilometers to the west of Trieste center,
on Via Giovanni Palatucci

This historic site on the outskirts of Trieste was originally a rice factory, or *risiera*. But it played two very different roles in the city's recent history. Toward the end of World War II, it became the only extermination camp in Italy, with its own crematorium. From the summer of 1944 through May 1945, about 150 prisoners were executed here every day—Gypsies, Jews, partisans, Slovenians, and Croats.

After the war, the *risiera* was converted into a refugee camp for those who fled to Trieste from communist Eastern Europe but could not be absorbed by the city or other parts of devastated Italy. And so, as my mother explains, this became her home and that of my uncle and my grandparents for two years, while they waited for their chance to immigrate to America and start a new life.

Today the *risiera* is a museum that speaks to both the atrocities committed here and the shelter provided to the flood of postwar refugees. It helps us remember the thousands who perished, and the thousands who gave up family, friends, and possessions in their flight toward freedom. Even if you don't have family ties to this terrible history, the *risiera* is an important place to visit.

FRIULI

Chapter 3

Velvety Cornmeal-Spinach Soup
PAPAROT

Frico with Potatoes and Montasio Cheese
FRICO CON LE PATATE

Frico with Apples and Montasio Cheese
FRICO CON LE MELE

Crispy Swiss Chard Cakes with Montasio
BIETOLE SOFFRITTE CON FORMAGGIO

Potato Gnocchi Friuli Style
GNOCCHI LUNGHI FRIULANI

Risotto with Spinach
RISOTTO CON SPINACI

Braised Pork Chops with Savoy Cabbage
COSTICINE DI MAIALE CON VERZE

Sautéed Spiced Beef Cutlets
BRACIOLE AROMATICHE

Roasted Lamb Shoulder
AGNELLO DI LATTE ARROSTO

Tangy Skillet Turnips and Potatoes
RAPE E PATATE ALL'ACETO

Apple Torte with Bread Crumb and Hazelnut Crust
TORTA DI MELE DI CARNIA

Friuli-Venezia Giulia is one region, but it consists of three counties, each county having a distinctly different dialect, different culture, and different food. There is the Friuli part, the Venezia part, and the Giulia part—hence the name. The capital of the region is Trieste.

Giulia is in the southeast, bordering on Slovenia and the Adriatic Sea. The food of this area has a strong Middle European flavor, and much of it comes from the seas. The port of Trieste was a stronghold for the Austro-Hungarian navy, and the Emperor Franz Joseph would often visit Trieste expecting to find the elegant desserts of his Vienna: strudel, Sacher torte, and Dobos, to name a few. These desserts are still favorites today, served both at home and in the pastry shops of Trieste.

The part referred to as Venezia is to the west and borders on the Veneto, where fertile plains spill into the Adriatic. This area is the richest agriculturally, with its lush pastures that feed the cows that give us the great Asiago cheese and Grana Padano, as well as its fertile fields that supply all of Italy with fresh vegetables and fruit. The cuisine here has been very much influenced by the long domain of the Serenissima, the Venetian Republic, which lasted more than seven hundred years and made Venezia an economic stronghold in the spice trade. Black pepper, cloves, cinnamon, ginger—all nonindigenous products—are very visible in the cooking of this area and throughout Friuli-Venezia Giulia.

Friuli and its food are at the heart of this chapter. There the plains are full of cornfields that extend to the north over the gently rolling hills of the Collio, where some of the best Italian white wines are produced. Grappa has also been made there for centuries. Grappa is the distillation of the pumice after the wine has been made, a clear liquid that delivers punch both in flavor and in alcohol. This tradition reflects a frugal people; the area saw many lean times as it was tossed between regimes.

Beyond these hills lies the rich tableland studded with little farms known as Le Malghe, where cows graze on wild herbs and flowers. From their milk comes one of the best-tasting cheeses, Montasio. Milky and mellow when young, it is used to make the national dish, *frico,* in which the cheese melts and crisps in a hot pan with a savory filling of potatoes or other vegetables or sausage, or a sweet filling of fruit, such as apples.

One staple, as important to the *friulani* as the potato is to the Irish, is polenta. Polenta is made from cornmeal—a recent arrival, introduced to the area after the discovery of the Americas, but you would never know it, for polenta is as Friulian as Udine, the capital city of Friuli.

Friuli holds a very special place in my heart. Thirty years after migrating from Trieste to America, we returned to buy in the Colli Orientali del Friuli, a vineyard and a home in Cividale del Friuli. But even before we opened a winery, I would come often to Friuli, searching for the best wines, the regional products that I could bring back and share in my restaurants with my American clientele. My children, Joseph and Tanya, would accompany me on my continuous quest for new recipes, new products, and good wines. We fell in love with the land and forged friendships with local producers.

Among them are Valter Scarbolo and his family. They run La Frasca, a wonderfully typical trattoria in Lauzzacco, and they produce a delicious and affordable selection of Scarbolo wines. In 1997, Joseph proposed that we buy a vineyard with the collaboration of Valter, who had the winemaking skills. Thus Azienda Agricola Bastianich was born. We now produce the whites Tocai Friulano, an indigenous varietal, and Vespa, a blend of Sauvignon, Chardonnay, and Picolit. Reds are the new frontier in Friuli, and our Vespa Rosso and Calabrone are a testament to the capabilities of producing great reds in Friuli. Our wines have been receiving yearly Tre Bicchieri, one of the most prestigious Italian wine awards, given by the Gambero Rosso, a renowned publishing house specializing in books on food and wine.

Velvety Cornmeal-Spinach Soup

PAPAROT

This is a poor man's simple recipe, a warm filler for cold winter days in Friuli. I use spinach, but any available green vegetable would have been used, and would be good. Cornmeal lovers will appreciate this; it has all the comforts of porridge, filled with the flavors of Friuli.

Serves 4

4 ounces (about ¾ cup) yellow polenta

3 tablespoons all-purpose flour

3 cups hot poultry or vegetable broth

2 garlic cloves, smashed and peeled

3 tablespoons butter

Coarse sea salt or kosher salt to taste

About ½ pound young spinach leaves, rinsed

Freshly ground black pepper to taste

Recommended Equipment
A heavy-bottomed 6-quart saucepan, 10 inches or wider

Whisk together the polenta and flour in the saucepan, then whisk in about ½ cup of the hot broth, to make a smooth, loose batter. Continue adding the rest of the broth, and bring to a moderate boil, whisking constantly.

Drop the garlic cloves and the butter into the pan, and salt lightly. Cook the soup at a bubbling simmer for about 25 minutes, whisking and stirring frequently, until the polenta has cooked and thickened. Stir in the spinach leaves, and cook 10 minutes more.

Remove from the heat, and season with more salt and freshly ground pepper to taste. Rest for 5 minutes, then serve hot, removing the garlic cloves if you like.

Velvety Cornmeal-Spinach Soup (Paparot) *with a slice of* Frico *(see recipe page 76)*

Frico with Potatoes and Montasio Cheese

FRICO CON LE PATATE

Serves 6 as an appetizer

1 medium baking potato (½ pound)

2 tablespoons extra-virgin olive oil

1 small onion, sliced (½ cup)

½ cup thinly sliced scallions

¼ teaspoon coarse sea salt or kosher salt

Freshly ground black pepper to taste

½ pound Montasio cheese, shredded

Recommended Equipment
A 10-inch nonstick skillet

Cook the potato in a pan of gently boiling water just until it is easily pierced with a sharp knife, all the way through, but is still intact and not mushy. Drain and cool the potato, remove the skin, and slice it into neat ¼-inch-thick rounds.

Pour the olive oil into the skillet, set over medium heat, and scatter in the sliced onion and scallions. Cook for a minute, then scatter the potato rounds in the pan. Toss and tumble the potatoes with the onion and scallions, and season with the salt and grinds of black pepper. Cook for about 5 minutes, tossing frequently, until the potato rounds are lightly crisped and golden.

Pile the shredded Montasio on top of the vegetables. Slide a metal spatula under some of the potatoes and flip them over, incorporating some of the cheese. Turn all the slices over and over this way, until the cheese shreds are well distributed. With the spatula, clean the sides of the skillet and smooth the vegetables and cheese into a neat pancakelike disk, filling the pan bottom.

Lower the heat, and let the *frico* cook undisturbed as the cheese melts and crisps, until the bottom is very brown and nicely crusted, about 5 minutes. Shake the pan to loosen the disk, put a large plate on top and invert, dropping the *frico* onto the plate, then slide it back in the skillet, top side down. Cook until the second side is crisp and brown, about 5 minutes more.

Slide (or invert) the *frico* onto the plate, and blot up excess oil from the cheese with a paper towel. Slice into six wedges, and serve immediately.

Frico with Apples and Montasio Cheese

FRICO CON LE MELE

Serves 6

2 Golden Delicious apples
or other firm apples (about
10 ounces)

1 tablespoon extra-virgin olive oil

½ pound Montasio cheese,
shredded

Recommended Equipment
A 10-inch nonstick skillet

Peel and core the apples, and slice into wedges about ½ inch thick. Pour the olive oil in the skillet, and set over medium heat. Scatter the apple wedges in the pan, and toss to coat with oil. Cook and caramelize the apples for about 8 minutes, tossing frequently, until tinged with brown and softened but not mushy. Spill the caramelized apples onto a plate.

Sprinkle half of the shredded Montasio in an even layer over the bottom of the skillet. Return the apples to the pan, spread them evenly on top of the cheese, then sprinkle the remainder of the shredded cheese over the apples.

Lower the heat, and let the *frico* cook undisturbed until the bottom is very brown and crisped, about 10 minutes. If the cheese releases a lot of fat in the pan, blot it up with paper towels. Shake the pan to loosen the disk, put a large plate on top and invert, dropping the *frico* onto the plate, then slide it back in the skillet, top side down. Cook until the second side is crisp and brown, about 7 minutes more.

Slide (or invert) the *frico* onto the plate, blot up oil, and slice into six wedges. Serve hot.

The Frico Way

Frico served with a slab of grilled polenta while everyone is seated around a *fogoler* with a crackling fire—this is Friuli. The *fogoler* is a four-sided open hearth with a central hood, from which the polenta cauldron hangs. As in most of the world today, these romantic traditions are disappearing, but if you travel to Friuli and wander off to a small-town restaurant or trattoria on a cold winter's day, chances are that you will find a *fogoler* with the fire raging and something perking on it.

Crispy Swiss Chard Cakes with Montasio

BIETOLE SOFFRITTE CON FORMAGGIO

These cheese-encrusted rounds of cooked chard, similar to *frico*, are from Carnia, a district of quaint cities and towns scattered along the Carnic Alps. The milk from the cows grazing on its high-altitude pastures makes some of the best Montasio in all of Friuli.

I like to serve these unusual and irresistible cakes as a highlight of lunch or brunch, topped with a poached egg, or in between slices of country bread, as a delectable vegetarian "cheeseburger." They're a marvelous accompaniment to grilled meats, or, cut into small wedges, a great party nibble.

Serves 6

2 pounds Swiss chard

4 tablespoons extra-virgin olive oil

1 medium onion, thinly sliced (1½ cups)

1½ teaspoons coarse sea salt or kosher salt, or to taste

3 tablespoons butter, in pieces

½ teaspoon freshly ground black pepper, or to taste

2 cups shredded Montasio (about 5 ounces)

1 egg, lightly beaten

Recommended Equipment
A heavy skillet or sauté pan, 12 inches or larger

Cut off the stem at the base of each chard leaf, and cut the central rib out of the leaf if thick and tough (save the stems and ribs for vegetable stock). Rinse the leaves, and drain in a colander.

Bring 5 or 6 quarts of water to the boil in a large pot, drop in the chard leaves, and stir to submerge them. Return to the boil, and cook for 20 minutes. Drain into a colander and let cool. Chop the cooked chard into small shreds, and drain once again in the colander. Press and squeeze the chard to remove as much liquid as you can.

Pour the olive oil into the skillet, and set over medium heat. Stir in the sliced onion and ½ teaspoon salt, and cook, stirring occasionally, until the onion wilts and barely colors, about 5 minutes. Scatter the chopped chard into the skillet, and drop in the butter pieces. Stir the chard with the onion and the melting butter; season with another ½ teaspoon salt. Cook over medium heat for 7 or 8 minutes, stirring and tossing frequently, until the chard is fairly dry—don't let it get brown or crispy.

Remove the chard to a big bowl; toss with the freshly ground pepper and more salt to taste. Spread it out in the bowl to cool. Let the skillet cool too, then wipe it clean and dry—you'll be using it again. Put the shredded Montasio in a plate or shallow bowl, and toss so the shreds are loose and separate.

When the chopped chard is lukewarm or cooler, pour the beaten egg over it, and mix in thoroughly with your fingers. Divide into six roughly equal parts, and form them into patties—just like hamburgers—3 to 4 inches across. Press each cake of chard firmly, so it holds together.

Set the dry skillet over medium-low heat. Hold a chard cake in one hand, and cover the top with 2 to 3 tablespoons of the shredded cheese. Press the shreds so they adhere, then turn and cover the bottom of the patty with a layer of Montasio. Lay the cake in the hot skillet (it should start to sizzle in a few seconds), and quickly coat 2 more patties with cheese and set them in the skillet, several inches apart. If there's room, start cooking another.

Fry on the first side for 3 minutes or longer, until the Montasio forms a crisp golden-brown crust. Shake the pan to loosen the cakes, slide a spatula underneath, and flip them over. Cook and crisp the second side, another 3 minutes or so. Lift out each patty with the spatula, blot up the oil released by the cheese with a folded paper towel, and set on a warm plate (placed in a low oven if you like).

Wipe the fat from the pan, return it to the heat, coat the remaining chard cakes with Montasio, and fry.

Serve the cakes warm and crispy, either whole or cut into bite-sized wedges.

Recommended Equipment

A meat mallet with toothed and smooth faces

Toothpicks

A fine-mesh sieve

A wide, heavy skillet or sauté pan, preferably 14-inch diameter

heating the butter until foaming (but don't let it brown). As the skillet heats, dredge 3 or 4 of the *braciole* in flour, shake off the excess, and drop them in the bowl of beaten eggs. Turn to coat well with egg and garlic, and sift a bit of the spice mixture over their tops.

When the butter is gently bubbling, lay the rolls in the skillet, spiced side down, and sift spices on the top side. Working quickly, dredge and coat the remaining rolls in batches, sprinkling the spices all over as they go into the skillet.

When all the *braciole* are in the pan, raise the heat a bit so the meat is sizzling gently. Slowly sauté the rolls, rotating them every few minutes, until nicely browned all over and cooked through, 10 minutes or longer. Slice into a roll to check for doneness; if it seems needed, give the thicker ones more time. As each roll is done, remove it to a platter and pull out the toothpick. Serve hot.

Roasted Lamb Shoulder

AGNELLO DA LATTE ARROSTO

Everybody is familiar with lamb chops and leg of lamb—but how about the shoulder? When is that used? Well, here I give you the recipe for a roasted lamb shoulder—and you will see why it is my favorite cut for roasting. The meat is sweeter on the blade bone, and, with lots of cartilage to melt during roasting, the meat is finger-sticking good. You might not get a clean, precise cut of meat from the shoulder, but it will be delicious.

Serves 6

6-pound lamb shoulder, cut by butcher into 4 very thick chops, about 1½ pounds each

2 celery ribs, cut in 1-inch chunks (about 2 cups)

2 medium carrots, cut in 1-inch chunks (about 2 cups)

2 medium onions, cut in large chunks (about 3 cups)

3-inch piece cinnamon stick

6 garlic cloves, crushed and peeled

4 small branches fresh rosemary

8 fresh sage leaves

½ teaspoon coarsely ground black pepper

1 teaspoon coarse sea salt or kosher salt, or more to taste

2 cups dry white wine

⅓ cup red wine vinegar

½ cup extra-virgin olive oil

Trim most of the fat from the chops, leaving only a very thin layer on the outside surfaces. With your fingers, pull apart each chop, roughly in half, along the natural break lines between the muscles.

Put the meat in a large bowl with all of the remaining ingredients except the stock. Toss well to distribute all the seasonings, and submerge the meat in the marinade. Seal the bowl with plastic wrap, and refrigerate for 24 hours. Turn the meat occasionally.

Heat the oven to 425°. Arrange the meat chunks in the roasting pan, spread the marinade all around them, and pour in the stock. Cover the pan with a tent of aluminum foil, and press it firmly against the sides. Pierce a few slits in the foil as steam vents.

Roast for 2 to 2½ hours, basting and turning the meat every 30 minutes or so. After the first hour, remove the foil, and continue roasting uncovered. As the pan liquid evaporates and the meat starts to caramelize, baste and turn more frequently. If the meat seems to be drying quickly, reduce the oven temperature. When the meat is very tender and nicely browned all over, and the pan juices have reduced by half, remove the pan from the oven and transfer the meat chunks to a warm platter.

To make the sauce, mash all the vegetables in the roasting pan, using a potato masher or a big spoon. Stir the pan juices around the sides and bottom of the pan to deglaze all the tasty caramelized bits. Pour everything into a sturdy wire-mesh sieve set over a bowl or large measuring cup. Press on the vegetables, releasing their juices, and force them through the sieve, scraping the purée into the bowl to thicken and flavor the sauce. Skim the fat from the surface, and adjust the seasoning to taste.

3 cups light stock (chicken, turkey, or vegetable broth), or more if needed

Recommended Equipment
A large, heavy-duty roasting pan, 17 by 20 inches preferred

Aluminum foil

When you are ready to serve, pour about half the sauce into a large skillet, along with the lamb pieces and any meat juices in the platter. Heat slowly to a simmer, turning the meat over and over until it is heated through. Return the meat to the platter, and drizzle over it the thickened sauce from the skillet. Serve right away, passing the remaining sauce at the table.

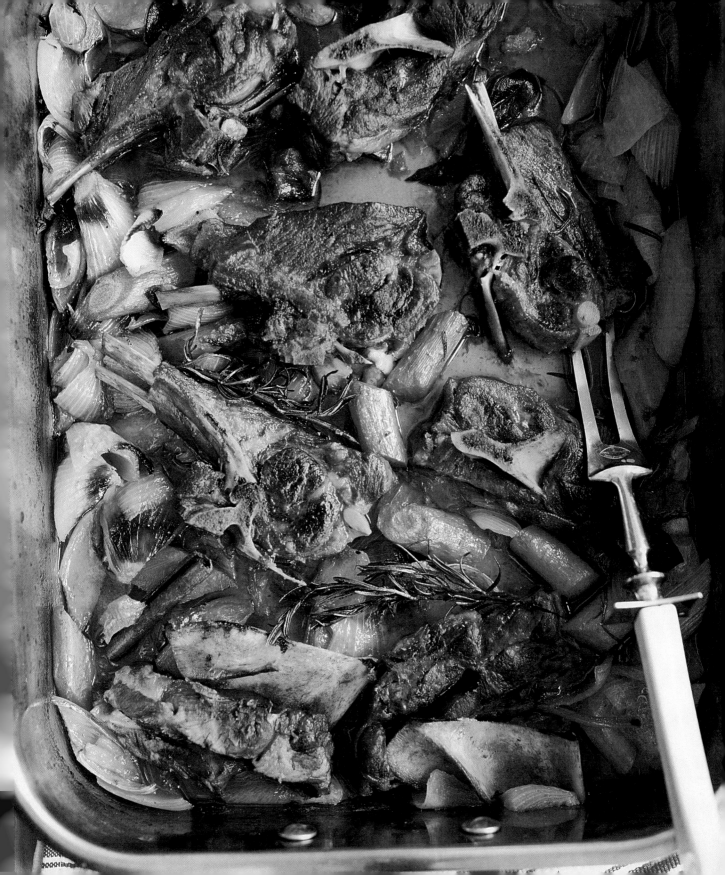

Tangy Skillet Turnips and Potatoes

RAPE E PATATE ALL'ACETO

Turnips play an important role in Friulian cuisine, especially in the form called *brovada*—turnips that have fermented for several months, as a way to preserve them and to develop a pronounced and appetizing acidity. *Brovada* is incorporated in many dishes, grated and braised with sausages and other meats, in soups, or just as a tangy and healthful vegetable.

This recipe, using fresh turnips, produces a side dish in the same vein as *brovada*, with distinctive acidity, well suited to accompany all sorts of cured and fresh meats. It is full of typical Friulian flavors, but you do not have to wait months for the turnip to ferment!

Serves 6

4 tablespoons extra-virgin olive oil

½ pound thick bacon slices, cut crosswise in 1-inch pieces

1 onion sliced (1 cup)

4 plump garlic cloves, crushed and peeled

1½ pounds white turnips, trimmed, peeled, cut in 1-inch chunks

1½ pounds waxy potatoes, peeled and cut in 1-inch chunks

1 teaspoon coarse sea salt

1 tablespoon red-wine vinegar

1 tablespoon sugar

¼ cup water

Freshly ground black pepper

1 tablespoon chopped fresh Italian parsley

Recommended Equipment
A heavy-bottomed skillet or sauté pan, 12-inch diameter or larger, with a cover

Pour 2 tablespoons of the olive oil in the big skillet, scatter in the bacon pieces, and set over medium-high heat. When the bacon starts to render fat, toss in the onion slices and garlic cloves. Cook, stirring and tossing, until the bacon is starting to crisp and the onion is just beginning to color.

Pile all the turnip and potato chunks in the pan, sprinkle with salt, and toss everything together well for a couple of minutes. Lower the heat, cover the pan, and cook for about 15 minutes, occasionally turning the turnips and potatoes over as they soften and start to color.

Stir together the vinegar, sugar, and ¼ cup water. Push aside the vegetables to clear a space on the skillet bottom. Pour the vinegar into the hot spot, and as it sizzles, toss and turn the vegetables to moisten them. Spread the chunks in a layer filling the pan, cover, and cook for several minutes, until they've crisped on the bottom, then toss well and spread out again.

Cook, covered, tossing and spreading every 4 minutes or so, until the potatoes and turnips are tender to the bite and caramelized all over, about 15 minutes. Season with more salt and freshly ground black pepper to taste. Serve right from the skillet, or heap the chunks in a warm bowl. Drizzle over the remaining 2 tablespoons olive oil, toss in the chopped parsley, and serve hot.

Apple Torte with Bread Crumb and Hazelnut Crust

TORTA DI MELE DI CARNIA

Apples grow well in the Carnic mountains, in the northern part of Friuli, and are used in many desserts. This delicious double-crusted tart reflects the deep-rooted frugality of cooks in this tough mountainous terrain. The crust is made with bread crumbs taken from stale bread, probably because of the scarcity of white flour and the time it takes to make a refined pastry dough. But the results, in the Carnic spirit, are delicious.

Makes a 9-inch tart, serving 8 or more

For the bread crumb crust
½ cup hazelnuts, toasted

1½ cups fine dry bread crumbs

6 tablespoons sugar

2 teaspoons freshly grated lemon zest

¾ cup milk

6 tablespoons butter, plus a bit for the tart pan

Flour for rolling out the dough

For the apple filling
2 pounds (or a bit more) tart, firm apples such as Granny Smith

⅓ cup sugar, or more to taste

1 cup hard (fermented) apple cider or dry white wine

Whipped cream or sour cream or ice cream or powdered sugar (optional)

Recommended Equipment
A wide, heavy-bottomed 3- or 4-quart saucepan, with a cover

To make the pastry dough, chop the toasted hazelnuts into small bits, about the size of barley or rice grains, using a chef's knife, or pulse in a food processor, in short bursts to avoid pulverizing. Mix the chopped nuts with the bread crumbs, sugar, and grated lemon zest in a big bowl.

Heat the milk and butter in a small saucepan just until the butter melts. Pour over the dry mixture, and stir until evenly moistened. Let the *very* sticky dough sit in the bowl for about 15 minutes, so the liquids are absorbed by the crumbs. Scrape dough onto a large piece of plastic wrap, enclose it, and press into a disk. Refrigerate the dough for an hour or more, until it is quite firm.

To make the filling, peel, core, and slice the apples; you should have 6 to 7 cups of slices. Spread them in the saucepan; pour the sugar and the cider or wine on top; cover the pan, and set it over medium heat. Cook covered for about 10 minutes, gently turning the apples every few minutes, as they wilt and release their juices. Uncover the pan; adjust the heat to keep the liquid perking and slowly reducing. Turn the slices over frequently but carefully, so they stay intact. When the liquid has all evaporated and the apples are soft and nicely glazed, turn off the heat and let the apples cool.

When you're ready to form the pastry and bake, arrange a rack in the middle of the oven (covered with a baking stone or tiles, preferably) and heat it to 375°. Lightly butter the tart ring and removable metal bottom.

Cut off a third of the chilled disk of dough for the top crust, and set it aside. On a well-floured surface, roll the remaining two-thirds of the dough to a 12-inch-diameter circle, almost ¼ inch thick—

A 9-inch tart pan with a removable bottom

A pizza stone or oven tiles, if available

more like a cookie dough than a pie crust. Flour the rolling pin and work surface as needed to prevent sticking. Lift the round and lay it, centered, on the tart pan. Press the dough down so it lines the pan bottom and sides, and trim the edges so there's an even ½ inch of dough over the rim of the tart ring, all around.

Spread the cooled apple slices on the bottom crust, in an even layer. Roll out the smaller piece of dough into a 9-inch round, the same thickness as the first. Lay it loosely over the filling, and trim the outside edges to fit snugly *inside* the bottom crust, covering the apples like a lid. Fold the overlapping bottom crust over the top piece, and pinch and smooth the dough layers together, sealing the apples inside.

Place the *torta* in the oven, and bake for an hour or longer, until the top crust is deep golden brown and the outer crust has separated slightly from the side ring. The top crust may crack open, and you should be able to see the apple filling bubbling inside. Set the pan on a wire rack to cool.

When the *torta* has cooled and the crust has firmed up, remove the side ring. If you wish, use a long metal spatula to separate the bottom crust from the metal disk, and slide the *torta* onto a board or cake plate. Serve cut in wedges, warm with ice cream, or completely cool with powdered sugar and some kind of cream.

Tanya's Tour

FRIULI

AQUILEIA: Roman Ruins and Christian Mosaics
Location: About 60 kilometers from Trieste on the way into Venice

The town of Aquileia was founded by the Romans in 181 B.C. and became one of the most important cities during the Roman Empire. Today it is full of archeological treasures and magnificent buildings from the classical and early-Christian eras. Along the Via Sacra, one can see the remains of the Roman city in the forum, circus, amphitheater, fortifications, sepulchers, and public and private buildings. The magnificent basilica contains the largest and some of the most interesting early-Christian mosaic floors in the Western world, dating from the fourth century, with a wonderful mix of Christian stories and pagan symbols. The Cripta degli Scavi (Crypt of Excavations) displays levels of excavated mosaics and decorations from different epochs layered one upon another, such as the mosaics of a Roman house and those of the basilica.

TIEPOLO'S FRESCOES IN UDINE: Watch Out for Falling Angels!
Location: Palazzo Patriarcale at Piazza Patriarcato 1; Oratory of the Purities
in Via di San Francesco

Udine has been the principal city of the Friuli region for centuries, and landmarks of its rich history are everywhere, starting with the Castle of Udine, which dominates the city center. At the heart of the castle, built by the Venetians in the early sixteenth century, is the Hall of Parliament, one of the oldest in Europe. The castle also houses several museums, including the archeological museum and the *pinacoteca* gallery.

For me (and all lovers of Baroque art), the great reward of a visit to Udine is found in the frescoes painted by the Venetian master Giambattista Tiepolo, early in his career. In 1726, before he became celebrated all over Europe, Tiepolo was brought to Udine by the local patrician Dionisio Delfino, to decorate the Parliament Hall and other buildings. These works, though not as spectacular as his most famous and monumental frescoes in the royal places of Würzburg and Madrid, are wonderful demonstrations of Tiepolo's mastery of foreshortening, and the use of color and light to imbue the scenes with powerful feeling.

Two of the frescoes in Udine will allow you to experience the power of this artist (without crowds of tourists). The first is in the Patriarchal Palace, where Tiepolo painted an important cycle of Biblical stories, including those of the Hebrew patriarchs Abraham, Isaac, and Jacob. Here you'll find Tiepolo's great genius beginning to blossom in the ceiling above the staircase, in his depiction of *The Banishment of the Rebel Angels.* Look upward and an intense panic fills you, for one of the angels is surely about to tumble off the ceiling, out of the frame, and onto you!

The second treasure is in the Oratory of the Purities, near the cathedral in the Piazza del Duomo. The oratory is closed, but you can ask the sacristan in the cathedral to open it (and a tip won't hurt). Inside, look up to witness the Assumption of the Virgin Mary. Tiepolo paints the scene with a great vertical force and a spinning vortex in which angels are caught in a tornado of clouds, their feet hanging out and swinging around. You feel not only that Mary is being swept up to heaven but that you are too.

CIVIDALE DEL FRIULI: The Legacy of the Lombard Kingdom
Location: 10 miles east of Udine

Perched above the Natisone River, the town of Cividale del Friuli was the capital of the Lombard Kingdom, the realm established by the Germanic Lombards (or Longobards), who invaded and then ruled northern Italy from the sixth to eighth century. A gem from that era is the Oratory of St. Mary in the Valley, more often known as the Longobard Temple or Tempietto di Cividale. It is a small and bizarre architectural masterpiece, decorated with magnificent yet haunting Byzantine stucco reliefs from the eighth century. The tiny space, with its pristine white decorations, is so simple, yet so rich in the details of the figures and saints. (It must be remembered, though, that originally the decorative patterns would have been filled in with colored-glass paste, and the stuccoes would likely have been painted, creating a different effect from what we experience today.)

Also of interest in Cividale is the Duomo, a fifteenth-century building, filled with wonderful Longobard art. The Church of St. Francis is one of the most significant examples of Gothic architecture in Friuli, with frescoes from the fourteenth to the sixteenth century. And a walk across the Devil's Bridge, over the Natisone, affords wonderfully panoramic views.

PALMANOVA: A Visit to a Venetian Fortress
Location: About 12 miles south of Udine

A national monument, the fortress town of Palmanova is a stellar example of the architectural and military prowess that allowed the Venetians to maintain their dominion over much of Friuli for nearly four centuries. And I mean "stellar" quite literally: the entire town is within a perimeter of fortress walls that form a nine-point star. Constructed at the end of the sixteenth century, along the eastern borders of the Venetian territory, the star shape of the outer walls marked an innovation in fortification design. It was a superb defense mechanism, allowing residents to see approaching enemies from all walls and to repel from two sides any attackers who got near the ramparts.

The star shape was repeated in a series of inner walls as a further protective measure, and entrance to the town was limited to three enormous gates. As the visitor today will discover, passage through the gate under the outer wall allows one only to walk across an exposed courtyard (surrounded by fortifications) to another enormous gate, which must be opened to actually enter the city.

PADOVA AND TREVISO

Chapter 4

Rice and Pea Soup
RISI E BISI

Fish Broth
BRODO DI PESCE

Marinated Winter Squash
ZUCCA GIALLA MARINATA

Homemade Bigoli Pasta

Bigoli with Chicken Livers
BIGOLI CON FEGATINI DI POLLO

Bigoli with Onion-Anchovy Sauce
BIGOLI CON SUGO DI CIPOLLA ED ACCIUGHE

Polenta

Beans and Sausages with Polenta
POLENTA E FASOI

Baked Radicchio
RADICCHIO TREVISANO AL FORNO

Risotto with Radicchio
RISOTTO AL RADICCHIO TREVISANO

Creamy Baked Salt Cod
BACCALÀ ALLA TREVIGIANA

Peach Tart with Cocoa-Almond Crust
CROSTATA DI AMARETTI AL CIOCCOLATO CON PESCHE

Limoncello Tiramisù
TIRAMISÙ AL LIMONCELLO

Cookie Crumble
FREGOLOTTA

Sandy Cake
TORTA SABBIOSA

Fried Ribbon Cookies
CROSTOLI

Padova and Treviso are in the region of the Veneto, both elegant cities where one still senses the mystique of a time past. The cupboards smell of spices not of this land, and pots of herbs hang in windows framed by curtains of silks from afar. Venice and its surroundings flourished and became a strong city-state, and a wealthy one thanks to the spice trade. To this day, spices from the Orient punctuate the cooking.

Rice reigns here, whether as the foundation for hearty soups or for creamy risottos accented with local flavors. Do not expect menus in restaurants in Padova or Treviso to boast pasta dishes, but the list of *minestre* is likely to be endless. Although rice is the starch of choice in the *minestra,* the flavorings could be celery, tomatoes, asparagus, fresh spring peas, fava beans, Savoy cabbage, squash, or whatever vegetables are in season. As an old Venetian saying goes, "Everything that the sea and the land bear should end up in a risotto or a *minestra."*

Beans are also basic to the cuisine. They are used as a base for *minestre,* and as a primary staple. The one pasta that is embraced is bigoli. Making bigoli is a tradition here, and you will not find them in any other part of Italy. White-flour bigoli or *bigoli scuri,* made with whole-wheat flour, is pasta that is extruded through a hand-operated press (*a torchio*), which shapes the pasta and gives it a chewy bite and a pleasant rough texture. Bigoli are usually dressed with a sauce of onions, anchovies, and black pepper, or with onions and chicken livers. Lots of onions, whether used to smother calves' liver or fish *in saor* (marinade)—that's what Venetians love.

There is a big garden culture here, and in the fertile lands around the Po (the largest river of Italy) Valley, with many canals that infiltrate and nourish the land, vegetable specialties abound.

In the beautiful market in Padova, or at the smaller but quaint markets in Treviso, you are bound to find in season mounds of radicchio from Treviso, Castelfranco, and surrounding areas. Piles of fresh peas, beans, squash, and Savoy cabbage fill the stalls in the morning at the *mercato,* but by noon most of the produce has ended up in some soup or risotto. This area also yields wonderful fruits—cherries, magnificent peaches, chestnuts in season, and grapes that make the deliciously fruity, sparkling Prosecco. Prosecco is a refreshing apéritif, but it is also delightful served with dessert, and there is a grand tradition of desserts in this area. After all, refined sugar was first used in Venice in the eighth century. And *tiramisù* is said to have been conceived in Treviso.

Venice overshadowed Padova and Treviso for centuries, and as a result, tourists visiting the Veneto region seldom end up in Padova or Treviso. Not I. I make regular pilgrimages to these two beautiful cities. In addition to its stupendous marketplace and art treasures, Padova harbors for me spiritual and sentimental values.

My first trip to the glorious city of Padova was to say goodbye to family, when we were heading for Rome to immigrate to the United States, and also to ask the blessings of San Antonio, the patron saint of Padova, known for his miracle-granting. On our way by train to Rome that distant day in early April 1958, we stopped in Padova to spend a few days with Anci Vocetti, my mother's first cousin, and her family. Nadia, her daughter, introduced me to the city, and it was glorious. But what I remember vividly is that in Padova I had the best peach I ever ate in my life.

Rice and Pea Soup

RISI E BISI

Everyone makes this classic soup a little differently, according to preference. I like my *risi e bisi* rather brothy, but others make theirs quite dense. This is controlled by the intensity of the boil, whether the pot is kept open or covered, and cooking time, all of which determine the rate of evaporation. (I cook my soup covered, at a slow boil.)

Either long- or short-grain rice can be used here. Traditionally, the soup was made with short-grain Carnaroli or Arborio rice, and I still think this gives the most authentic flavor and texture. It cooks faster too, but if you need to cook the soup longer or reheat it, the rice tends to dissolve. Long-grain rice, on the other hand, stays more intact in a long-cooking or reheated soup. But as it does not release starch like short-grain rices, the soup will be thinner.

Makes about 3 quarts, serving 8

3 tablespoons extra-virgin olive oil, plus more for serving

¼ pound bacon (about 4 thick-cut strips), cut in ⅓-inch pieces

2 cups ½-inch-diced leek

1 tablespoon coarse sea salt or kosher salt, plus more to taste

1 pound frozen peas, or 3 cups shucked fresh peas

¾ to 1 cup rice

4 tablespoons chopped fresh Italian parsley

½ cup freshly grated Grana Padano or Parmigiano-Reggiano for serving, and more for passing

Freshly ground black pepper

Recommended Equipment
A 5-quart pot for heating the water

A heavy-bottomed stockpot or large saucepan, at least 10 inches wide and 8-quart capacity

Pour the olive oil into the heavy pot and set over medium heat. Stir in the bacon pieces, and cook for several minutes to render the fat. When the bacon starts to crisp, stir in the leek (and fresh peas, if using). Cook, stirring frequently, until the leek is wilted and the bacon is caramelized, about 6 minutes.

Meanwhile, heat 3 quarts water to a simmer. Pour into the pot with the leek and bacon, add the tablespoon salt, and stir well. Rapidly bring to a boil, then adjust the heat to maintain active bubbling, and cook for an hour or longer, to build flavor in the soup base. Cook covered or uncovered, to reduce the soup rapidly or slowly, to a consistency you prefer (see headnote).

Stir in the frozen peas, if using. Return the soup to a bubbling simmer, and cook for 20 minutes before adding the rice. (If fresh peas are already cooking in the pot, stir in the rice after the hour or so of cooking, when the volume has reduced.) Use ¾ cup rice for a looser soup, or a full cup of rice for a denser one. Return the soup to the active simmer, taste, and stir in ½ teaspoon or more salt—remember that more rice needs more seasoning.

Cook the rice for 10 minutes or so, stirring occasionally, until the grains are cooked through but not mushy. Turn off the heat; stir in the parsley and grated cheese; season the soup with lots of freshly ground black pepper. Serve immediately, passing more cheese and olive oil at the table.

Fish Broth

BRODO DI PESCE

This soup is common in all of the regions hugging the Adriatic, where fish trimmings of one sort or another are always available to cook into a light, flavorful broth. We had it often when we lived in Istria, whenever someone in the family was not feeling well, for its supposed restorative powers. And although children sometimes disdain "fishy"-tasting food, I recall vividly savoring this broth, which had the taste of the sea but was sweet and elegant too.

In those days, we would take the fish heads and tails out of the soup pot and pluck the hidden morsels of whitefish meat off the bones. In the version that follows, you'll strain the bones out of the broth and briefly cook some meaty (but boneless) trimmings just before serving the soup.

Makes about 3 quarts of broth, serving 8 or more

3 pounds fish trimmings (such as bones, heads, tails, and belly flaps), from black or striped bass, red snapper, fluke, or other nonoily fish

2 large onions (about 1¼ pounds), peeled and cut in half

1 garlic head, cloves peeled

3 or 4 carrots (about 12 ounces), peeled and cut in 4-inch chunks

4 big celery stalks (about 12 ounces), trimmed and cut in 4-inch chunks

A big handful of fresh Italian parsley stalks with lots of leaves

2 tablespoons tomato paste

2 tablespoons coarse sea salt or kosher salt, plus more to taste

2 teaspoons whole black peppercorns

Rinse all the fish trimmings, put them in the stockpot, and add 6 quarts cold water. Set over medium-low flame to heat gradually.

Set the onion halves, cut side down, directly on the grate of a stove burner over a medium flame for several minutes, until dark brown. (Alternatively, brown the cut sides in a dry heavy skillet.) Drop the browned onions into the stockpot along with all the other broth ingredients. Cover the pot, leaving it open a crack, and bring the water to a boil. Adjust the heat to keep it bubbling gently, and cook the broth, with the lid set ajar, for 3 hours or so, until the level of the broth has reduced by about one-quarter. If it is not reducing steadily, raise the heat and remove the cover.

When the broth is full-flavored, turn off the heat. Strain the broth well through a colander and then a fine-meshed sieve. Press on the solids gently to release broth, and then discard all the fish bones and seasonings. Serve as is or with rice and fish as described on the following page.

Variation: Fish Broth with Rice and Fish

1½ to 2 cups Arborio rice

About ½ pound skinless fish fillet, cut in small pieces

⅓ cup chopped fresh Italian parsley

Recommended Equipment
An 8-quart stockpot with a cover

Return the preceding fish broth (or as much of it as you want to serve) to the pot, and heat to a simmer. Stir in ½ cup of rice for every quart of broth (or more rice for denser consistency) and the pieces of fish fillet. Simmer for 10 to 15 minutes, until the rice is cooked (but not mushy) and the fish is tender and flakes apart in the broth. Adjust the seasoning to taste, sprinkle on the chopped parsley, and serve very hot, in warm bowls.

Special Treats from the Market in Padova— Piazza delle Erbe and Piazza della Frutta

The two piazzas are the markets, one to the north and one to the south of the magnificent Palazzo della Ragione in the center of Padova.

There are loggias facing the piazzas, underneath the Palazzo della Ragione, with long arched corridors; they look like beehives and harbor specialty-food shops. *Salumeria* (the cured-meat shop), *maccelleria* (the butcher), *norcineria* (the pork-only butcher), *latteria* (the cheese shop), *maccelleria carne equine* (the horse-meat butcher), *pescheria* (the fish market)—you could navigate this vaulted loggia by aromas that waft from every shop door, luring you toward the perfectly ripe, aged, and seasoned merchandise.

Marinated Winter Squash

ZUCCA GIALLA MARINATA

Squash is not one of the most popular vegetables, but I love it and love cooking with it. It is nutritious, versatile, and delicious. Northern Italy consumes more *zucca*—winter squash—than southern Italy, especially in the areas near Modena in Emilia-Romagna, and Padova in the Veneto.

This is a great side dish or appetizer. Traditionally, the *zucca* is fried before it is marinated, as I do here, but the dish is also delicious when made with grilled or boiled *zucca*. I recommend butternut squash, but acorn, Hubbard, and other varieties will work as well.

Serves 6 or more as an appetizer or side dish

1 cup apple-cider vinegar or white vinegar

1 tablespoon sugar

½ teaspoon coarse sea salt or kosher salt, or more to taste

6 garlic cloves, peeled and sliced

1 tablespoon extra-virgin olive oil

1 butternut squash, about 2 pounds

1 cup vegetable oil, or as needed

10 to 20 fresh basil leaves

Recommended Equipment
A heavy-bottomed skillet or sauté pan, 12-inch diameter or larger

A 6-cup glass or ceramic casserole dish, preferably about 6 inches wide, to marinate the squash in several layers

Mix the vinegar, sugar, and ¼ teaspoon salt together in a small saucepan. Over high heat, reduce by half. Remove from the heat, drop in the garlic slices, and let the marinade cool. Stir in the olive oil.

Slice the squash in half lengthwise, and scrape out all the seeds. Peel the halves, place cut side down, and cut crosswise, into ⅓-inch-thick half-rounds.

Pour vegetable oil into the skillet to the depth of ⅛ inch, and set over medium-high heat. When the oil sizzles on contact with squash, fill the pan with a layer of slices, spaced slightly apart. Fry for about 3 minutes on the first side, then flip the slices over. Fry on the second side another 2 or 3 minutes, until the slices are cooked through (easy to pierce with the tines of a fork), crisped on the surface, and caramelized on the edges.

Lift out the slices with a slotted spoon, draining off oil, and lay them on paper towels. Sprinkle salt lightly on the hot slices. Fry up all the squash in batches, the same way.

Arrange a single layer of fried squash in the bottom of the marinating dish, and scatter 4 or 5 basil leaves on top. Stir up the marinade, and drizzle a couple of spoonfuls over the layer of squash. Scatter some of the garlic slices on the squash too. Layer all the squash in the dish this way, topping each layer with basil leaves, garlic, and marinade. All the seasonings should be used—drizzle any remaining marinade over the top layer of squash.

Wrap the dish in plastic, and marinate the squash for at least 3 hours, preferably overnight in the refrigerator. If chilled, let the squash return to room temperature before serving.

Homemade Bigoli Pasta

Thick and chewy, with the nuttiness of whole wheat, bigoli is the signature pasta of the Veneto. At Ristorante Celeste in Venegazzu, outside of Treviso, Giuliano Tonon taught me how to extrude fresh dough into strands with a *torchio*, the traditional hand press. But bigoli is not only a restaurant treat—most home cooks in the region have a *torchio* in the kitchen and make bigoli every week! Happily, this pleasure is now available to Americans since I have found a genuine *torchio* for sale on the Internet (see Sources, page 340). Bigoli can also be made with an electric pasta-extruder or a meat grinder.

The two traditional sauces on the following pages are packed with flavor. With homemade bigoli, they each make a big, gutsy pasta, very worth the effort and very Venetian. (And if you can't make your own bigoli, whole wheat spaghetti will be delicious with either sauce.)

Makes 2 pounds of fresh bigoli, serving 6 to 8

4 cups all-purpose flour, or 3 cups all-purpose flour and 1 cup whole-wheat flour, plus more all-purpose flour for working with the dough

½ teaspoon salt

1 tablespoon soft butter

½ cup warm milk, or more as needed

3 large eggs, lightly beaten

Recommended Equipment
A food processor fitted with steel blade for mixing the dough

A genuine *torchio* hand press (see Sources, page 340), or a home pasta-extruder (stand-alone machine or electric-mixer attachment) or meat grinder (machine or mixer attachment)

To mix the dough in the food processor, put the flour (all-purpose and whole-wheat, if using) and salt in the work bowl and process briefly to blend. Drop the butter into the ½ cup warm milk; stir to melt the butter, then mix the beaten eggs into the milk.

Start the food processor running, then pour in the liquids through the feed tube. Process for 30 to 40 seconds, until a dough forms and gathers on the blade, leaving the sides and bottom of the bowl clean. The dough should be soft but not sticky. If it is dry and crumbly, add a bit more milk, and process. Turn the dough out of the bowl, and knead into a smooth ball. Wrap the dough in plastic, and let it rest at room temperature for ½ hour before extruding the dough.

If you have a *torchio*, fit it with the large-hole bigoli die. With a pasta-extruding machine or attachment—or a meat grinder—use a disk with ¼-inch holes, or as close to that size as you have. If using a meat grinder or attachment, be sure to remove the rotary cutting blade before extruding the dough. Put the dough through your extrusion device, and cut the strands of pasta into 8-inch lengths as they emerge. Immediately dust them with flour and lay

Marinated Winter Squash (see recipe page 103)

them flat, not touching, on a floured tray or baking sheet. Keep covered with a floured towel until you cook them. (You can freeze the strands on the sheet pan, then wrap them together in plastic wrap, in portions for cooking. Keep in a plastic container to protect from breakage. Cook without thawing.)

Finds on the Bridge in Treviso

As much as Padova shines in its art, Treviso glistens on its waterways and is called Città d'Acqua, City of Water. The Sile is the river that, like a gentle serpent, curves its way through the city. There are balconies full of blossoming geraniums spilling onto the running river below, and with each turn of the winding street there is yet another balcony where occasionally one finds old paddle wheels still clinging to buildings that once harbored polenta mills. But the fish market in the center of town, with its modern design and aquacolored tiles, perched on a wide bridge, seems to be at odds with the rest of the architecture. The locals were not too happy about it when it was built, but on my last visit the market was bustling in the morning hours with fish buyers while flocks of ducks paddled in the river below, awaiting a treat from the fishmonger.

Bigoli with Chicken Livers

BIGOLI CON FEGATINI DI POLLO

Serves 6 as a main course, 8 or more
as a first course

1 pound chicken livers

6 tablespoons extra-virgin olive oil

3 tablespoons butter

1 medium onion, finely chopped
(1¼ cups)

2 bay leaves

1 teaspoon coarse sea salt or
kosher salt, or to taste, plus more
for the pasta water

3 cups hot stock (Poultry Broth,
page 8, or chicken, turkey, or
vegetable stock)

1 tablespoon tomato paste

1 cup frozen peas

Freshly ground black pepper
to taste

1 recipe (2 pounds) fresh bigoli,
page 105

⅓ cup chopped fresh Italian
parsley

1½ cups freshly grated
Grana Padano or
Parmigiano-Reggiano

Recommended Equipment
A heavy-bottomed skillet or sauté
pan, 14-inch diameter or larger

A large pot, 10-quart capacity, to
cook the bigoli

Clean the chicken livers, removing all the fat, veins, and membranes. Chop them into small bits with a chef's knife.

Heat 3 tablespoons of the olive oil and all the butter in the large skillet over medium heat. Stir in the onion and the bay leaves, and season with ¼ teaspoon salt. When the onion is wilted and translucent, stir in the chopped chicken livers, and salt again lightly.

Pour in ¼ cup hot stock, raise the heat, and cook, stirring, until the moisture is nearly evaporated. Clear a space in the skillet, drop in the tomato paste, toast it in the hot spot for a minute, then stir the paste in with the chopped livers and onion. Scatter the frozen peas into the skillet, stir, then pour in the remaining stock.

Bring the liquid to a boil, and adjust the heat to keep it bubbling steadily. Season with ½ teaspoon salt and generous grinds of black pepper. Let the sauce cook and reduce, stirring occasionally, until most of the moisture is gone and it has a thick, flowing consistency, 10 minutes or so. Adjust the seasonings, and have the sauce simmering when the pasta is dressed.

Meanwhile, fill the large pot with 8 quarts of water, add 2 tablespoons salt, cover, and heat to a rolling boil. Shake excess flour off the bigoli, drop into the pot, and return rapidly to the boil. Cook, occasionally stirring, until the pasta is nearly *al dente* (time will vary with the thickness of the strands). Lift bigoli from the water with a spider, drain briefly, and turn it into the simmering sauce. Toss together until the pasta is fully cooked and dressed with sauce.

Turn off the heat, toss in the parsley, the remaining 3 tablespoons olive oil, and a cup of the grated cheese. Serve immediately, passing more cheese at the table.

Bigoli with Onion-Anchovy Sauce

BIGOLI CON SUGO DI CIPOLLA ED ACCIUGHE

Serves 6 as a main course, 8 or more
as a first course

½ cup extra-virgin olive oil

8 tablespoons (1 stick) butter

2 large onions, peeled and
sliced in ¼-inch-thick half-moon
shapes (about 6 cups)

3 plump garlic cloves, peeled
and chopped

½ teaspoon coarse sea salt or
kosher salt, or to taste, plus
more for the pasta water

2-ounce can anchovy fillets,
drained and finely chopped

1 cup hot stock (Poultry Broth,
page 8, or chicken, turkey, or
vegetable stock)

Freshly ground black pepper
to taste

1 recipe (2 pounds) fresh bigoli,
page 105

⅓ cup chopped fresh Italian
parsley

Recommended Equipment
A heavy-bottomed skillet or
sauté pan, 14-inch diameter
or larger

A large pot, 10-quart capacity,
to cook the bigoli

Heat the olive oil and butter in the large skillet over medium heat. When the butter is melted, stir in the onions and garlic, season with ½ teaspoon salt, and cover the pan. Let the onions cook slowly, stirring now and then, to release their liquid, soften, and shrink. After 15 to 20 minutes, when the onions are concentrated, golden, and edged with brown, add the chopped anchovies, raise the heat, and cook, stirring, for a couple of minutes, as the anchovies melt in the hot oil.

Pour in the stock, bring to a bubbling boil, and cook, stirring, to amalgamate the sauce and thicken it slightly. Season generously with freshly ground black pepper, and adjust salt to taste. Remove from the heat; return to the simmer before you add the bigoli.

Cook the bigoli until nearly *al dente* in 8 quarts of boiling salted water, as detailed in the preceding recipe. Drop the pasta into the simmering onion-anchovy sauce, and toss together for a minute to finish cooking and coat the bigoli. Turn off the heat, toss in the parsley, and serve immediately.

Polenta

Serves 6 or more

10 cups water

¼ cup extra-virgin olive oil

1 tablespoon salt, plus more
if needed

4 bay leaves, preferably fresh

2 cups yellow polenta,
medium-grind

Optional enrichments
1 cup freshly grated Grana
Padano or Parmigiano-Reggiano,
or more to taste

¼ pound (1 stick) butter, or to taste

Recommended Equipment
A heavy-bottomed saucepan or
French oven, 10 inches or wider, at
least 6-quart capacity, with a cover

A sturdy wire whisk

Pour the water and olive oil into the heavy pot, add the salt and bay leaves, and bring to a boil over high heat. With the water bubbling steadily, pick up the polenta by handfuls and let it rain into the water through your fingers, whisking steadily to avoid lumps, until it is all incorporated.

Bring the polenta to a boil over medium heat, whisking frequently. When big bubbles start bursting, lower the heat a bit and set the cover ajar. Keep the polenta perking, and stir frequently, scraping the thickening cereal from the bottom and corners of the pot.

Cook for about 30 minutes, until the polenta is glossy and pulls away from the sides as you stir. If you like the consistency, turn off the heat, or cook longer for greater density. Taste (carefully—it's hot!), and add salt if needed. Remove all the bay leaves. To enrich the polenta, stir in grated cheese or butter—or both—to taste, then cover the pan until you are ready to serve.

To serve, dip a large spoon in water and use it to scoop polenta from the pot, mounding it in a warm pasta bowl.

Set aside some of the freshly cooked polenta to prepare Baked Polenta later (page 111).

Beans and Sausages with Polenta

POLENTA E FASOI

Serves 6

For the beans
1 pound dried cannellini beans

4 bay leaves, preferably fresh

2 tablespoons extra-virgin olive oil

½ teaspoon coarse sea salt or kosher salt

For the sausages
4 tablespoons extra-virgin olive oil, plus more for finishing

¾ cup bacon chopped in ½-inch pieces (3 thick-cut strips)

6 sweet Italian sausages (about 1½ pounds), in casings

1 small onion, chopped (1 cup)

2 bay leaves, preferably fresh

3 tablespoons tomato paste

2 tablespoons red wine vinegar

2 cups hot water

3 cups (or a 28-ounce can) canned Italian plum tomatoes, preferably San Marzano, crushed by hand

1 teaspoon coarse sea salt or kosher salt, or to taste

Freshly ground black pepper to taste

Polenta, freshly cooked and soft, page 109

Rinse the beans, and soak them in plenty of cold water for 8 hours or overnight. Drain, and place the beans in a 4-quart saucepan with fresh cold water, covering them by an inch or more, along with the four bay leaves and 2 tablespoons olive oil. Bring to a boil, partially cover the pot, and adjust the heat to maintain a bubbling simmer. When the beans are almost tender but still slightly undercooked, after about 40 minutes, remove from the heat. Drain through a colander. Stir in the ½ teaspoon salt and let cool; discard the bay leaves.

To cook the sausages and tomato sauce, pour the 4 tablespoons olive oil into the wide saucepan, scatter the bacon pieces into it, and set over medium-high heat. Cook, stirring, until the bacon starts rendering fat, then drop in the sausages; let them sizzle and begin to brown. Add the chopped onion and the two bay leaves, and stir them around the pan bottom; meanwhile, keep rolling over the sausages so they color on all sides.

Cook for several minutes to allow the onion and meat to caramelize, then clear a space on the pan bottom and drop in the tomato paste. Stir it in the clear spot for a minute, until sizzling, then spread the paste all around the pan, stirring and tumbling the sausages so they're coated. Pour the red wine vinegar into a clear space in the pan, let it sizzle and evaporate for a few moments, then stir and tumble everything again.

Pour 1 cup of hot water into the saucepan, raise the heat, and deglaze the caramelization as the water bubbles. Pour in the crushed tomatoes and stir well. Rinse the tomato containers with a second cup of water, and pour that in too. Season with ½ teaspoon salt, stir everything together, and bring to a boil.

Keep the tomato sauce bubbling gently for about 10 minutes, then spill the beans into the pan. Stir in the beans while the sauce returns to the boil. Stir in water, if needed, so the sauce is loose and nearly covers the sausages and beans. Cook at a gentle boil, stirring now and then, until the beans are tender and the sauce has nicely thickened, 10 minutes or more. (Add water if the beans need longer cooking; or, if the sauce seems too loose, reduce it quickly over

Recommended Equipment

A 4-quart saucepan for cooking the cannellini

A wide, heavy-bottomed saucepan, 6-quart capacity, about 12-inch diameter, for the sausages in tomato sauce

high heat.) Turn off the heat, and adjust the seasoning with salt and lots of freshly ground black pepper to taste. Cover the pan to keep the beans warm until the polenta is ready to serve.

Meanwhile, cook the polenta following the procedure on page 109, until it is thick and glossy and just starts to pull away from the sides of the pot when stirred, about 30 minutes. For this dish, polenta should be soft rather than dense—add a bit of water, and stir well to loosen if necessary. Turn off the heat, remove and discard the bay leaves; taste, and add salt if needed.

Assemble individual portions in warm wide pasta bowls. First dip a large spoon in water, and with it scoop up polenta and mound it in each bowl. Spoon over a generous helping of beans in sauce, and lay a sausage on top. Drizzle olive oil over, grind on more black pepper, and serve immediately.

Baked Polenta

Polenta, after it has set, is baked and served as an accompaniment to many dishes in the Veneto and other northern regions of Italy. Here's a basic procedure to follow, starting with freshly cooked soft polenta in any amount—as prepared in the recipe on page 109.

While the polenta is still warm, pour it into a bowl, loaf pan, or other mold, lightly coated with olive oil. Lay plastic wrap right on top of the polenta to minimize crusting. Let it cool thoroughly at room temperature until firm. For longer keeping, refrigerate, up to 2 days.

When ready to bake, preheat the oven to 400° and set a rack in the center. Coat a baking dish or sheet pan lightly with butter. Unmold the polenta, and cut it in ½-inch-thick slices. Cut the slices into any size and shape you like—smaller for hors d'oeuvres or appetizers, or larger to serve as an accompaniment to a main course.

Arrange the pieces in the dish or baking sheet spaced apart, so they will crisp all around. Dot the top of each piece with bits of butter, and, if you like, mound a bit of cheese on top as well: grated Grana Padano or Parmigiano-Reggiano; shredded fontina (imported), mozzarella (dry-packed), Muenster, or Cheddar; or a combination of cheeses. Bake until the polenta is crispy and golden and the cheese has toasted to a dark-gold crust, 15 to 20 minutes.

Baked Radicchio

RADICCHIO TREVISANO AL FORNO

Although it is great in a salad—sweet and bitter at the same time—in the cold winter months *radicchio trevisano* is better cooked, and has a more resilient texture. Traditionally paired with speck—boneless, smoked prosciutto—radicchio makes a great risotto (see page 115) and a great sauce for pasta. In those dishes, the radicchio serves a secondary role as a distinctive flavoring, but when baked this way, it is the main protagonist. I enjoy baked radicchio by the mouthful, savoring its taste and texture, sweet, bitter, and crunchy.

The best variety for baking is the long thin *radicchio trevisano* or *spadone* (as shown in the photos), but the small round heads most often found in the supermarket or the kind with long but wide leaves (resembling purple romaine lettuce) are also delicious baked this way. Serve as an antipasto or a vegetable course, over soft or baked polenta.

Serves 6

1½ pounds round or long radicchio, 2 or 3 firm heads

4 tablespoons butter

4 tablespoons extra-virgin olive oil

1 medium-large onion, peeled and sliced in ¼-inch-thick half-moons (2 cups)

3 plump garlic cloves, smashed and peeled

1 teaspoon coarse sea salt or kosher salt, or to taste

1 tablespoon red wine vinegar

Freshly ground black pepper to taste

1 cup freshly grated Grana Padano or Parmigiano-Reggiano

Trim the radicchio heads, discarding wilted or bruised outer leaves and slicing off the very bottom if tough and discolored (don't remove the core). Slice the heads in quarters or sixths, into wedges about 3 inches wide. Cut through the core, so the leaves are held together. Arrange a rack in the center of the oven, and heat to 375°.

Put the butter and 2 tablespoons of the olive oil in the skillet, and set over moderate heat. When the butter is melted and foaming, stir in the onion and garlic and cook for a minute, then lay in all the radicchio wedges in one layer. Sprinkle on the salt, cover the pan, and cook slowly, turning the wedges over and stirring the onion every couple of minutes.

After 10 minutes or so, when the radicchio is softened slightly but still firmly holding its shape, stir the vinegar with ½ cup water and pour into the pan. Raise the heat a bit and bring the liquid to the boil, turning the wedges and stirring. Cook for a couple more minutes, until the pan juices are reduced and syrupy and the wedges are lightly caramelized.

Remove the skillet from the heat, and arrange the radicchio wedges in the baking dish in one layer. Spoon the onion all around, and pour the skillet liquid over. Drizzle on the remaining 2 table-

Recommended Equipment
A heavy sauté pan, 12-inch diameter or wider, with a cover

A baking dish or shallow casserole, 9 by 13 inches or similar size

spoons olive oil, season with freshly ground black pepper, and sprinkle the grated cheese in an even layer, covering the radicchio.

Tent the dish with aluminum foil, pressing it against the sides. Bake covered for about 20 minutes, remove the foil, and bake another 5 minutes or more, until the radicchio wedges are tender and moist and glazed golden on top.

Treats from Treviso—Radicchio Spada

The true birthplace of radicchio is Treviso, and as you meander through the curved streets of Treviso, following the running streams—for Treviso is full of streams and bridges—you are bound to find little markets and specialty-food stores that, when it is in season, sell nothing but different renditions of radicchio: radicchio in a jar pickled, under oil, a pesto of radicchio, a radicchio chutney, and, of course, piles upon piles of fresh radicchio or "the sword"—*spada,* as the *radicchio trevisano* is called. These are heads of radicchio that look like hands cupped together with long purple fingers and a white backbone, the tips of the radicchio curving in like the long fingernails of Mortitia, of the Addams family.

The *radicchio trevisano* is always sold still attached to the root, and it is always cooked with the root attached, whereas for a salad only the leaves are used. On the other hand, the round heads of radicchio that are mostly yellow and speckled with purple, *la rosa,* are from Castelfranco, a city close to Treviso. The round heads of red radicchio that you find in your supermarket are either from Verona or Chioggia, a seaside town in the Veneto. Today this varietal of radicchio is produced in California and other states.

Risotto with Radicchio

RISOTTO AL RADICCHIO TREVISANO

Radicchio trevisano will yield the best risotto with the most authentic Italian flavor, but this recipe will be very good with radicchio grown in the United States, either the small round heads, or heads with long wide leaves. Endive, a distant cousin of the radicchio, will also make a good risotto.

Serves 6 or more

1 pound round or long radicchio, 2 small heads or 1 large head

¼ cup extra-virgin olive oil

¼ pound bacon (3 or 4 thick-cut strips), cut crosswise in ⅓-inch pieces

2 medium onions, chopped

1 teaspoon salt, plus more to taste

2 cups Arborio or Carnaroli rice

1 cup white wine

For finishing
6 tablespoons butter, in tablespoon-sized pieces

½ cup grated Grana Padano or Parmigiano-Reggiano, plus more for passing

Recommended Equipment
A 3-quart pot for hot water

A heavy saucepan, such as an enameled cast-iron French oven, 10 inches wide, with 3-to-4-quart capacity

Separate the radicchio leaves, discarding the outer leaves and any that are wilted or damaged. Trim and discard the thick leaf bottoms and tough sections of the central ribs. Slice the leaves in long shreds, about ½ inch thick. Heat 8 cups water almost to the boil. Keep it very hot, simmering near the risotto pan.

Put the olive oil in the saucepan, and set over medium heat. Scatter in the bacon pieces and cook briefly, until the fat renders, then stir in the onions and ½ teaspoon salt. Cook, stirring frequently, until the onions are wilted and lightly colored and the bacon is slightly crisped, 8 minutes or so.

Pour in the rice all at once, raise the heat, and stir continuously for about 2 minutes, until the rice grains are toasted (but not browned). Pour in the wine and cook, stirring continuously, until nearly all the liquid has been absorbed.

Drop all of the shredded radicchio into the saucepan, and stir in with the rice for a couple of minutes, as the shreds wilt and release liquid. Then ladle in 2 cups of the simmering water and cook, stirring, until the water is almost absorbed, 5 minutes or more. Quickly ladle in another couple of cups of water, add another ½ teaspoon salt, and keep stirring, as the rice releases its starches and a thick, creamy suspension starts to form. Again, when the water is almost absorbed—and you can see the bottom of the saucepan as you stir—ladle in another cup or so of water. Continue this process.

After the risotto has cooked for 15 to 20 minutes and incorporated 6 cups of water, taste for texture and seasoning: add more salt and/or incorporate more hot water as needed. When the risotto is *al dente* and creamy, turn off the heat. Drop in the butter pieces and stir in vigorously, along with the ½ cup of grated cheese.

Serve without delay, heaping the risotto in warm pasta bowls, and pass more grated cheese at the table.

Creamy Baked Salt Cod

BACCALÀ ALLA TREVIGIANA

I love dishes made from preserved codfish, and in the Veneto they make marvelous use of cod preserved by different methods. *Baccalà* is codfish that has been salted, and this is made into *baccalà alla trevigiana*, which I share with you here. Then there is *stoccafisso*, codfish that has been air-dried and that is used for *baccalà manteccato*, whipped with olive oil and garlic.

Today salted cod—*baccalà*—is available in many supermarkets, and your fishmonger should carry it. It comes in boneless sides, and it is best to get center cuts, which are meatier and less salty. In any case, thorough soaking, as detailed in the recipe, is vital to the success of the dish. In Treviso, *baccalà alla trevigiana* is always served with Baked Polenta (page 111), and the combination of flavors and textures is so delicious I never break tradition. Do the preliminary cooking of the polenta the day before you cook the *baccalà*, and you can finish both in the oven at the same time.

Serves 6 or more

2 pounds boneless *baccalà* (salt cod)

1 cup or more flour, for dredging

4 tablespoons butter

4 tablespoons extra-virgin olive oil

2 medium onions (1 pound), peeled, halved, and sliced ¼ inch thick

1 quart milk, or more if needed

1 cup grated Grana Padano or Parmigiano-Reggiano, or more as needed

Baked Polenta, page 111 (finish and serve with *baccalà* per instructions below)

To remove the salt from the salt cod, put it in a large, deep container that fits in your sink, under the faucet. Run fresh cold water over the fish, filling the container completely so water is spilling over the brim. Keep a slow, steady drip of fresh water going as you soak the *baccalà* for at least 12 hours, up to a couple of days. Occasionally drain the water and refresh (which you can do whenever you need the sink). If you can't keep the drip going, change the water every 4 hours. To decide when *baccalà* has been soaked sufficiently, lift the fish out of the water, press a finger against it at a thick part, and touch it to the tongue. If it's palatably salty, it is ready to be cooked. Drain the *baccalà*, pat dry, and cook within a day or so; meanwhile, store it in the refrigerator, well wrapped.

Cut the *baccalà* into chunks about 3 inches square, and dredge on all sides in flour. Put the butter and olive oil in the saucepan, and set over medium heat. When the butter is foaming, lay in a batch of floured codfish chunks in one layer, not crowded. Cook and color the underside for several minutes, turn the chunks, and crisp and color the other sides. When lightly browned all over, remove to a platter. Fry the remaining chunks the same way.

Recommended Equipment

A heavy-bottomed saucepan or high-sided sauté pan, 10-to-12-inch diameter, with a cover

A baking dish or shallow casserole, 9 by 13 inches or similar size

Dump the onion slices into the pan, and toss well in the remaining fat. As the onions start to sizzle and wilt, pour in ½ cup water, and stir and scrape up the browned bits on the pan bottom. Cook the onions, stirring frequently, until wilted and translucent, 8 to 10 minutes. Meanwhile, heat the milk in a separate pan, almost to a simmer.

Lay the *baccalà* chunks on top of the caramelized onions, nestling all the chunks in one layer. Pour in any juices from the fish platter, and enough hot milk to cover the fish completely. Over medium heat, bring the milk to a gentle bubbling simmer. Set the cover slightly ajar, and simmer the *baccalà* for about an hour and a half, until the fish chunks break apart when stirred.

Uncover the pan, and maintain the slow simmer to gradually reduce the milk (which by now has curdled and separated—no cause for concern). Stir the fish occasionally, and break up the flakes into smaller pieces. As the moisture evaporates, lower the heat and scrape up any crust on the pan bottom, to avoid burning.

Cook uncovered, slowly, for 2 to 2½ hours, until the *baccalà* and milk have melded into a thick sauce, about half the original volume. (If you need to shorten the cooking time, boil the milk over higher heat, but be sure to stir the *baccalà* and scrape the saucepan frequently.)

When it is fully cooked and thickened in the saucepan, pour the hot *baccalà* into the baking dish and spread it in an even layer. Heat the oven to 350°, and set a rack in the center. Sprinkle the grated Grana Padano or Parmigiano-Reggiano over the top of the *baccalà*, and bake for about an hour, or until the top is crusty and browned.

Bake slices of firm polenta, topped with grated cheese, during the last 15 or 20 minutes that the *baccalà* is in the oven. To serve, put a slice or more of crisp polenta in a plate, and spoon some hot *baccalà* alongside.

Peach Tart with Cocoa-Almond Crust

CROSTATA DI AMARETTI AL CIOCCOLATO CON PESCHE

Decades after the fateful bite that I took of the peach when I was in Padova at the age of twelve, I still think there is nothing more sensuous than biting into a perfectly ripe peach. When the same peach is baked, though, it takes on an additional element of complexity in flavor. Bake the peaches on an amaretto crust, with a hint of chocolate, and you have a delectable Italian flavor harmony.

Makes an 8- or 9-inch tart, serving 6 or more

For the filling
4 or 5 ripe peaches (1 pound or a bit more)

¾ cup sugar

1 tablespoon freshly squeezed lemon juice

1 cup sliced almonds, lightly toasted

For the dough
½ cup sugar

1 teaspoon cocoa powder

3½ tablespoons all-purpose flour, plus a bit for the tart pan

1 large egg white

1½ tablespoons soft butter, plus 1 teaspoon or more for the tart pan

1 tablespoon apricot jam

Garnish: vanilla ice cream or whipped cream or crème fraîche

Rinse and dry the peaches, cut them in half through the stem, and remove the pits. Spread the ¾ cup sugar in the bottom of the sauté pan, drizzle the lemon juice all over, and fit in all the peach halves, cut side down, on top of the sugar.

Set the pan over medium heat, and, without disturbing the contents, let the sugar dissolve in the juices released by the peaches. Raise the heat and bring this syrup to a boil, partially cover the pan, and cook the peaches in place for about 5 minutes, then turn them over and cook for a couple of minutes. Turn them over again to cook the skin side for 2 minutes.

Keep cooking and turning the peaches until they're tender and glistening with the syrup they've absorbed, about 15 minutes or more, depending on ripeness. Cover the pan if the peaches seem hard; otherwise, cook uncovered. Keep the syrup bubbling and thickening, but don't let it burn. Turn off the heat, and let the peaches cool in syrup while you prepare the crust dough.

Put the almonds and ½ cup sugar in the food-processor bowl and process; add cocoa and flour and blend with the almond powder. Drop in the egg white, and process until incorporated. Scrape down the sides of the bowl, add the butter, and process. Clean the sides again; process once more to form a stiff, smooth, and somewhat sticky dough.

Butter and flour the tart pan. Scrape all of the dough into the pan bottom. Moisten your fingers with water, and press the dough, spreading it over the pan bottom in an even layer, with a rim of dough up against the fluted side ring. Blot up any moisture on the dough—from your wet fingers—with a sheet of paper towel.

Recommended Equipment

A skillet or sauté pan, about 10 inches wide, or just big enough to hold the peach halves in 1 layer

A food processor

A 9-inch fluted tart pan

Arrange a rack in the center of the oven, with a baking stone if you have one, and heat to 375°.

Spread the apricot jam in an even layer on the dough. Cut the cooled peach halves in two, so you have sixteen or twenty wedge-shaped fruit pieces, and place them in a flower-petal pattern, or some other neat arrangement, completely filling the crust. Spoon some of the remaining peach syrup all over the fruit.

Set the tart on a cookie sheet or a sheet of heavy-duty foil (to catch the juices), and bake for 45 minutes, or until the peaches are nicely caramelized and the crust is deeply browned. Cool briefly on a wire rack, and separate the side ring from the crust before any caramelized juices are set.

While the peaches are still warm, drizzle over them the last of the peach syrup, and, if you like, top with a scoop of vanilla ice cream or dollops of whipped cream or crème fraîche. Serve right away, as the ice cream melts.

Limoncello Tiramisù

TIRAMISÙ AL LIMONCELLO

Though Treviso is recognized as the birthplace of *tiramisù*, the precise origins of this phenomenally popular dessert are shrouded in mystery. Imagine my excitement, then, when my friend Celeste Tonon, proprietor of Ristorante da Celeste, passed on to me the original procedures for making this luscious assemblage of ladyfingers (*savoiardi*) and mascarpone cream, which Celeste learned from his mentor Speranza Garatti, the true mother of *tiramisù*, he claims. Her creation was made and served in individual protions, in a goblet or *coppa*, which I suspect gave rise to its name, which means "pick me up" in the Venetian dialect.

One of the delights of making *tiramisù* is its versatility. This recipe makes a family-style dessert in a large dish, but you can easily compose single servings in dessert glasses, wine goblets, or even elegant teacups for a more impressive presentation, in the style of Signora Garatti's original "*coppa imperiale*." And while the conventional version of *tiramisù* calls for espresso-soaked *savoiardi*, I've found that other flavors can be incorporated into the dessert with great success. Here, the brightness of fresh lemons and limoncello liqueur lace the cream and soaking syrup to make for a *tiramisù* that is refreshing and irresistible.

5 large eggs

5 or 6 lemons

1 cup sugar

1½ cups limoncello liqueur

1 cup water

1 pound (2 cups) mascarpone, at room temperature

40 ladyfingers (preferably imported Italian *savoiardi*), or more as needed

Makes a 12- or 13-inch *tiramisù*, serving 12 or more

Pour just enough water in the double-boiler pan so the water level is right below the bottom of the mixing bowl when it is sitting in the pan. Separate the eggs, putting yolks into the large bowl of the double boiler and the whites into another stainless-steel bowl for whipping by hand or with an electric mixer.

Remove the zest of two or more of the lemons, using a fine grater, to get 2 tablespoons of zest. Squeeze out and strain the juice of these and the other lemons to get ¾ cup of fresh lemon juice.

To make the base for the *tiramisù*, heat the water in the double boiler to a steady simmer. Off the heat, beat the egg yolks with ¼ cup of the sugar and ½ cup of the limoncello until well blended. Set the bowl over the simmering water, and whisk constantly, frequently scraping the whisk around the sides and bottom of the bowl, as the egg mixture expands and heats into a frothy sponge, 5 minutes or longer. When the sponge has thickened enough to

Recommended Equipment

A double boiler, with a large stainless-steel bowl and a wide saucepan to hold it

A large flexible wire whisk

A shallow-rimmed pan for moistening the *savoiardi* with syrup

For assembling the *tiramisù,* a shallow casserole or baking dish with 3-quart capacity, such as a 9-by-13-inch Pyrex pan

form a ribbon when it drops on the surface, take the bowl off the double-boiler pan and let it cool.

Meanwhile, pour the remaining cup of limoncello, all of the lemon juice, 1 cup water, and ½ cup of the sugar in a saucepan. Bring to a boil, stirring to dissolve the sugar, and cook for 5 minutes, evaporating the alcohol. Let the syrup cool completely.

In another large bowl, stir the mascarpone with a wooden spoon to soften it, then drop in the grated lemon zest and beat until light and creamy. Whip the egg whites with the remaining ¼ cup sugar, by hand or by machine, until it holds moderately firm peaks.

When the cooked limoncello sponge (or zabaglione) is cooled, scrape about a third of it over the mascarpone, and fold it in with a large rubber spatula. Fold in the rest of the zabaglione in two or three additions. Now fold in the whipped egg whites in several additions, until the limoncello-mascarpone cream is light and evenly blended.

Pour some of the cooled syrup, no deeper than ¼ inch, into the shallow-rimmed pan to moisten the ladyfingers (*savoiardi*). One at a time, roll a ladyfinger in the syrup and place it in the casserole or baking dish. Wet each cookie briefly—if it soaks up too much syrup, it will fall apart. Arrange the moistened ladyfingers in neat, tight rows, filling the bottom of the pan completely. You should be able to fit about twenty ladyfingers in a single layer.

Scoop half of the limoncello-mascarpone cream onto the ladyfingers, and smooth it to fill the pan and cover them. Dip and arrange a second layer of ladyfingers in the pan, and cover it completely with the remainder of the cream.

Smooth the cream with the spatula, and seal the *tiramisù* airtight in plastic wrap. Before serving, refrigerate for 6 hours (or up to 2 days), or put it in the freezer for 2 hours. To serve, cut portions of *tiramisù* in any size you like, and lift each out of the pan onto dessert plates.

Cookie Crumble

FREGOLOTTA

Fregola means "crumb," and *fregolotta* means "one big crumb:" for this delightful treat, you make and bake lots of little crumbs into two round cookie crumbles.

This is an ideal cake/cookie: it keeps for days in a tin, and is delightful after dinner with some ice cream or whipped cream. It is the quintessential cookie to have with your espresso to finish a true Italian meal.

Makes two 9-inch cookies for crumbling, serving 12 to 14

2 tablespoons soft butter for the pans

6 ounces (about 1¼ cups) whole unblanched almonds, toasted

1 cup plus 3 tablespoons all-purpose flour

1 scant cup sugar

¼ teaspoon salt

3 large egg yolks

6 tablespoons heavy cream, or more if needed

Recommended Equipment
Two 9-inch springform pans

Preheat the oven to 350°. Assemble the springform pans, and butter the bottom disks and about an inch up the sides.

Set aside two or three whole almonds, and chop all the rest coarsely into chunks the size of chocolate chips. Stir the flour, sugar, and salt together in a mixing bowl, and toss in the chopped almonds.

Beat the yolks together briefly, and drizzle all over the dry ingredients. Toss with a fork to blend. Drizzle the cream over by tablespoons, tossing and stirring to moisten the nut mixture evenly. It should be crumbly but not floury; add a small amount more cream if necessary.

Pour half of the crumb mixture into each buttered cake pan. Spread and press the crumbs down lightly in an even thick layer covering the bottom of the pan.

Bake for about 25 minutes or more, until the cookie rounds are nicely browned and starting to shrink from the side ring of the pan. Let them cool, then remove the springform side rings and bottom disk.

To serve, set the *fregolotta* in front of your guests on the table, with one of the reserved whole almonds underneath it. Smack the *fregolotta* in the center with the back of a spoon.

Serve as garnish with poached fruits or ice cream, or enjoy a crunchy piece all by itself with a cup of espresso. The leftovers are great for breakfast with *caffè latte*.

Sandy Cake

TORTA SABBIOSA

Sabbiosa means "sandy," and that's a good description of this delightful cake. At first bite it seems dry, but then it melts in your mouth, and you will love its golden hue as well. The cake can be enjoyed plain, simply dusted with confectioners' sugar, or doused with amaretto or limoncello and a topping of cream and/or fruit and berries. Serve it warm right from the oven; freeze it to pull out when unexpected guests drop in—or (as I do) have a piece for breakfast with cappuccino. All in all, this is a recipe you need to try.

Makes a 9-inch cake, serving 8 to 12

7 ounces (14 tablespoons) soft butter, plus more for the cake pan

¼ cup all-purpose flour, plus more for the cake pan

⅔ cup finely milled corn flour or cornmeal

¼ cup potato starch

½ packet (1 teaspoon) active dry yeast

1 cup sugar

2 eggs, separated

⅛ teaspoon salt

Powdered sugar for dusting the cake, or other toppings (optional)

Recommended Equipment
An electric mixer with paddle beaters

A 9-inch cake pan, conventional or springform, and a parchment circle for the bottom

Butter the cake-pan bottom, cover it with a parchment circle, then butter and flour the entire inside of the pan. Arrange a rack in the center of the oven, and preheat to 350°.

Sift together the corn flour, white flour, and potato starch.

Sprinkle yeast over ¼ cup warm water, and let it dissolve.

In the bowl of the mixer, cream together the sugar and 7 ounces butter for several minutes on high speed, scraping down the bowl several times, until light and smooth.

Beat in the egg yolks one at a time; scrape down the bowl, and fluff up the batter on high speed. Lower the speed, and incorporate the dry ingredients, alternating with the yeast water, in two or three additions. Mix only briefly after adding the flours, but scrape the bowl and beaters well, and fold the batter over with a rubber spatula—it will be stiff—to be sure the dry ingredients are evenly moistened.

With the whisk attachment or a hand whisk, whip the egg whites in a clean bowl, with the ⅛ teaspoon salt, to firm peaks. Stir a third of the whites into the batter to lighten it, then gently fold in the remainder. Scrape the batter into the prepared pan, and spread it in an even layer.

Bake for about 40 minutes, or until the top is golden brown and springs back to the touch, and the cake is starting to pull away from the sides of the pan.

Let it cool on a wire rack for an hour, then remove from the pan and dust with powdered sugar if you wish. Cut the cake in wedges, and serve warm or at room temperature (or reheated in a low oven, if you like), plain or fancy. (Wrap well and freeze for a month or so; defrost at room temperature before removing the wrappings.)

Fried Ribbon Cookies

CROSTOLI

In Padova, Treviso, and Venice (and elsewhere in Italy), sugar-dusted mounds of these fried cookies are served at weddings and holiday celebrations. They're essential at pre-Lenten festivities. In the Veneto, it just wouldn't be Carnevale without lots of *crostoli*!

At our house, these are a favorite treat all year around. The dough is easy to mix in the food processor, and it's fun for the whole family to make little ribbons and tie them in a knot. Make the cookies a few days in advance if you prefer, and powder with sugar just before serving.

Makes about 40 cookies

6 tablespoons very soft butter

⅓ cup sugar

½ teaspoon salt

¼ cup milk

1 large egg

1 egg yolk

3 tablespoons dark rum

1½ tablespoons fresh lemon juice

Finely grated zest of 1 lemon (about 2 teaspoons)

Finely grated zest of 1 orange (about 2 tablespoons)

2¼ cups all-purpose flour, plus more as needed

6 to 8 cups vegetable oil for frying, or as needed

2 tablespoons powdered sugar, or as needed

Blend the butter, sugar, and salt in the food processor. Add the milk, egg and yolk, rum, lemon juice, and citrus zests, and process everything together until smooth. Scrape down the sides of the bowl, dump in all of the flour, and process in pulses until the dough comes together. Clean the bowl again, and pulse a few more times to mix thoroughly.

Scrape the dough out onto a lightly floured work surface, and knead briefly into a soft, smooth ball. If it is sticky, knead in more flour in small amounts. Wrap the dough tightly in plastic, and chill for 30 minutes to an hour. (You can keep it refrigerated up to a day, but let it return to room temperature before rolling.)

Cut the chilled dough in half, and work with one piece at a time. Flatten the dough on a lightly floured work surface, and roll it out to a rough square shape, approximately 16 inches on a side. Trim the edges of the square, and with the fluted cutter divide it into ten strips, about 1½ inches wide. Cut across all the strips in the middle to form twenty ribbons, each about 7 inches long (though they shrink after you cut them).

One at a time, tie each ribbon into a simple overhand knot. If necessary, stretch the ends gently so they're long enough to knot. Place the knotted *crostoli* on a sheet pan lined with parchment or wax paper as you work, leaving room between them so they don't stick to each other. Roll out the second piece of dough; cut and tie ribbons the same way.

Fried Ribbon Cookies (continued)

Recommended Equipment
A food processor, a rolling pin, and a fluted pastry cutter for mixing and rolling the dough

A 10-inch saucepan or sauté pan with 4-inch sides for frying the *crostoli*

Meanwhile, pour vegetable oil in the pan to a depth of 2 inches or a bit more. Set over medium heat to reach frying temperature gradually. When you're ready to start frying, raise the heat, and test the oil by dropping in a scrap piece of dough; the fat should bubble actively around the dough, but it shouldn't get dark quickly. (If you have a frying thermometer, heat the oil to 350°. And be sure to use long-handled tools, hot pads, and caution when deep-frying.)

Using long-handled tongs, quickly drop the first batch of *crostoli* into the fryer—raise the heat to return the oil to frying temperature. Don't crowd the cookies—fry only ten or twelve at a time in a 10-inch-diameter pan. The cookies first drop to the bottom, but soon float to the surface. Turn them frequently with tongs and a spider or slotted spoon, to cook evenly.

Fry the *crostoli* for 4 minutes or so, as they color gradually to dark gold. Adjust the heat as needed to maintain oil temperature and prevent too rapid browning. When crisp and golden all over, lift them from the oil with a spider or spoon, drain off oil, then lay them on layers of paper towel to cool. Fry the remaining *crostoli* in batches the same way; drain and cool. Store in a sealed cookie tin or plastic container, and keep them dry.

To serve, pile the cooled *crostoli* on a serving plate in a heaping mound. Put the powdered sugar in a small mesh sieve, and dust generously over the cookies.

Tanya's Tour

PADOVA AND TREVISO

BAPTISTERY: Visited by Few, Populated by Many
Location: In Padua (Padova), near the Piazza Monte di Pieta, next to the Duomo

Padua's Baptistery is a simple yet pleasant structure with small decorative Romanesque arches. Inside is one of the most complete medieval fresco cycles in Italy, masterfully painted in 1378 by Giusto de'Menabuoi and his workshop, depicting stories from the Old and New Testaments. Some are told in sequences of small scenes, like comic strips; other parables are fully illustrated in one large frame. With every bit of available wall space covered by painted vignettes, it is as if you're enclosed in a magnificent patchwork quilt (which can be a bit claustrophobic). There are too many wonderful details to describe here: just sit down and let your eyes move slowly, alighting on such dramatic scenes as the banishment of Adam and Eve from the Garden of Eden or the amazing architectural details of Sodom and Gomorrah burning, with small licks of flame coming out of each window. Most striking is the vortex created in the central dome by the multitude of figures swirling upward to heaven.

BASILICA DI SAN ANTONIO: The Many Miracles
Location: In Padua, southeast of the Piazza delle Erbe, on the Piazza del Santo

From the outside, the basilica that houses the body of St. Anthony looks like a small version of St. Mark's in Venice, with similar eastern architectural influences. Inside, the silence is absolute, as most visitors head straight for St. Anthony's tomb to invoke its miraculous powers. You can (and should) see the many artworks, including Donatello's bronze reliefs and his wonderful *Gattamelata* statue, and the chapel painted by Altichiero.

Even if you are not a religious or spiritual person, it is fascinating and moving to see how deeply St. Anthony is revered, and how powerfully drawn so many people are to his tomb. By custom, visitors process around the back of the tomb and touch the dark slab of stone nearest the saint's body. Many stop and pray, and the shrine is covered with photos or ex-votos, small silver hearts framed on velvet, left by those asking for a miracle (or in thanks for one already received). People also ask the saint for guidance and other forms of help. I know that my *nonna* Erminia came here to ask St. Anthony to provide safety for her family as they began their journey to America.

CAFFÈ PEDROCCHI: A Caffè That Never Sleeps
Location: In Padua, on the Piazza Cavour, a short way to the northeast of the Piazza delle Erbe

From the moment it opened its doors in 1848, Caffè Pedrocchi has been a caffeine-fueled chat room for the intense intellectuals of Padova, many of them students at the famous University of Padova, and for radicals to engage in political discussions. Today the *caffè* still exhibits some of that youthful revolutionary energy and charm. And even its Art Deco décor, in Egyptian or Greek style on the second floor (or *piano nobile*), will provide some diversion when you stop for a coffee.

THE SCROVEGNI CHAPEL: Where the Renaissance Was Born
Location: In Padua, northeast of the Piazza delle Erbe, along the Corso Garibaldi

The huge forward movement in art history contained in the word "Renaissance" is visible in this tiny chapel. Under an azure starry sky—the fresco color almost as vivid as when it was painted—you can see the many ways in which Giotto redefined the conventions of art, in spatial definition, emotional expression, and anatomical representation. Here, in *The Flight to Egypt*, Mary is riding a very realistic donkey, and Giotto captures an emotional intensity in Judas' betraying kiss and in the anguish over Christ's dead body that had never been seen before. I am always impressed at the spatial prowess demonstrated in *The Pentecost*; there we not only see the seated disciples but can somehow sense the weight of their bodies firmly planted on the wooden plank upon which they are seated. History was made in this room, and I urge you to take time to observe all the details of the genius of Giotto displayed here in the Scrovegni chapel.

SALA DEI GIGANTI: Giants from the Past and One Small Master
Location: In the Palazzo Bo at the University of Padova

The *sala* is decorated with a cycle of large fresco portraits of *uomini illustri*, or illustrious men, which I tell you about on page 161.

You will also see a small portrait in the corner of the room, not one of the *uomini illustri*. This is an extremely rare depiction of the great poet Petrarch, at his desk writing, painted around the time of his death in 1374.

TREVISO'S PAINTED HOUSES: Ghosts of the Past
Location: Painted houses will surprise you here and there around Treviso (hints below). The Museo Civico is at Borgo Cavour 24, along Via Riccati

A stroll through the narrow streets of Treviso is full of delightful surprises and a wonderful sense that things are not what they seem at first glance. Begin walking at the fish market, along the canals with gorgeous, antique paddle wheels gently lapping at the water, shadowed by rows of narrow towerhouses—multistoried medieval homes, usually with arched loggias on ground level. You'll think you're in a medieval hamlet, cramped and concentrated. Then all of a sudden you'll walk into the large expanse around the cathedral in the Piazza dei Signori, with its monumental buildings and broad vista, and your whole perspective on the city will change.

Most exciting to me is to come upon the rare towerhouse with faded yet enchanting traces of decoration over its entire façade—lines and panels of a geometric pattern, swatches of tapestry design or remnants of a fresco with mythological themes. Once nearly every tower in the town displayed a brilliant, colorful face to the public but time has almost completely erased and eroded them. Today muted colors remain on only a handful of structures, ghostly but thrilling reminders of how grand and colorful medieval Treviso must have been. It is a particular delight to stumble on one of these faded beauties when you don't expect it, so I suggest strolling along Via Riccati, Via Canova, and Via della Poggia with your eyes open. There are also treasures to be found on Via Pescheria, near the fish market island as you walk south toward the station—hint: look for Casa Quaglia.

If you don't trust your luck, just head for the painted houses that are part of the Museo Civico and enjoy its collection of paintings and archeological finds as well. Several of the artworks are outstanding, such as Titian's portrait of philosopher Sperone Speroni, Lorenzo Lotto's *Portrait of a Dominican*, and Sebastiano Florigero's *Castragatti* (Cat Fixer).

IL DUOMO: Richness and Simplicity
Location: In Treviso, on Via Duomo, northwest of the main Piazza dei Signori

When we arrive in Treviso by train, I like to start walking toward the Piazza dei Signori, which has some of the city's most impressive architecture, notably the Palazzo dei Trecento and the Palazzo del Podestà. You can make your way down the Calmaggiore, an arcaded street, to the Duomo, which has undergone many changes since its Romanesque beginnings (from which two lions remain). Its temple-front neoclassical façade, with seven domes, is distinct from the rest of the city's architecture. The crypt, from 1100, is the only original part of the cathedral, with fragments of frescoes in the vaults and Romanesque zoomorphic mosaic on the floors. I love the Pordenone fresco cycle, a huge jumble of figures, enormous expressive bodies with saturated hues. Finally, I always spend some time in front of Titian's *Annunciation* in the chapel—sometimes enjoying the rare good fortune of having a Titian all to myself. The natural lighting of the room mimics the soft lighting that illuminates the veil like robes and supple skin in the painting.

SAN NICCOLÒ: Power in Numbers

Location: In the southwest of Treviso, just inside the city walls,
on Via San Niccolò

The large Dominican church of San Niccolò is an impressive structure with a colossal fresco of St. Christopher and enormous columns frescoed with representations of saints by Tomaso da Modena, a little-known but wonderful fourteenth-century artist. An extraordinary display of his work can be seen in the seminary adjoining the church, on Via San Niccolò. Few visitors know of this treasure, so ring the bell and ask to enter the chapter house. Here, the upper arches of the walls are covered with Tomaso's portraits of famous Dominican monks, forty in all. These revered scholar-priests, including St. Thomas Aquinas, are all portrayed at their desks, a typical setting for members of this intellectual order, yet the artist has captured the individual personality of each man.

PIEMONTE

Chapter 5

Roasted Pepper Rolls Stuffed with Tuna
PEPERONI RIPIENI CON TONNO ED ACCIUGHE

Quince and Hazelnut Chutney
CUNJA

Warm Garlic Anchovy Dip
BAGNA CAUDA

Scrambled Eggs with Truffle
UOVA STRAPAZZATE AL TARTUFO

Tajarin Pasta with Truffle Butter
TAJARIN AL BURRO E TARTUFO

Agnolotti with Roast Meat and Spinach Stuffing
AGNOLOTTI DEL PLIN

Truffle Risotto
RISOTTO AL TARTUFO

Baked Cardoons My Way
CARDI ALLA LIDIA

Beef Braised in Barolo
STUFATO AL BAROLO

Espresso Zabaglione
ZABAGLIONE AL CAFFÈ NERO

Cornmeal Cookies
CRUMIRI

Hazelnut Torte
TORTA DI NOCCIOLE

In my constant pursuit of new food experiences, I often go to the region of Piemonte. There some of the world's best red wines are made. Barolo is one of them and is considered the king of Italian reds. It is made from the Nebbiolo varietals, as is the Barbaresco, both bearing the names of the local towns. In Italy, cuisine is all about the right product—using the best primary ingredients is the guarantee of good results in cooking. So it is no surprise that in Barolo their own robust wine is the essential liquid for traditional *stufato al Barolo,* a deliciously complex, fork-tender braised beef. Though the finest Barolo is never used for cooking—that would be considered sacrilege—a bottle or two of respectable Barolo is readily poured into the braising pot, for nothing less will give the *stufato* (or stew) the flavor that makes it special and worthy of the Barolo name.

Where there is good wine, good food is sure to be found. And nowhere is this more true than in the Langhe, the area around Alba, a wonderful town right between the Barolo and Barbaresco wine districts. This hilly countryside harbors many little towns and food delights that draw me back to make new discoveries.

Most prized of all the local products, certainly, are the white truffles, or *Tuber magnatum,* of the Langhe. Considered by many to be the most aromatic of all truffles, these white *tartufi* are genuine buried treasures, a small number unearthed each year during a short foraging season from October to December. Memorable meals in Alba have taught me that simple dishes are the best for enjoying the ethereal flavor and fragrance of truffle. Piedmontese cooks just shave paper-thin flakes of raw truffle over steaming risotto, or homemade *tajarin,* a traditional rich egg pasta cut like tagliatelle. Simplest of all, and my favorite, is *uova strapazzate,* lightly scrambled eggs with truffle shavings dropped on at the last second. It is heaven on a plate.

In the area of Nizza Monferrato, the *cardi gobbi* ("hunchbacked cardoons" is the literal translation) are king, and they are used in many dishes, from soup to pasta filling, or turned into a glorious baked vegetable dish. Cardoons are from the thistle family, hence cousin to the artichoke, and though they might be a little tough on the outside, they are deliciously crunchy and tasty. The *cardi gobbi* are called "hunchbacked" because, as with endive and white asparagus, the young shoots are pressed back close to the ground and covered with straw so they remain white, and in the process develop a hump. Without the sunlight, the chlorophyll does not develop, so, instead of turning green, they stay white and tender.

Strangely enough for a landlocked region of Italy, Piemonte has a lot of fish on its menu: roasted peppers stuffed with tuna (the peppers used are the meaty horn-shaped *corno di bue* from Carmagnola); *bagna cauda,* a garlic-and-anchovy dip for raw vegetables or a sauce for cooked; and *vitello tonnato,* to name a few. Liguria is just to the south of Piemonte, and since it is coastal there is a lot of fishing. The Ligurians for centuries came up to Piemonte, and still do today, to buy Barolo. But in earlier times they bartered fish for wine, and so fish permeated the cuisine of Piemonte.

Roasted Pepper Rolls Stuffed with Tuna

PEPERONI RIPIENI CON TONNO ED ACCIUGHE

Antipasti are, for me, the best part of a Piedmontese meal. At any family gathering (and in restaurants as well), the platters of different antipasti just never stop coming. And at some point in the procession, roasted peppers stuffed with tuna will arrive at the table. The combination of sweet, meaty peppers and well-seasoned oil-cured tuna is always delightful.

In Piemonte, cooks are discriminating about the peppers they roast, and most sought are those from Carmagnola, a town in the countryside south of Torino. Carmagnola peppers are justly famous, for wonderful flavor as well as their vivid colors and distinctive shapes, like the *corno di bue* (ox horn) and *trottola* (spinning top). Carmagnola also is well known for *il coniglio grigio di Carmagnola*—the gray rabbit from Carmagnola—considered to be one of the best in Italy.

Here in the States, any fresh, meaty sweet bell-type peppers are suitable—different colors make a nice presentation. And peppers are always best roasted and peeled at home, though a jar of roasted red peppers can be substituted if you are short on time. (If you have no peppers at all, this tuna filling is delicious on crostini or crackers—it makes a world-class tuna-fish sandwich too.)

Makes about 15 small rolls, serving 6 as an hors d'oeuvre

3 or 4 sweet red or assorted-color peppers (about 1½ pounds total)

⅓ cup or so extra-virgin olive oil

1 teaspoon coarse sea salt or kosher salt, or to taste

Two 6-ounce cans tuna packed in olive oil (preferably imported from Italy)

2 small anchovy fillets, drained and finely chopped

2 tablespoons small capers, drained and finely chopped

1 tablespoon apple-cider vinegar

Preheat the oven to 350°. Rub the peppers all over with 2 tablespoons olive oil, season with ½ teaspoon salt, and place on a parchment-lined baking sheet. Roast for 30 minutes or so, turning the peppers occasionally, until their skins are wrinkled and slightly charred.

Let the peppers cool completely. Slice in half (through the stem end), discard the stem, peel off the skin, and slice the halves lengthwise into strips 2 inches wide. Scrape the seeds from the strips, and lay them in a sieve to drain and dry.

To make the stuffing, drain the tuna and break it into flakes in a medium-sized bowl. One at a time, mix the seasonings into the tuna with a fork: chopped anchovies, capers, vinegar, mustard, mayonnaise, parsley, 2 tablespoons olive oil, and about ½ teaspoon salt. Stir vigorously, breaking up lumps of fish, until the stuffing is soft and fairly smooth. Add more of any seasoning to taste.

Roasted Pepper Rolls Stuffed with Tuna (continued)

1 tablespoon prepared mustard

⅓ cup mayonnaise

1 tablespoon chopped fresh Italian parsley

Drop a scant tablespoon of stuffing at one end of each roast pepper strip and roll it up snugly, creating a neat cylinder. Press the pepper as you wrap, so it adheres to itself and stays closed.

To serve, arrange all the rolls on a platter, drizzle a bit more olive oil all over, and sprinkle lightly with coarse salt.

Seeds of a Food Revolution from Piemonte

An hour south of Torino, just a few kilometers from Alba, is the rural town of Bra. In the past, it was perhaps best known as the trading center for the cheeses of the Cuneo province of Piemonte, and for the fine cheeses that took the town's name, such as Bra Tenero, Bra Duro, and Bra d'Alpeggio.

Today, though, Bra is becoming more famous as the birthplace and headquarters of the influential Slow Food Movement, first organized in 1986 by Carlo Petrini. The philosophy of Slow Food—which now has associations in a hundred countries worldwide—is the restoration of the fundamental importance of conviviality and the right to the true values and pleasures of the table. The movement believes that any traditional product encapsulates the flavors of its region of origin, of the local customs and the ancient techniques of producing it. The Slow Food movement is playing an important role in saving the traditional artisan products of Italy and other nations.

Among Slow Food's activities worldwide, one of the most successful is an international festival of artisanal cheeses, held every two years in Bra. When I attended this event in 2005, more than a hundred thousand people from around the world descended on the little town—cheesemakers, farmers, dairy experts, and cheese lovers—to sample and learn about more than 150 distinctive cheeses. If you love cheese (and other traditional food products) you must make a trip to Piemonte for future festivals. For more information, visit the Slow Food Web site: www.slowfood.com.

Quince and Hazelnut Chutney

CUNJA

I love chutneys, for both their concentrated flavor and the convenience. You make them and store them, and whenever you want that special treat you can just pull them from the fridge or pantry. All you need is a spoonful to enjoy the essence of whatever ingredients you put into them.

Cunja is just such a treasured condiment from Piemonte. Quince is a primary ingredient (as it is in *cotognata*, another traditional Italian chutney), but *cunja* incorporates the indigenous flavors of late autumn in Piemonte: the local San Martino pears, the *mosto* of pressed Nebbiolo grapes, and its famed hazelnuts.

Though these particular ingredients will probably not be in your market, my recipe produces a thoroughly delicious and long-lasting chutney with much of the layered complexity of *cunja*. In place of *cotto mosto*, the cooking liquid here is bottled Concord-grape juice (always made from concentrate); organic juice is highly recommended.

Unfortunately, we can't get small sweet San Martino pears in the United States. These are the last pears to be harvested, in early November, at the same time as the Feast of San Martino—hence their name. Our Seckel pears are an excellent alternative, and Granny Smith apples will also work well. Packed in jars and refrigerated, this will keep for a couple of months. As I explain, *cunja* is meant to be enjoyed with a creamy Piemontese cheese, but I serve it with pork roast and other meats. I am sure you will find many delicious uses for it.

Makes 2 to 3 cups of dense fruit condiment

8 cups organic Concord-grape juice

1 lemon, zest removed in ribbons, and juiced

4-inch piece stick cinnamon

4 whole cloves

4 dried figs, cut in quarters

4 ripe quince (about 1¼ pounds), cored and cut into 1½-inch chunks

Pour the grape juice into the pan with the ribbons of lemon zest, strained lemon juice, cinnamon stick, and cloves. Bring to a steady boil, and cook uncovered until reduced by half.

Strain the thickened grape juice (discard the spices and lemon peel), and return to the clean saucepan with the cut fruit. Heat to a gently bubbling boil, and cook, partially covered, for 15 minutes or so, to soften the fruit.

Remove the cover, and simmer slowly, frequently turning and stirring the fruit chunks, as the juices concentrate and are absorbed. Lower the heat if necessary to avoid burning. Cook, stirring almost constantly at the end, until there's no liquid in the pan and the *cunja* is quite dense (40 minutes or more).

1 pound firm Seckel pears (preferred) or Granny Smith apples, cored and cut into 1½-inch chunks

¼ cup coarsely chopped toasted walnuts

½ cup coarsely chopped toasted hazelnuts

Recommended Equipment
A heavy-bottomed 4- or 5-quart saucepan or enameled French oven

Cool completely, then fold in the chopped toasted nuts. Pack into jars. It will keep for a month or two refrigerated.

Serve at room temperature with cheese (preferably ripened Toma Piemontese).

Cunja and Cheese from Piemonte— a Match to Die For

As I have learned in my visits to Piemonte, traditionalists insist that there is only one way to serve and enjoy *cunja*, page 139 (though I admit to you it does have *many* delicious uses). For them, *cunja* is made to accompany the great creamy local cheeses, a morsel of condiment with each taste of cheese. The depth of feeling about this marriage of seasonal treasures is frequently expressed in the Italian phrase *"questo è la sua morte"*—which I roughly translate for you to mean, "This is the ultimate way it should be enjoyed!"

What cheese is best with *cunja*? I particularly like soft Toma Piemontese, a DOP (protected origin) cow's-milk cheese with a creamy interior. Toma is ripened for at least a couple of weeks, but it grows more flavorful and deeper yellow in color as it ages. After a couple of months, when I can taste the mountain pasture in the cheese, Toma is at its best. Another fine cheese is Robiola, produced mainly in the Langhe. It is creamy with a slight acidic finish and delicious with *cunja.* (Both cheeses are usually available in season from one of the fine Italian cheese importers listed in Sources, page 340.)

Warm Garlic Anchovy Dip

BAGNA CAUDA

Bagna cauda is one of Piemonte's best-known dishes. The name means "warm bath," and that's what it is: a sauce of garlic, butter, oil, and anchovy heated in a deep earthenware container set on the table over a little flame, like a fondue pot. Also on the table are arrayed a great variety of cut vegetables, raw and cooked, to be dipped in the piping-hot sauce, eaten, and savored. In Piemonte, *bagna cauda* will always include some of the fabulous vegetables for which the region is renowned, such as *cardi gobbi* from Nizza Monferrato, and the gorgeous long peppers of Carmagnola.

At home I serve an assortment of seasonal vegetables: You'll find some suggestions on the next page. This is a great starter on the table or for a buffet. To make more sauce for a crowd, simply multiply the ingredient amounts given in the recipe.

Makes about 1 cup of dipping sauce, for 6 appetizer servings with vegetables

4 to 6 plump garlic cloves, peeled

6 tablespoons extra-virgin olive oil, plus more as needed

2-ounce can anchovy fillets packed in olive oil, drained (2 tablespoons packed)

4 tablespoons butter

Recommended Equipment
A deep earthenware saucepan or terra-cotta fondue pot with heat source

In a mortar and pestle or mini-chopper, mash the garlic cloves and 1 tablespoon olive oil into a smooth paste, and transfer to a small bowl. Mash (or chop) the anchovy fillets into a smooth paste. (Alternatively, chop or slice the garlic and anchovy by hand, separately.)

Put the garlic (crushed, chopped, or sliced) in the saucepan with the butter, and set over medium-low heat or a tabletop heat source. Cook slowly until the garlic is thoroughly softened and melted in the butter. Stir in the anchovies and the remaining olive oil, and heat over a low flame, mashing the anchovies with the back of a spoon until thoroughly disintegrated.

When the *bagna cauda* is piping hot, whisk the sauce briefly to blend and emulsify, and serve with cut vegetables alongside (see box on following page).

Vegetables for Dipping in Bagna Cauda

Here are some of the vegetables that I enjoy with *bagna cauda* at home. You don't need to have every one and can certainly include other vegetables you love and that reflect the season. Before cutting the vegetables, squeeze the juice of one lemon into a quart or so of cold water. Then, to prevent oxidation, immerse the cut pieces of cardoon, Jerusalem artichoke, turnip, and other raw vegetables in the acidulated water. Cut raw vegetables thin for pleasant munching: $\frac{1}{4}$-inch sticks are a good size. Drain and dry just before serving.

- Raw celery stalks, cut in sticks
- Raw carrots, cut in sticks
- Fresh sweet pepper, red or yellow, cut in wide sticks
- Raw cardoon, trimmed and peeled (see page 152), cut in $\frac{1}{2}$-inch sticks
- Raw Jerusalem artichoke, peeled and cut in thin slices
- Raw cauliflower, cut in small florets
- Fingerling potatoes, boiled and peeled (or thin rounds of cooked larger potatoes)
- Tender center leaves of raw Savoy cabbage, uncooked, cut in wide shreds
- Small turnips, cooked or raw, peeled and cut in thin sticks

Scrambled Eggs with Truffle

UOVA STRAPAZZATE AL TARTUFO

This is one of the simplest recipes in this book, and it is one of the most sublime. Yes, truffles add a mystique—but even without them this is my favorite way to cook eggs.

Essential to this procedure is never to allow the olive oil to reach temperatures at which heat alters and degrades the flavors. Hence, you will ultimately have the full presence of fresh olive oil in a natural state intermingled with the egg and truffle flavors. Thus, the quality of the olive oil is paramount here, more than in most cooked dishes. I like using lighter and more vegetal olive oils from the Lago di Garda district, Friuli-Venezia Giulia, or Istria.

Another important point is to keep the curd of the egg large and soft. The steady but gentle dragging of the curds—*strapazzati* means "dragged"—and controlled heat prevents any part from cooking solid, and in this moist state all the natural flavor of the egg comes through. As with olive oil, the best-quality eggs are essential—as fresh as can be, and organic if possible.

There is a basic lesson to be learned in this recipe that applies to Italian cooking—for that matter, to all cooking—get the best ingredients, do not overcrowd the flavors, and work the food as little as possible. Along with this lesson, I am sure, you'll get some of the best scrambled eggs you've ever tasted—even without truffles.

Serves 4 as a light meal or 6 as an appetizer

12 large eggs

¾ teaspoon salt

6 tablespoons extra-virgin olive oil

1-ounce or larger white truffle, brushed clean

Recommended Equipment

A sturdy 12-inch nonstick skillet with a cover

A heat-proof rubber spatula

A truffle shaver or sharp vegetable peeler

Beat the eggs and the salt very well in a large bowl.

Pour the olive oil into the skillet, swirl it to coat the bottom and sides, and set on a stove burner, heat off.

Pour and scrape all the eggs into the skillet. Turn the heat on high. Wait a few seconds, just until the heat starts to permeate the pan and reach the eggs. Gently slide the spatula from the side of the pan into the center, dragging the first coagulated eggs with it. Repeat the motion, drawing in eggs from another spot.

Steadily move around the pan, constantly pulling in cooked eggs with the spatula blade, as uncooked eggs flow into the cleared space. As you drag them, the eggs will form long rippling sheets. Don't break them up, but keep gathering them gently, into a soft mass of ruffles.

Lower the heat if the eggs sizzle—don't let them brown. As soon as the sides stay clear and no loose egg is flowing, turn off the

Scrambled Eggs with Truffle (continued)

heat. If there's a lot of wet, uncooked egg caught in the ruffles—more than you like—tumble the mass over gently to cook them, but don't break it up. Or leave the eggs wet and soft, as I like them.

Quickly divide the eggs in equal portions on warm plates, and immediately shave paper-thin flakes of truffle, a dozen or so, on top of each one. Serve right away, as the heat releases the aroma of truffle.

Tajarin Pasta with Truffle Butter

TAJARIN AL BURRO E TARTUFO

When you have a white truffle, enjoy it just as they do in Alba, with golden *tajarin*. If fresh truffle is unavailable, packaged truffle butter makes a nice dressing for the pasta too (see Sources, page 340). Should you have no truffle at all, *tajarin* with only butter and Grana Padano or Parmigiano-Reggiano will be simply luxurious, if not quite ethereal.

Makes 1 pound of fresh pasta, serving 6 as a first course

For the pasta
2 cups all-purpose flour, plus more for working

9 large egg yolks (about ⅔ cup)

2 tablespoons extra-virgin olive oil

3 tablespoons ice water, plus more as needed

For cooking and dressing the pasta
1 tablespoon coarse sea salt or kosher salt, or more if needed

½ pound (2 sticks) butter

1 cup freshly grated Grana Padano or Parmigiano-Reggiano

1-ounce or larger white truffle, brushed clean

Recommended Equipment
A food processor and a pasta-rolling machine

An 8-quart pot for cooking the pasta

A heavy, wide skillet for dressing the pasta

A truffle shaver or sharp vegetable peeler

To mix the *tajarin* dough, put the 2 cups flour in the food processor, fitted with the metal blade, and process for a few seconds to aerate. Mix together the egg yolks, olive oil, and 3 tablespoons of the water in a measuring cup or other spouted container. Start the food processor running, and pour in the liquids through the feed tube (scrape in *all* the drippings). Process for 30 to 40 seconds, until a dough forms and gathers on the blade. If the dough does *not* gather on the blade or process easily, it is too wet or too dry. Feel the dough, then work in either more flour or ice water, in small amounts, using the machine or kneading by hand.

Turn the dough out on a lightly floured surface, and knead by hand for a minute, until it's smooth, soft, and stretchy. Press it into a disk, wrap well in plastic wrap, and let rest at room temperature for ½ hour. (You can refrigerate the dough for up to a day, or freeze it for a month or more. Defrost in the refrigerator and return to room temperature before rolling.)

Cut the dough in four equal pieces. Keeping the dough lightly floured, roll each piece through a pasta machine at progressively narrower settings into sheets that are 5 inches wide (or as wide as your machine allows) and at least 20 inches long. Cut each strip crosswise into three shorter rectangles, about 7 inches long.

Flour the rectangles, and roll them up the long way, into loose cylinders, like fat cigars. With a sharp knife, cut cleanly through the rolled dough *crosswise* at ⅛-to-¼-inch intervals. Shake and unroll the cut pieces, opening them into *tajarin* ribbons, each about 7 inches long and ¼ inch wide. Dust them liberally with flour, and set them on a floured towel or tray.

To cook the *tajarin*, bring to the boil 6 quarts of water with the tablespoon salt. Meanwhile, melt the butter in the large skillet, and dilute it with ⅓ cup of the hot pasta water. Heat until barely simmering.

When the pasta water is at a rolling boil, shake the *tajarin* in a colander to remove excess flour, and drop them all at once into the pot. Stir well to separate the ribbons, and bring back to the boil. Cook for only a minute, or until the pasta is just *al dente*, then lift it from the water with a spider, drain briefly, and drop it into the skillet.

Over low heat, toss the *tajarin* until well coated with butter. Turn off the heat, and toss in half the grated cheese. Shave coin-sized flakes of truffle—using half the piece—over the pasta, and toss in.

Heap individual portions of pasta into warm bowls. Quickly shave the remaining truffle, in equal shares, on top of each mound of *tajarin*, and serve immediately.

Opposite: *Agnolotti (left);*
cutting fettuccine (right)

Agnolotti with Roast Meat and Spinach Stuffing

AGNOLOTTI DEL PLIN

Agnolotti del plin, or agnolotti with a pinch, is the quintessential Piedmontese stuffed pasta, served in starred restaurants and the simplest of trattorias throughout the year. But if you happen to be in the Alba area in the late autumn, don't fail to order the agnolotti, because every eating establishment will be shaving white truffle over them. And when blanketed with white Alba truffles, this always delicious dish is raised to an even greater height of flavor.

In Piedmontese homes, *agnolotti del plin* is often made with small amounts of any roast-meat leftovers, whether beef or pork, poultry or game, chopped and seasoned to serve as an impromptu filling for golden *tajarin* dough. For big occasions (and in restaurants, of course), meat is roasted specifically for the filling, as in the recipe here. But if you happen to have one or more kinds of tasty leftover roast, by all means use it (you'll need a couple of cups of shredded meat, trimmed of gristle, to make a full batch). And even if you don't have a white truffle, a simple dressing of sage-infused butter is a lovely complement to the flavors of the meat filling and the rich egg pasta.

Makes about 50 agnolotti

1 batch *tajarin* pasta dough (preceding recipe)

For the filling
8-to-10-ounce chunk boneless pork shoulder or butt, veal shoulder, or beef chuck

2 chicken thighs or 1 rabbit leg, on the bone (½ pound or so)

1 tablespoon extra-virgin olive oil

1 small onion, peeled and cut in chunks

2 garlic cloves, peeled

1 sprig rosemary

⅓ cup light stock (chicken, turkey, or vegetable broth)

Mix the pasta dough in advance, following the instructions in the preceding recipe. Refrigerate or freeze the dough. Return it to room temperature before rolling.

Several hours in advance, roast the meats, to allow them to cool at room temperature. Preheat the oven to 425°. Pour the tablespoon olive oil in the bottom of a small roasting pan. Cut the pork, veal, or beef chunk in 1-inch pieces, and put the pieces in the pan with the chicken (or rabbit) pieces, onion chunks, garlic, and rosemary. Pour in the stock, and season with ¼ teaspoon of the salt. Cover the pan with aluminum foil, roast for about ½ hour, and remove the foil. Continue roasting, turning the pieces occasionally, until all are tender and caramelized and there's only a small amount of liquid left in the pan. Remove from the oven, and let the meat cool completely in the roasting juices.

Rinse and drain the spinach leaves, and slice into thin shreds. Melt the tablespoon butter in a skillet over medium-high heat until foaming, add the spinach, season with ½ teaspoon of the salt, and stir to wilt the shreds. Cover the pan and cook for a minute or so, until the spinach releases its liquid, then cook uncovered over

1 teaspoon coarse sea salt or
kosher salt

1 pound tender fresh
spinach leaves

1 tablespoon butter

1 large egg

Freshly grated nutmeg

Freshly ground black pepper
to taste

⅓ cup freshly grated
Grana Padano or
Parmigiano-Reggiano

*For cooking and dressing the
agnolotti*
1 tablespoon coarse sea salt or
kosher salt for the pasta pot

12 tablespoons (1½ sticks) butter

8 large fresh sage leaves (or
more smaller leaves)

1 cup freshly grated
Grana Padano or
Parmigiano-Reggiano

Recommended Equipment
A pasta-rolling machine and a
rotary pastry cutter or pizza wheel

A large pot for cooking
the agnolotti

A 14-inch-wide sauté pan or deep
skillet for dressing the agnolotti

A pastry brush

medium heat until the liquid has all cooked off and the spinach is
tender. Turn the spinach into a colander set over a bowl, spreading
it out to drain and cool quickly. Do not squeeze it.

When the meats are cool, pour off and strain the pan juices.
Pull the chicken or rabbit meat off the bones; remove and discard
all fat, gristle, and skin. Shred the meat chunks, then chop into very
fine bits with a sharp knife. Finely chop the onions and mix into the
chopped meat, along with the pan juices. When the spinach is cool,
blend with the meat in a mixing bowl. Beat the egg, and stir it into
the filling along with the final ¼ teaspoon of the salt, gratings of
nutmeg and black pepper, and the ⅓ cup of grated cheese. Chill the
filling for several hours or overnight.

When ready to make the agnolotti, cut the pasta dough in
quarters. Roll each piece through a pasta machine at progressively
narrower settings into strips 4 to 5 inches wide and at least 24 inches
long. Lay the long strips flat on a floured surface and keep covered.

Fill and form agnolotti one strip at a time. With the dough running left to right in front of you, drop a scant tablespoon of filling in a mound, about 1 inch in from the end of the strip, then
drop more mounds at 2-inch intervals along its entire length. You
should have at least a dozen mounds in a straight line.

Dip the pastry brush in water, and moisten the long edges of the
dough strips, above and below the row of mounds. Pick up the top
long edge of each strip, fold it over the filling mounds, align it with
the bottom edge of dough, and press the moistened edges together.

To seal the agnolotti, pinch the dough on either side of every
filling mound, bringing the top and bottom edges of the folded
strip together, with your forefinger and thumb. Finally, run the
pastry wheel up and down through the pinched dough, separating
individual plump agnolotti. Lay them, spaced apart, in a single layer
on a floured tray. Repeat the entire process with the remaining
long strips of dough.

Cook the agnolotti right away, or refrigerate for a few hours, on
the tray, sealed with plastic wrap. For longer storage, freeze them
solid on the tray, then pack in freezer bags.

Fill the big pot with at least 6 quarts of water, with 1 tablespoon
salt, and bring to the boil. Meanwhile, put the butter in the sauté
pan or skillet, set it over low heat to melt, then toss in the sage

leaves. Keep the sauce warm—but not cooking—so the sage leaves infuse the melted butter.

Cook only two dozen or so agnolotti at a time. When the water is at a rolling boil, shake excess flour from the agnolotti and drop them into the pot. Stir well, and return to the boil rapidly. The agnolotti will drop to the bottom, then rise to the surface; keep moving and stirring them so they cook evenly and don't stick. Cook for about 4 minutes, and check for doneness, biting into the thickest edge of dough.

When they are fully cooked, lift out the agnolotti with a spider, drain briefly, and spill them into the warm butter in the pan, gently stirring and tumbling so all are coated. Meanwhile, return the water to the rolling boil and cook the remaining agnolotti. Drain and drop them in the pan, on top of the first batch. Raise the heat slightly, and turn and tumble the agnolotti until all are hot and coated with sage butter.

Turn off the heat and sprinkle half of the grated cheese on top. Spoon portions of agnolotti onto warm plates, drizzle a bit of the hot sage butter left in the pan over each portion, and serve right away. Pass more cheese at the table.

Truffle Risotto

RISOTTO AL TARTUFO

6 to 8 cups water

4 tablespoons extra-virgin olive oil

2 cups chopped onion

1 teaspoon salt, plus more to taste

2 cups Arborio or Carnaroli rice

1 cup white wine

For finishing
6 tablespoons butter, in tablespoon-sized pieces

½ cup freshly grated Grana Padano or Parmigiano-Reggiano

1-ounce or larger white truffle, brushed clean

Recommended Equipment
A 3-quart pot for hot water

A heavy saucepan, such as an enameled cast-iron French oven, 10 inches wide, with 3-to-4-quart capacity

A truffle shaver or sharp vegetable peeler

Heat the water in the pot almost to the boil. Cover and keep it very hot on the stove, near the risotto pan.

Put the olive oil, onion, and ½ teaspoon salt in the saucepan, and set over medium heat. Stir well as the onion starts to heat and soften; stir frequently and cook until it's wilted and just starting to color, 8 minutes or so.

Pour in the rice all at once, raise the heat, and stir the rice and onion continuously, toasting the grains (but not browning them!), until they make a clicking sound as you turn them in the pan, 2 minutes or more. Now pour in the wine, and keep stirring for another couple of minutes, all around the pan, until the moisture has evaporated and the rice is dry.

Immediately ladle in 2 cups of the almost simmering water, enough to cover the rice, and lower the heat. Cook, stirring steadily, until the water is almost totally absorbed, 4 to 6 minutes. Quickly ladle in more water to cover the rice, add another ½ teaspoon salt, and keep stirring, as the rice swells and releases its starches and a thick creamy suspension starts to form. Again, when the water is almost completely absorbed—and you can see the bottom of the saucepan as you stir—ladle in another cup or so of water.

Remember how much water you add: after incorporating 6 cups (or a bit more) over a period of 15 to 20 minutes, taste the rice for texture and seasoning—add more salt and/or incorporate more hot water if needed. When the risotto is perfectly cooked—at once *al dente* and creamy—turn off the heat.

Without delay, drop the butter pieces into the saucepan, and stir vigorously to mount—or amalgamate—the risotto with butter. Stir in the ½ cup of grated cheese. For each serving, spoon a mound of risotto into a warm pasta bowl, and immediately shave paper-thin flakes of truffle over the top. Serve right away, as the heat releases the aroma of truffle into the air, and dish up the next portion.

Baked Cardoons My Way

CARDI ALLA LIDIA

Cardi are popular all over Italy, but especially in Sicily and in Piemonte, at opposite ends of the country. In Sicily it is cooked as a side dish (*contorno*) and served with pasta, whereas in Piemonte it is used in soups and stuffings and dipped in *bagna cauda*. In truffle season, all *cardi* dishes are served with shavings of white truffles. The prized cardoon of Piemonte—essential if serving with truffle—is the *cardo gobbo di Nizza*, the tender white cardoon that never sees light.

Here is the baked cardoon *gratinate* I prepare at home with the conventionally grown cardoons available in American markets. The dish is delightful as is, but if you happen to have a white truffle lying around, give it a shave over the *gratinate* before serving.

Serves 4 to 6

1 lemon

2 pounds cardoon, 1 small head or the inner stalks of a large head

6 tablespoons butter, or as needed

1 teaspoon coarse sea salt or kosher salt, or as needed

About ⅔ cup freshly grated Grana Padano or Parmigiano-Reggiano, or as needed

Recommended Equipment
A sharp knife and vegetable peeler for trimming cardoon stalks

A 2-quart baking dish or shallow casserole, 8 by 11 inches or similar size

Before trimming the cardoon head, fill a large bowl with 1½ quarts cold water, squeeze in the juice of the lemon, and drop in the cut lemon halves.

Snap off the outer stalks at the base, discarding any bruised or tough and overmature stalks (usually 4 inches or wider). Keep separating stalks until you get to the heart, a pale cluster of tender stalks and leaves. Trim the base of the heart stalks so they separate, cut crosswise in 3-inch pieces, and drop in the acidulated water.

Now trim the larger, separated stalks one at a time. First peel or cut the long edges, removing all the sharp-pointed leaves (they get softer on inner stalks). Trim the top and base of the stalk, as with celery, and pull up the strings that run along the outside. Shave off the remaining fuzzy skin with the vegetable peeler. Finally, remove the pale, transparent skin that covers the inside: lift it at one end with the knife point, and peel away in long ribbons. Cut the trimmed stalk crosswise into 3-inch pieces, and immerse them in the lemon water while you cut up the rest.

Bring 3 quarts water to the boil in a large saucepan. Lift the cardoon pieces from the lemon water, drop into the pot, and cook until soft and tender (and to extract some bitterness), at least 30 minutes, and an hour or more for thick pieces. Remove the pieces as each is done (heart pieces first), and drain in a colander. Preheat the oven to 375°. Smear 2 tablespoons or so of the butter

on the bottom and sides of the baking dish, coating it generously. Melt the remaining butter. Lay cardoon pieces flat in the dish, covering the bottom in a single layer; sprinkle about ¼ teaspoon salt and 4 tablespoons grated cheese all over, and drizzle 2 tablespoons melted butter over that. Make another layer of cardoon (or two more, if you have lots of pieces), and top with salt, cheese, and butter. Sprinkle ⅓ cup grated cheese on the top layer of cardoon, or more, covering it completely.

Lay a sheet of aluminum foil over the dish, and crimp it loosely against the sides. Bake for 30 minutes, remove the foil, and bake another 10 minutes, until the cardoon is lightly caramelized and bubbling and the *gratinate* topping is golden. Serve hot.

Cardoons in Our Markets

California-grown cardoons (sometimes called *cardone*) appear in our supermarkets in the winter months. The large heads are gray-green and resemble giant heads of celery. They won't be crisp like celery, but should look fresh and feel heavy and moist. However, they often have many tough stalks, which I discard completely.

A rough rule of thumb is to buy 1 pound of *cardi* for each two portions. To minimize discard, try to buy several lighter cardoon heads, 2½ pounds or under, rather than one big head, to get a greater proportion of slender, inner stalks. In any case, you'll need to trim the stalks and parcook them as detailed in the recipe.

Beef Braised in Barolo

STUFATO AL BAROLO

Barolo is the king of Italian reds, a big wine, full of flavors, aromas, and lots of tannins. When you braise a beef shoulder or other big roast in a good Barolo, these elements permeate the meat and create a distinctive and complex sauce. Even if you are thousands of miles away, there's no doubt you will be transported to Piemonte for a few hours while the beef cooks to melting tenderness.

When you actually get to visit Piemonte, be sure to enjoy the region's renowned beef, from the Fassone breed of cattle, which yields lean and yet delicious meat. In addition to *stufato al Barolo*, Fassone beef served raw in carpaccio or steak tartare will be often on menus. In the fall, when the white truffle is in season, these dishes will be served with shavings of *tartufo*. This is food that we just can't replicate at home—I hope you get to Piemonte and savor it *in situ*.

Serves 6 or more

5-pound boneless beef roast, chuck or bottom round, trimmed of fat

2 teaspoons coarse sea salt or kosher salt, or to taste

⅓ cup extra-virgin olive oil

2 medium onions (1 pound total), peeled and quartered

3 big carrots (about ½ pound), peeled and cut in 2-inch wedges

4 big celery stalks (½ pound total), cut in 2-inch chunks

6 plump garlic cloves, peeled

2 branches fresh rosemary with lots of needles

6 large fresh sage leaves

Heat the oven, with a rack in the center, to 250°.

Season all surfaces of the roast with 1 teaspoon salt. Pour the olive oil into the big pan, and set over medium-high heat. Lay the roast in, and brown it on each side for a minute or two, without moving, until caramelized all over. Remove to a platter.

Still over medium-high heat, drop in the cut vegetables and garlic cloves, toss to coat with oil, and spread out in the pan. Drop in the rosemary, sage leaves, grated nutmeg, peppercorns, dried porcini, and remaining teaspoon salt, and toss all together. Cook for 3 or 4 minutes, stirring frequently and scraping up the browned meat bits on the pan bottom, just until the vegetables soften, then lower the heat.

Push the vegetables to the sides, and return the roast to the pan, laying flat on the bottom. Pour in the two bottles of wine and any meat juices that collected on the platter. The roast should be at least half submerged—add beef stock as needed.

Cover the pot, and heat until the wine is steaming but not boiling. Uncover the pan, and place it in the oven. After 30 minutes, rotate the roast so the exposed meat is submerged in the braising liquid. Braise this way, turning the meat in the pan every 30 minutes,

¼ teaspoon freshly grated nutmeg

1 teaspoon whole black peppercorns

1 ounce dried porcini slices (about 1 cup, loosely packed)

Two 750-milliliter bottles Barolo, or as needed

2 cups beef stock, or as needed

Freshly ground black pepper to taste

Recommended Equipment
A heavy 6-quart saucepan or enameled cast-iron French oven, round or oval, with a cover; select a pot in which the roast will fit with no more than 2 inches of space around it—the less space in the pot, the less wine you'll need

A meat thermometer

for about 3 hours, until fork-tender. The liquid should not boil—if it does, pour in some cold water to stop the bubbling, and lower the oven temperature.

After 2½ hours or so, check the beef with a meat thermometer. When its internal temperature reaches 180°—it should be easily pierced with a fork—take the pan from the oven. Remove the meat to a platter, with intact carrot and celery pieces to serve as a garnish.

Skim any fat from the braising juices, heat to a boil, and reduce to a saucy consistency that coats the back of a spoon. Pour through a sieve set over a clean container. Press in the juices from the strained herbs and vegetable pieces. Pour in any juices from the meat platter, and season the sauce to taste with salt and freshly ground black pepper. (If you are not going to serve right away, put the meat and reserved vegetables in the sauce to rest and cool, for a couple of hours or overnight.)

To serve, slice the meat crosswise (easier when it is cool). Pour a shallow layer of sauce in a wide skillet, and lay the slices in, overlapping. Heat the sauce to bubbling, spooning it over the beef, so the slices are lightly coated. Lift them with a broad spatula, and slide onto a warm platter, fanned out. Heat the carrots and celery in the sauce too, if you've saved them, and arrange on the platter. Serve, passing more heated sauce at the table.

Espresso Zabaglione

ZABAGLIONE AL CAFFÈ NERO

There's no way to exaggerate Italians' deep love of coffee, and nowhere is this more true than in Piemonte, where the *caffè*s are filled at every hour. And however many *tazzine* of potent espresso one might have gulped down during the day, a true Piedmontese will likely choose a coffee-flavored dessert after supper, be it *tiramisù*, gelato, or this light zabaglione laced with dark-roasted coffee.

This recipe is simple and delicious, whether freshly whipped and warm, or enriched with whipped cream and chilled. Serve with biscotti, *crumiri*, or over the *Torta di Nocciole* (on page 158).

Serves 6

6 large egg yolks

½ cup sugar

½ cup very strong brewed espresso, at room temperature

¼ cup dry Marsala

1 cup whipping cream, chilled

Recommended Equipment
A double boiler with a large stainless-steel bowl and a wide saucepan to hold it, to whip the zabaglione

A large flexible wire whisk

Tall glasses for serving

Fill the double-boiler pan with enough water to come just below the bottom of the mixing bowl without touching it. Remove the bowl, and heat the water to a steady simmer.

While the bowl is still cold, drop in the egg yolks, sugar, espresso, and Marsala, and whisk together until well blended. Set the bowl over the gently bubbling water, and immediately start whisking at a moderate speed. Beat the egg mixture with large strokes, frequently scraping the whisk around the sides and bottom of the bowl, to heat the zabaglione evenly (and avoid scrambled eggs).

Whisk steadily as the zabaglione expands into a frothy sponge, 5 minutes or longer. When the sponge is very warm to the touch and thickened enough to form a ribbon when it drops back on the surface, take the bowl off the double-boiler pan.

To serve the zabaglione warm, quickly whip the cream (with a whisk or an electric mixer) until it holds soft peaks. Ladle the zabaglione into tall glasses, spoon a dollop of whipped cream on the top of each portion, and serve immediately.

For a chilled dessert, set the bowl of warm zabaglione into a larger bowl partly filled with ice cubes and enough water to cool the inner bowl but not splash over. Whisk for several minutes, until the zabaglione is cool to the touch.

Whip the cream until it holds soft peaks, and fold it into the cooled zabaglione with a large rubber spatula. Cover the bowl with plastic wrap, and refrigerate for 2 hours or longer, then spoon it into glasses or dessert bowls.

Cornmeal Cookies

CRUMIRI

Cornmeal cookies are a favorite all over northern Italy: the Veneto has its *zaletti*, in Friuli we have *gialetti*. In Piemonte, you will find *crumiri*, piped into distinctive crescent-moon shapes. They are deliciously crumbly and just sweet enough.

Makes about 30 cookies

1 cup yellow polenta, medium-grind

1 cup all-purpose flour

⅔ cup sugar

Pinch of salt

6 ounces (12 tablespoons) soft butter, plus some for the baking sheet

4 large egg yolks

1 teaspoon vanilla extract

Recommended Equipment
A food processor fitted with the metal blade

A 12-by-18-inch half–sheet pan or other large baking sheet

A pastry bag with a ½-inch star tip

Put the polenta, flour, sugar, and salt in food-processor bowl, and process to blend.

Drop in the soft butter, and process continuously until the butter is completely incorporated, scraping down the sides of the bowl.

Stir together the egg yolks and vanilla, pour over the dry mixture, and process briefly, until a soft dough forms.

Arrange a rack in the center of the oven, and preheat to 350°. Lightly butter the sheet pan.

Fill the pastry bag with *crumiri* dough, and pipe U-shaped cookies 3 inches wide in rows, filling the pan.

Bake for about 20 minutes, or until the cookies are firm and golden, with a hint of brown on the piped ridges. Cool on a wire rack, and store for up to a week in an airtight container.

Hazelnut Torte

TORTA DI NOCCIOLE

This is a wonderfully easy cake with flavors for which Piemonte is known. The best hazelnuts in Piemonte are called *tonda gentile delle Langhe*—the "gentle round one of the Langhe"—and with a bit of chocolate, you have the match made famous in Torino, *gianduja*.

I love this torte for its versatility as well. I serve it simply with powdered sugar or whipped cream, or you can flank it with a scoop of chocolate ice cream or give it a drizzle of warm chocolate sauce. In Piemonte, I've had the torte with zabaglione—and if you turn to page 156, you'll find a perfect partner in *Zabaglione al Caffè Nero*.

Makes a 10-inch cake, serving 10 or more

1½ cups hazelnuts, toasted and with skins rubbed off

1½ cups all-purpose flour, plus some for the cake pan

1 teaspoon baking powder

¼ teaspoon salt

6 tablespoons soft butter, plus a bit for the cake pan

1 cup plus 2 tablespoons sugar

3 large eggs

1 tablespoon extra-virgin olive oil

½ tablespoon finely grated orange zest

Chop the hazelnuts in a food processor or mini-chopper to small bits—not to a powder. Set aside. Whisk or sift together the flour, baking powder, and salt. Butter and flour the cake pan. Preheat the oven to 350° with a rack in the center.

In the mixer, cream the butter and sugar together until light, smooth, and fluffy; scrape the sides of the bowl as needed. Incorporate the eggs, olive oil, and orange zest in several additions, blending each in at slow speed, scraping the bowl, then beating at high speed for a couple of minutes to lighten.

On slow speed, incorporate the dry mix in several additions, alternating with splashes of milk. Scrape the bowl when both are added, and beat briefly on high. Fold in the chopped nuts and chocolate by hand, and blend in well.

1 cup milk at room temperature

4 tablespoons semisweet chocolate, chopped by hand in small pieces

Garnish: powdered sugar or whipped cream

Recommended Equipment
A 10-inch springform cake pan

A heavy-duty electric mixer fitted with the whisk

Scrape the batter into the cake pan, and smooth the top. Bake until a cake tester comes out clean, about 45 minutes. The top should be lightly browned and just spring back to a light touch.

Cool on a wire rack for 30 minutes or so, remove the side ring of the springform, and let the cake cool completely. Cut in wedges, and serve topped with powdered sugar or whipped cream.

The torte will keep in the refrigerator for a week, well wrapped in plastic, or you can freeze it for longer storage. When serving torte that has been chilled or frozen, toast the cut pieces in the oven (or toaster oven) to bring out the flavors.

A Tradition of Chocolate, Hazelnuts, and Caffès

Most tourists are lured to the Langhe and nearby Asti (where Asti Spumante comes from), but you should not bypass the city of Torino. Torino has been dubbed the Detroit of Italy, and, yes, it is the home of Fiat, which employs 40 percent of its population. But Torino is much more than that. In 2006, Torino hosted the Winter Olympics, and it is the home of some of the most influential Italian royal families, Casa Savoia being the most important one, having produced several Italian kings who shaped Italy's history. Torino has been the seed for Italian intellectualism and revolutionary ideas. It is here that the movement for the unification of Italy began, which became a reality in 1861.

Torino is a seedbed for culinary ideas and innovations as well. Both vermouth and bitters had their genesis in and around Torino. It is also the birthplace of torrone, almond nougat, and has long been known for its chocolate confec-

tions. One of Torino's most famous (and my most favorite) chocolate creations is *gianduja,* a blend of chocolate and Piemonte's wonderful hazelnuts. *Gianduja* (named for the hat of a traditional puppet and carnival character) in turn led Pietro Ferrero, a confectioner in Alba, to invent Nutella, the chocolate-hazelnic sandwich spread now sold around the world, more popular than peanut butter.

For adult tastes, Torino offers the *bicerin,* a glass of espresso with an equal amount of intense hot chocolate, invented in Caffè Bicerin, packed full of clients every day. There is a grand tradition of *caffès* in the city, serving generations of thinkers and revolutionaries as gathering places. Whenever I'm in a Torinese *caffè,* enjoying a coffee or a *bicerin,* I can still feel the spirit of those before me, who lingered for hours in these very seats, to sip their drinks and philosophize.

Tanya's Tour

PIEMONTE

CASTELLO REALE DI RACCONIGI: A Royal Household
Location: About 25 miles south of Torino

The kings of Italy of the Savoia family reigned from Piemonte—and maintained many royal residences in Torino and around the region—until 1946, when Italians voted an official end to the monarchy. Whenever I visit the Racconigi Castle, the king's summer residence, I am drawn to the grand entrance with its magnificent stucco decoration, and to the royal bedroom, and I find myself imagining what it would be like to live there. I particularly enjoy the intact nineteenth-century kitchen, a rather rare survival with its antique iceboxes, a small glassed-in kitchen manager's office, and huge cooking hearths.

CASTELLO DELLA MANTA: My Fresco Heaven
Location: About 40 miles southwest of Torino, near Saluzzo

Set in a small village in the province of Cuneo (where great Piedmontese cheese comes from), this fortified palace from the thirteenth century houses one of the most beautiful fresco cycles in all of Italy. Specifically, it is a magnificent *uomini-illustri* cycle—a fascinating genre of decorative art in grand residences during the Middle Ages and Renaissance. The works in these cycles depict admirable and illustrious men in such a way that the whole display conveys a message, a tribute to an individual or acclamation of a moral ideal. (They are so fascinating, in fact, that I spent a few years moving slowly through the halls of Italian castles, studying *uomini-illustri* cycles, for my doctoral thesis in art history.)

The frescoes in the Castle of Manta were painted, it is believed, by Giacomo Jaquerio of Torino roughly from 1420 to 1430, commissioned by the nobleman Valerano to honor his father, Thomas III, prince of the local realm of Saluzzo. Thomas was the author of a medieval romance called *The Knight Errant*, and the entire fresco cycle is based on the romance, expressing its ideals of chivalry. To do this, Jaquerio depicts figures from Hebrew, Christian, and pagan history, in an elegant courtly dance along the walls. I have spent hours tracing such details as the precisely rendered flora and fauna decorating the ladies' gowns. Jaquerio also entertains with a humorous illustration of the Fountain of Youth, around which figures are hurriedly disrobing to bathe. After their immersion, in the bushes nearby, the men are seen to be enjoying their rediscovered youthful prowess. This is truly fresco heaven!

THE ABBAZIA DI STAFFARDA: Architectural Marvel in the Mountains
Location: About 35 miles southwest of Torino

A marvel of Romanesque and Gothic architecture, this Cistercian abbey is one of the most important monuments in Piemonte. Built in the twelfth and thirteenth centuries, the abbey was an important producer of food and housed the area's largest market in its Loggia del Mercato. This magnificent creation always makes me stop, sit, and look. Upon first glance, the decoration and architecture of the loggia appear uniform. But close perusal reveals that every capital atop the columns has a different face or zoomorphic image. Parts of the decoration are elongated and warped—others not. The doors are different, the arches are different, yet the entirety is completed in harmony. When I've satisfied myself with this man-made beauty, I wander outside to take in the spellbinding panorama of the abbey with white-dusted Alpine peaks behind it.

CASTELLO D'ISSOGNE AND CASTELLO DI VERRES: Medieval Magic
Location: About 50 miles north of Torino, in the Valle d'Aosta

North of Torino, in the Valle d'Aosta region, the countryside is dotted with feudal castles, and two of my favorites are in the neighboring towns of Issogne and Verres.

Both castles are spectacular to behold amid the gorgeous Alpine scenery, but what draws me back to the Castello d'Issogne is its marvelous and unusual fresco cycle. The scenes of daily life in a medieval city are almost magical in the setting. In the courtyard of the castle, stroll through the portico, under the arched vaults, with their colorful checkerboard-painted ribs. In the lunette of each vault (the half-circle of wall) is a fresco depicting a different spot in town—a bakery, a cobbler, a produce seller, a tavern where soldiers have hung their armor. It's a rare and vivid view of what life was truly like, and since you'll probably be the only visitor, it's easy to imagine yourself back in the twelfth century.

Across the valley lies the town of Verres, and perched high above it, almost teetering on a steep hilltop, is the *castello*, a massive military stronghold. This is the castle of fairy tales, a place to bring children and let their imaginations run wild. The stone construction, especially the monster interior staircase, is a monumental feat. The stone chambers, barely illuminated by daylight, are full of mystery too. Do you think, I ask my kids, that someone was left behind in the dungeon when the soldiers moved out?

CASTELLO DI FENIS: A Dance of Chivalry and Saints
Location: About 60 miles north of Torino, in the Valle d'Aosta

The Castle of Fenis is very different from the many others in the region, as it is not placed up high for defensive purposes but set on a gentle plateau. In fact, it was built as the official residence of the Challant family, and the many towers and walls were primarily to project the image of a powerful family. The decoration in the interior courtyard projected an image of intelligence, saintliness, and strength— the way in which the family wanted to be perceived by visitors. The semicircular stairway and the wooden balcony were a stage for the public appearance of the rich and powerful. At the top of the staircase in the center is an image of St. George slaying the dragon, but most of the walls are covered by important religious and historical figures holding words in antique French about good deeds and virtue.

TORINO: My Favorite Caffè
Location: Piazza del Castello, Torino

I don't need to tell you about the myriad cultural masterpieces in Torino—there are countless sources for that. But I do want to add my own opinion to Lidia's, about where to enjoy the city's great coffee and lively intellectual and social scene. My mother, as you might guess (see page 159), prefers the famous Caffè Bicerin, but my favorite is Caffè Mulassano, with its gorgeous wooden décor and view of the lively Piazza del Castello. It is a superb place for people-watching, and I am always delighted to look at the huge castle in the center, which appears to have been simply plopped down in that spot.

MAREMMA

Chapter 6

Alma's Cooked Water Soup
ACQUACOTTA DI ALMA

Chickpea Soup with Porcini Mushrooms
ZUPPA DI CECI CON FUNGHI PORCINI

Crespelle Stuffed with Mushrooms
CIAFFAGNONI RIPIENI CON I FUNGHI

Braised Swiss Chard and Cannellini Beans
ZIMINO DI BIETOLE E FAGIOLI

Gramigna with Spinach, Chickpeas, and Bacon
GRAMIGNA AL VERDE RUSTICO

Tortelli Filled with Chicken Liver, Spinach, and Ricotta
TORTELLI MAREMMANI

Tuscan Meat and Tomato Ragù
RAGÙ MAREMMANO

Pappardelle with Long-Cooked Duck Sugo
PAPPARDELLE AL SUGO D'ANATRA

Fresh Pasta for Pappardelle (and Tortelli Maremmani)

Pappardelle with Long-Cooked Rabbit Sugo
PAPPARDELLE AL SUGO DI CONIGLIO

Hunter's-Style Chicken with Rosemary
POLLO ALLA CACCIATORA

Spicy Braised Pork
MAIALE ALL'ARRABBIATA

Filet of Wild Boar with Prune and Apple Sauce
CINGHIALE CON LE PRUGNE

Beef Braised with Black Peppercorns
ANTICO PEPOSO

Beefsteak Maremma Style
BISTECCA CHIANINA ALLA MAREMMANA

Poached Fresh Figs
FICHI AL GALOPPO

Roasted Chestnuts with Red Wine
CASTAGNE AL VINO

Sage Pudding
BUDINO ALLA SALVIA

For me, Tuscany always meant Florence, Chianti, and Siena. Then, in 1999, it happened that I was introduced to Maremma, and I discovered the other Tuscany. The oenologist for our Azienda Agricola Bastianich vineyard in Friuli, Maurizio Castelli, a Tuscan from Pistoia, invited my son, Joseph, and me to see a potential vineyard in Maremma. According to him, Maremma was undiscovered, and it offered a wonderful opportunity to buy a vineyard with good potential in a beautiful setting. He and his son Simone had bought land and were making wine, and this property was attached to theirs.

The thought of making wine in Tuscany piqued our interest. We knew that the hills of the Maremma produce delightful wines that have been receiving considerable attention lately, particularly the crispy Vermentino and the aromatic Malvasia whites, and the Ciliegiolo and Morellino, the fruity, cherry reds. My favorite is the Morellino, and some of the best comes from the area around Scansano, just north of La Mozza, the locale that Maurizio showed us. It all seemed like a heaven-sent opportunity, and having a friend whom we trusted on the property would make it feasible. Before we knew it, we, along with Mario Batali, had bought the forty-acre winery.

What we didn't realize was that a few hundred yards down the road from the winery lived Alma Amaddi, an excellent home cook who, I soon discovered, knew all about the region. La Mozza is not a town per se but a group of houses, some clustered and some scattered. In order to socialize, you have to knock on someone's door, and I find myself paying a visit to Alma as often as I can whenever I am in La Mozza.

Alma is a widow in her late seventies; her children live in Florence, where she stays during the winter, but every spring she returns to La Mozza, like the swallows. I sit with her for hours while she shares enthusiastically with me the stories and recipes of this harsh terrain. All the time she is talking she cooks, and I taste eagerly and enjoy the traditional dishes she prepares. According to her, game and foraging have long been the primary sources of food in Maremma. Everyone had courtyard animals and a garden, but foraging and hunting were free and so became a big part of the *cucina maremmana.*

The hills of Maremma, besides producing great wines, are quite intriguing and beautiful. Standing on one, you can see hundreds of others, which look like green dragons frolicking in the big valley with the Etruscan/medieval towns perched on top as their heads. Periodic lines of cypress and pine trees on their crest seem like their spiny backbones, and the vineyards and olive groves are like the speckled scales of these mighty dragons. The landscape of Maremma is mesmerizing—gentle, with rolling, cultivated hills framed by impenetrable brush and evergreen forests.

Maremma is also known for its coastline, with magnificent sandy dunes and imposing reefs reflected in the silvery sea. But I was more fascinated by the internal part of Maremma, full of mystique, an inviting place where one can find peace and a different kind of food experience. There the customs as well as the culinary traditions are *montanare*—of the mountain.

And most of the recipes that follow reflect a cuisine that is as unadorned as Alma, but at the same time elegant. In every dish you can taste the complexity of the terrain and the intensity of its flavors.

Alma's Cooked Water Soup

ACQUACOTTA DI ALMA

Acquacotta literally means "cooked water," a traditional term for a soup of just a few ingredients cooked in boiling water. But the pale name in no way reflects the savor and satisfaction of this vegetable soup. It has great depth of flavor, and when served Alma's way, with a poached egg and country bread in the bowl, it is a complete meal.

In country fashion, Alma cracks a raw egg right into each portion of hot soup and inverts another bowl on top, as a cover. You have to wait (mouth watering) for a minute or two before removing the top bowl, to find a beautifully cooked egg. Here I transfer the soup to a skillet and poach the eggs over low heat, to be sure they have cooked thoroughly.

Since this soup is so quick, inexpensive, and nourishing, local women would make it often, especially when extra farmhands came to help to harvest the grapes and olives and to work the land.

Serves 6

2 pounds Swiss chard

1 onion, chopped (about 1 cup)

2 celery stalks, trimmed, peeled, and cut into chunks (about 1½ cups)

⅓ cup fresh Italian parsley leaves

8 fresh basil leaves

⅓ cup extra-virgin olive oil

½ teaspoon peperoncino flakes, or to taste

1 tablespoon tomato paste

9 cups water

2 teaspoons salt, or to taste

¼ teaspoon freshly ground black pepper, or to taste

Wash and drain the chard, and tear out the long stems from the leafy parts. Stack the leaves, and slice crosswise into 1-inch strips. Cut off the tough base of each stem, and discard. Chop the trimmed stems into ½-inch pieces.

Using a food processor, mince the onion, celery, parsley, and basil into a fine-textured paste (*pestata*). Heat the oil in the saucepan over medium heat, scrape in the *pestata*, and stir it all around the pan as it starts to steam and sizzle. Sprinkle in the peperoncino and cook, stirring, until the *pestata* has dried and starts to stick, 4 minutes or so. Drop in the tomato paste, and stir to toast it for a minute.

Pour in 9 cups water, raise the heat to high, and stir up all the cooked seasonings, while adding 2 teaspoons of salt and some freshly ground pepper to taste. Bring the water to the boil, and dump in all of the cut chard leaves and chopped stems. Return to the boil, cover partially, and cook at a steady simmer for about 40 minutes, until the chard is very tender and the broth is quite flavorful. Turn off the heat until you're ready to serve.

Ladle about 1⅓ cups of soup per serving into the skillet. Heat to a simmer; crack and carefully slip into the soup one egg for each serving. Turn the heat down very low, cover the skillet tightly,

For each serving of soup
1 egg

½ slice day-old country bread,
or 3 or 4 large croutons

Freshly grated pecorino to taste

Recommended Equipment
A food processor

A heavy-bottomed saucepan or
soup pot, 5- or 6-quart capacity,
with a cover

A skillet or sauté pan, 3-inch
sides or deeper, with a cover, for
poaching eggs

and poach the eggs for 2 minutes or longer. Put a bread slice or croutons in each warm soup bowl, and when the eggs are done as you like them, lift them out one at a time with a slotted spoon or spatula, taking some cooked greens too. Lay the egg and greens on the bread, and ladle in hot broth to cover. Sprinkle pecorino over the egg and broth, and serve immediately, passing more cheese at the table.

Chickpea Soup with Porcini Mushrooms

ZUPPA DI CECI CON FUNGHI PORCINI

This hearty vegetarian soup gets superb flavor and texture from the long-cooking chickpeas and dried and fresh mushrooms. But the secret to the great taste is the paste (*pestata*) of aromatic vegetables and herbs, ground in the food processor. Before adding it to the soup however, you give the *pestata* even more flavor by browning it in a skillet—which makes it, in culinary Italian, a *soffritto*. As you will see in the coming pages, this *pestata/soffritto* step is used in many Maremma recipes, in sauces and stews as well as soups.

In the country, such a soup is often served with grilled bread, making a whole meal. Adding rice or small pasta to the soup pot during the final 10 minutes of cooking is another way to enhance it. Or drop some good Italian sausages into soup for the last 20 minutes of cooking. Slice them right into the soup, or serve the sausages separately as a second course.

Makes 5 to 6 quarts, serving 12 or more

1 pound dried chickpeas

½ ounce (about ½ cup) ½-inch pieces dried porcini

1 small onion, coarsely chopped (about ½ cup)

2 garlic cloves, peeled

1 or 2 tender celery stalks with leaves, coarsely chopped (about 1 cup)

¼ cup fresh flat Italian-parsley leaves

2 tablespoons fresh marjoram or oregano leaves

2 tablespoons fresh rosemary needles, stripped from the branch

2 tablespoons coarse sea salt or kosher salt, or to taste

6 tablespoons extra-virgin olive oil

Rinse the chickpeas, and put them in a bowl with enough cold water to cover by at least 4 inches. Let soak for 12 to 24 hours in a cool place.

Drain and rinse the beans, put them in the soup pot with 5 quarts of fresh cold water, and bring to the boil over high heat. Drop in the dried porcini pieces, partially cover the pot, and adjust the heat to maintain steady but gentle bubbling while you prepare the *pestata*.

Put the onion, garlic, celery, all the herbs, and 1 teaspoon of the salt in the work bowl of the food processor. Process to chop everything to small bits, scrape down the bowl, and process again into a finely minced paste.

Pour the olive oil into the skillet, and set over medium-high heat. Scrape and stir in all of the *pestata*, and cook for 2 or 3 minutes, stirring frequently, until it starts to color and stick to the pan. Add the crushed tomatoes.

Scrape the paste into the boiling soup. Slosh a cup or two of the soup liquid into the skillet to deglaze, scraping up any browned bits stuck to the bottom; pour this into the soup too. Now let the soup perk along steadily for about an hour, uncovered, to develop flavor and reduce slightly.

Dump in all the sliced mushrooms and another teaspoon salt,

1½ cups canned Italian plum tomatoes, preferably San Marzano, crushed by hand

2 pounds mixed fresh mushrooms (such as porcini, shiitake, cremini, and common white mushrooms), cleaned and sliced

½ teaspoon coarsely ground black pepper

Freshly grated Grana Padano or Parmigiano-Reggiano, for serving

Extra-virgin olive oil, best quality, for serving

Recommended Equipment
A heavy-bottomed soup- or stockpot, 8-quart capacity or larger

A food processor

A large skillet for cooking the *pestata*

stir well, and let the soup bubble and reduce for another hour, or until the chickpeas are tender and the broth has thickened slightly with a velvety sheen. Taste and adjust the seasoning. Serve right away, or let it cool and use later.

Ladle portions of hot soup into warm bowls, sprinkle freshly grated cheese over, and give each portion a flourish of excellent olive oil. Pass more cheese at the table.

Crespelle Stuffed with Mushrooms

CIAFFAGNONI RIPIENI CON I FUNGHI

Crespelle (Italian for "crêpes") are easy, delicious, and versatile. You can fill and bake them with almost any stuffing. Here's a favorite of mine, *crespelle* filled with a creamy mushroom ragù, as they do it in Maremma.

Many wonderful dishes can be made using *crespelle* in place of pasta. If you have all the ingredients for a filling for lasagna, for example, but do not want to make pasta, crêpes are ideal.

Makes 12 stuffed *crespelle*, serving 6 or more

For the crespelle
5 large eggs

4 tablespoons extra-virgin olive oil

1½ cups water

⅓ teaspoon salt, plus more for the stuffing

1½ teaspoons sugar

1½ cups all-purpose flour

4 tablespoons melted butter for the pans, or more if needed

For stuffing and baking the crespelle
5 tablespoons butter

1 medium-large onion, chopped (1½ cups)

4 garlic cloves, crushed and peeled

1½ teaspoons all-purpose flour

1½ pounds mixed fresh mushrooms (such as porcini, shiitake, cremini, and common white mushrooms), cleaned and sliced

To make the *crespelle* batter, whisk together the eggs, olive oil, and 1½ cups water in a large bowl until well blended. Mix in the salt and sugar, then sift the flour on top, a bit at a time, whisking each addition well to avoid lumps. You should have 3 cups of thin batter—beat in more water if necessary. Let it rest for 30 minutes.

To fry the crêpes, brush the crêpe-pan bottom with a light coating of melted butter, and set it over medium heat until hot but not smoking. Ladle ¼ cup of batter into the pan, quickly tilt and swirl the pan so the batter coats the bottom, and cook for about 30 seconds, until the underside is lightly browned. Flip the *crespella* over with a spatula, and fry for another ½ minute, until the second side is lightly browned, then remove it to a plate.

Cook all the *crespelle* the same way, brushing the pan with melted butter if it seems dry or the *crespelle* are sticking. Stack them on the plate. (You can make them a day ahead; cover in plastic wrap and refrigerate.) Pour the remaining melted butter in the baking dish, and brush it all over the bottom and sides.

To make the stuffing, melt the 5 tablespoons of butter in the big skillet over medium heat, and stir in the onion and garlic. Raise the heat a bit, and cook for a few minutes, stirring and tossing, until the onion is wilted and starting to color, then sprinkle over it the flour, stir in well, and cook for a minute or so.

Dump in all the sliced mushrooms, season with salt, and stir and toss everything together. Cook the mushrooms for about 10 minutes, stirring frequently, until they've released their juices, wilted, and started to caramelize. Pour in the cream, bring it to the boil, stirring, and cook for a couple of minutes to thicken. Turn off

1½ cups heavy cream

3 tablespoons chopped fresh Italian parsley

2 cups freshly grated Pecorino Romano

Recommended Equipment
A 9-inch crêpe pan

A heavy-bottomed skillet or sauté pan, 12-inch diameter or larger

A large baking dish or shallow casserole, 10 by 15 inches, or similar size

the heat and stir in the chopped parsley; adjust the seasoning to taste and let the stuffing cool a bit.

When you're ready to stuff and bake the *crespelle*, preheat the oven to 400°.

Spread 3 or 4 tablespoons of the filling on each open crêpe; fold it in half and then into quarter-rounds. Arrange the filled and folded *crespelle* in rows in the buttered baking dish, overlapping like fish scales, filling the entire pan. Scatter any remaining mushroom stuffing on top. (If you wish, seal the dish with plastic wrap, and refrigerate for a day before baking.)

Sprinkle the grated cheese over the *crespelle* in a light, even layer. Cover the pan with aluminum foil, making sure it doesn't touch the cheese and pressing it against the sides.

Bake the *crespelle* for about ½ hour and remove the foil. Bake for another 20 minutes, or until the filling is bubbling and the *crespelle* are beautifully browned on top and crisp on the edges. Let them sit for a few minutes before serving.

Braised Swiss Chard and Cannellini Beans

ZIMINO DI BIETOLE E FAGIOLI

Swiss chard is a vegetable that is much appreciated in Maremma. Even though it is readily available in most supermarkets, it is not much used in the States. I love it, and suggest that whenever you are thinking spinach you should think of substituting Swiss chard. It usually comes in a bunch tied around the stalks. Look for young, tender bright-green leaves and thin stalks. This recipe, cooked with cannellini beans, makes almost a complete meal.

In Maremma, this dish is served with grilled meats. I love grilled sausages with it, but I also like it topped with a poached egg, a slab of grilled crusty Tuscan bread, and a drizzle of olive oil—it makes a great lunch. This dish is good just off the stove, but it gets better when it rests a bit and is reheated. It will keep in the refrigerator for a few days, and also freezes very well.

Serves 6

½ pound dried cannellini beans, or 3 cups canned cannellini, drained and rinsed

1 teaspoon coarse sea salt or kosher salt, or to taste

2 pounds or more big unblemished Swiss chard leaves

6 tablespoons extra-virgin olive oil, or more to taste

4 garlic cloves, sliced thin

1 tablespoon tomato paste

½ teaspoon peperoncino flakes, or to taste

1 cup canned Italian plum tomatoes, preferably San Marzano, crushed by hand

Recommended Equipment
An 8-quart soup- or stockpot for cooking the Swiss chard

Rinse the beans (unless you are using canned), and put them in a bowl with cold water to cover by at least 4 inches. Let soak in a cool place for 8 hours or overnight. Drain the beans, and transfer them to a large saucepan with fresh cold water to cover by two fingers. Bring to a boil, partially covered, and cook the beans about 40 minutes, until tender but not mushy. Turn off the heat and stir in ½ teaspoon salt, then let the beans cool to absorb the cooking liquid. Taste, and adjust the salt if needed.

Bring 6 quarts of water to the boil in the stockpot. Meanwhile, rinse and drain the Swiss-chard leaves. Cut off the stems at the base of the leafy part. Slice the leaves crosswise every 2 inches or so, into long strips.

When the water is boiling, drop in all the cut chard at once, stir, and cover the pot. Bring the water back to the boil, and cook the chard for about 15 minutes, until thoroughly tender—check a piece with a thick middle vein to be sure. Drain the cooked chard well in a colander. Drain the cannellini (and rinse them too, if using canned beans).

Heat ¼ cup of the olive oil and the sliced garlic in the skillet over medium-high heat, stirring frequently, until the garlic is sizzling, about 2 minutes. Drop the spoonful of tomato paste into a clear spot in the pan, stir, and toast it for a minute. Toast the peper-

A heavy-bottomed skillet or sauté pan, 12 inches in diameter or larger

oncino in a hot spot too, then pour in the crushed tomatoes and stir everything together.

Bring the tomatoes to a boil, and spill in all the beans. Stir, season well with salt, and heat the beans rapidly, stirring constantly. When they're simmering, stir in the chard and bring to a boil over high heat. Cook rapidly for a couple of minutes to reduce the liquid, tossing the beans and greens over and over. As the juices thicken, drizzle the remaining 2 tablespoons olive oil all over, toss it in with the vegetables, and simmer for another 2 or 3 minutes, until most of the liquid has evaporated.

Serve right away, or set aside the skillet, covered, and reheat later.

Gramigna with Spinach, Chickpeas, and Bacon

GRAMIGNA AL VERDE RUSTICO

This skillet pasta is the epitome of good everyday Italian cooking. It is fast—everything, including the dried *gramigna* pasta, cooks in less than 10 minutes. The ingredients are right out of the pantry and fridge. And when you put them all together—the textures and tastes are in perfect balance.

When dishes are so simple, every ingredient is very important. Here the feel and texture of curly *gramigna* pasta plays an important role, so do try to find it (see Sources, page 340). Other pastas, such as elbows, shells, or small pennette, will be delicious, but *gramigna* is used in Maremma, and I love it.

Serves 6

¼ teaspoon coarse sea salt or kosher salt, plus 1 tablespoon for the pasta pot

3 to 6 tablespoons extra-virgin olive oil, plus more for finishing

6 garlic cloves, peeled and sliced

4 ounces pancetta or bacon, cut in matchstick strips

½ teaspoon peperoncino flakes, or to taste

1½ cups cooked chickpeas, or 1-pound can *ceci,* drained and rinsed

3 cups tender spinach leaves, rinsed and trimmed

1 pound *gramigna* pasta

1 cup freshly grated authentic Italian pecorino

Recommended Equipment
A heavy-bottomed skillet or sauté pan, 12-inch diameter or larger

Start heating 6 quarts of water with 1 tablespoon of salt in a large pot. (If it comes to a rolling boil while you are cooking the dressing, you can drop in the *gramigna* to cook at the same time or wait until you've added the spinach, as described below.)

Pour 3 tablespoons olive oil into the skillet, and set over medium-high heat. Strew the garlic slices in the oil, and cook for a couple of minutes, stirring. Scatter the pancetta or bacon strips in the pan, stir, and cook for 3 minutes or so, to render their fat. (If the pork is very lean and releases little fat, add more olive oil to the skillet.) Sprinkle in the peperoncino.

When the pancetta is sizzling, dump in the chickpeas. Stir and toss them for a minute or so, then scatter the spinach leaves on top. Turn and toss as the leaves wilt in the heat. Season with ¼ teaspoon salt; ladle about ½ cup of boiling pasta water into the pan, and simmer the beans and greens for a couple of minutes. If the *gramigna* are not already cooking, turn off the heat and cover the skillet to keep the dressing hot until the pasta is ready.

Boil the *gramigna* until *al dente*, lift the pasta from the pot, drain briefly, and drop into the skillet of *ceci* and spinach, which should be simmering. Toss together for a minute or two, or longer if necessary, until the *gramigna* are amalgamated with the dressing. If the dish is dry, ladle in a bit of hot pasta water from the cooking pot. If there's too much liquid, reduce by tossing rapidly over high heat.

Take the skillet off the heat, toss the pecorino in, and drizzle a final flourish of olive oil over the *gramigna*. Serve right away.

Tortelli Filled with Chicken Liver, Spinach, and Ricotta

TORTELLI MAREMMANI

Tortelli are ravioli by another name—a square, filled pasta. And though they vary greatly, like all pastas, tortelli often are filled with fresh ricotta and spinach or other greens, herbs, or vegetables. In Maremma, where carnivorous appetites rule, such a meatless approach is not typical. As you'll find in this set of recipes, *tortelli maremmani* have meat inside and outside—and lots of it. Fried chopped chicken livers plump up the tortelli, in addition to ricotta and spinach. Once cooked, the tortelli are dressed with a typical *ragù maremmano*, made with three chopped meats slowly cooked in tomatoes. My friend Alma likes best boar, chicken, and pork, but here I call for veal, pork, and sausage, because I find that combination comes close to the complexity of the boar. Of course, if you can get boar, by all means use it.

This is a great pasta, and worth all the stirring and stuffing. However, it is not necessary to make everything here and put the ingredients together in just one way. The components of *tortelli maremmani* give many options for delicious meals (and convenient advance preparation). For instance, it's fine to make the filling and the pasta for the tortelli and leave the ragù for another day. You can sauce your tortelli simply with sage butter, pages 49–50, or just shower them with Tuscan olive oil and Pecorino Toscano.

On the other hand, go right to the ragù recipe—skip the tortelli—and make this marvelous sauce to dress any pasta, fresh or dry, or polenta or gnocchi. Indeed, the ragù recipe makes enough for two or more meals. Toss a couple of cups of ragù with spaghetti for a fabulous (and fast) supper one night, and freeze the rest. It will still be perfect whenever you do get a chance to roll and fill those plump *tortelli maremmani*.

Makes 24 or more tortelli, serving 4 to 6

For the tortelli
1 pound fresh pasta dough, page 185

For the tortelli filling
½ pound fresh ricotta

1 pound tender spinach leaves, tough stems removed

½ cup chicken livers

Prepare the fresh pasta dough and chill it.

Drain the ricotta in a mesh sieve set over a bowl for 8 hours or overnight.

Bring a large pot of water to the boil, dump in all the spinach, and return to the boil. Blanch for 5 minutes, then drain through a colander. When the spinach is cool, forcefully squeeze out all the moisture, and chop fine.

1½ tablespoons extra-virgin olive oil

½ cup chopped onion

⅓ teaspoon salt, or to taste

1 large egg, beaten

2 teaspoons chopped fresh basil

¼ teaspoon freshly ground black pepper

⅛ teaspoon freshly grated nutmeg

½ cup freshly grated Grana Padano or Parmigiano-Reggiano

For serving
4 cups Meat and Tomato Ragù (recipe follows)

Freshly grated Grana Padano or Parmigiano-Reggiano

Extra-virgin olive oil, best-quality

Recommended Equipment
A pasta-rolling machine and fluted pastry cutter to make the tortelli

A wide pot, 8-to-10-quart capacity, for cooking the tortelli

A heavy skillet, 14-inch diameter, or two 12-inch skillets, to sauce the full batch of tortelli

Remove the membranes, fat, and veins from the chicken livers with a paring knife. Rinse them, and pat dry. Heat the olive oil in a small skillet, stir in the onion, and cook over medium heat until wilted. Add the chicken livers, season lightly with salt, and cook for about 5 minutes over moderate heat, turning frequently. When livers are cooked through but still moist, turn off the heat and let them cool a bit. Spoon the livers and onion out of the skillet, and chop them fine with a chef's knife.

Beat the egg in a large bowl. Stir in the chopped livers and the meat juices and oil from the small skillet. Stir in the chopped basil, ¼ teaspoon salt or more to taste, the ground pepper and nutmeg. Fold in the chopped spinach, drained ricotta, and grated cheese. Chill thoroughly in a sealed container.

To make tortelli, cut the pasta dough into four pieces, and roll them all through the pasta machine at progressively narrower settings into sheets 6 inches wide, or as wide as your machine allows. Cut the sheets (crosswise) when they stretch longer than 20 inches. Roll the shorter sheets until the pasta is quite thin, always keeping the sheets about 6 inches wide.

Lay one sheet of dough on a lightly floured surface with the long edge running left to right in front of you. With your hands or a rolling pin, stretch the dough gently *top to bottom*—that is, make it a bit *wider* than 6 inches, so you can fold it over the filling.

Drop a rounded tablespoon of filling on the bottom half of the sheet every 3 inches, from left to right. With a pastry brush dipped in water, moisten the edges of the sheet and in between the mounds of filling, to help the dough stick together. Now fold the sheet over the filling so the top edge aligns with the bottom. Press the dough lightly so it adheres and encloses the filling. Run the pastry cutter in between the mounds, creating 3-inch-square tortelli. Press the edges of the squares to make sure the pasta has sealed. Set the tortelli on a lightly floured tray; stretch and fill all the rolled sheets in the same way.

To cook the tortelli, bring 8 quarts of salted water to the boil in a wide pot. Pour the *ragù maremmano* (recipe follows) or other sauce into one or two skillets (depending on the size of your pans). For the whole batch of tortelli, heat 4 to 5 cups of sauce; about 2 cups sauce for a half-batch. If the sauce is thick, loosen it with hot water from the pasta-cooking pot. Have the sauce already simmering when you cook the tortelli.

Drop the tortelli into the boiling water and return it to the boil. Cook for 3 to 4 minutes, gently stirring and turning the tortelli to keep them from sticking. When they're cooked through (test a thick edge of pasta), lift them from the pot with a spider, drain off excess water, and slide them into the sauce.

Spread the tortelli in one layer in the skillet, spooning over the hot sauce and shaking the pan, to coat them thoroughly. Remove the pan from the heat, sprinkle grated cheese over the tortelli, and drizzle a final flourish of good olive oil. Arrange tortelli on warm plates and spoon over hot sauce from the skillet.

Tuscan Meat and Tomato Ragù

RAGÙ MAREMMANO

Makes about 9 cups

½ cup dried porcini

1 medium onion, in chunks
(1 cup or more)

2 celery ribs, in chunks
(about 2 cups)

⅓ cup extra-virgin olive oil

1 pound ground veal

1 pound ground pork

1 pound sweet Italian sausage,
removed from the casing and
crumbled

2 teaspoons salt, or to taste

2 cups red wine

3 cups (or a 28-ounce can)
canned Italian plum tomatoes,
preferably San Marzano, crushed
by hand

Meat, poultry, or vegetable stock,
or water, as needed

Freshly ground black pepper
to taste

Recommended Equipment
A food processor

A heavy-bottomed 5-quart
saucepan with a cover, 12 inches
or wider

Soak the dried porcini in a cup or so of hot water for at least ½ hour.

Using the food processor, purée the onion and celery to a paste. Heat the oil in the saucepan over medium-high heat, scrape in the paste, and stir it for 3 or 4 minutes as it steams and starts to caramelize.

Add all the meats to the pan, raise the heat, and continuously turn and loosen the chopped meat as it sears and browns. Sprinkle 2 teaspoons salt over the meat, and keep tossing and breaking up any lumps, until all the meat is colored and has started to release moisture. Cook, stirring frequently, to evaporate all the liquid in the pan, about 15 minutes or more.

When the meat is dry, pour in the wine, stir well, and bring it to the boil. Cook, frequently stirring, to evaporate the wine. Meanwhile, lift the reconstituted porcini pieces from the soaking water, squeeze them dry, and chop into bits. Stir the porcini into the sizzling meats. When the wine has almost evaporated, pour in the porcini water (but not the sediment), stir, and cook until it too has disappeared into the meat.

Pour the tomatoes into the pan, slosh the containers with 2 cups of water, and stir that in. Cook, covered, until the tomato juices are bubbling, then lower the heat and simmer the sauce, partially covered, for 2 to 3 hours—the longer it perks the better! As the sauce reduces, add stock or water as needed to keep the meat covered by liquid.

Taste, and season with salt and freshly ground black pepper. Use right away or—for best flavor—let the sauce sit for a couple of hours or up to 2 days (refrigerated). Loosen sauce with water or stock, if necessary, when reheating.

Pappardelle with Long-Cooked Duck Sugo

PAPPARDELLE AL SUGO D'ANATRA

When duck is braised for sauce in Maremma, pappardelle is the pasta of choice. Therefore, I encourage you to make your own fresh pappardelle, following my recipe here. (Of course, the sauce will be delicious on other fresh pastas, gnocchi, or polenta; and pappardelle is great with other dressings too!)

I also recommend using duck legs for this dish rather than a whole duck, as I think they're tastier and make a better sauce. If you don't see packaged duck legs, ask your butcher to special-order them for you.

Serves 4 to 6

1 pound fresh pappardelle (recipe follows)

4 pounds duck legs (5 or 6 legs) or 1 whole duck cut up

6 cups poultry or vegetable stock, or as needed

½ cup dried porcini

1 large onion, chopped (2 cups)

1 cup celery cut in 1-inch chunks

4 garlic cloves, peeled

6 fresh sage leaves

1 cup fresh Italian parsley leaves, loosely packed

2 tablespoons fresh rosemary needles, stripped from the stem

6 tablespoons extra-virgin olive oil, plus more for serving

1 teaspoon coarse sea salt or kosher salt, or to taste

1 cup dry white wine

Prepare the pasta dough and chill it.

Trim all the excess skin and fat from the duck legs. Heat 2 cups of the stock, and pour it over the dried porcini. Let soak for ½ hour or longer. When the mushrooms have softened, drain and squeeze them, reserving all the soaking liquid; chop the porcini into ½-inch pieces.

Using the food processor, mince the onion, celery, garlic, and all the fresh herbs for 20 to 30 seconds, to a moist paste, or *pestata*.

Set the big pan over medium-high heat, and film the bottom with 2 tablespoons of the olive oil. Lay all the duck legs in the pan, skin side down; sprinkle on ½ teaspoon salt, and sizzle for a couple of minutes, until the skin side is browned. Flip the legs over and continue cooking, adjusting the heat and moving the meat as needed, until nicely browned all over, then remove them to a bowl or platter.

If you want to continue cooking with the duck fat, leave 4 tablespoons of it in the pan. Otherwise, pour it all out and use 4 tablespoons of olive oil instead. Return the saucepan to the heat, and scrape in all of the paste from the food-processor bowl. Stir it all over the hot pan, scraping up the browned bits, for 2 minutes or so, until it is nearly dry and toasting.

Return all the duck legs to the pan, and tumble them in the hot *pestata*. Scatter in the chopped porcini, stir and toss with the legs, and cook for several minutes, until everything is sizzling.

Freshly ground black pepper
to taste

1 cup freshly grated Grana
Padano or Parmigiano-Reggiano

Recommended Equipment
A food processor

A large, heavy-bottomed sauté
pan, wide enough to hold all the
duck legs in 1 layer, with a cover

Pour in the wine, raise the heat, and turn and tumble the duck and seasonings until the wine has almost cooked away. Pour in the porcini-soaking liquid (leave any mushroom sediment in the container), and sprinkle another ½ teaspoon salt all over. Heat to a boil, turning the duck legs and stirring to amalgamate all the seasonings in the broth.

Set the cover ajar—leaving a crack for evaporation—and cook at an actively bubbling simmer, turning the duck frequently. Add stock every 20 minutes or whenever needed, so the liquid level is about two-thirds of the way up the meat. After 1½ hours or so, when the duck is quite tender and loose on the bone, turn off the heat, and let the legs cool completely in the covered pan.

Remove the duck legs from the saucepan, and pull all the meat off the bones. Discard the bones and cartilage; tear the meat into good-sized shreds. Spoon fat from the sauce, and stir in the meat. If the sauce is dense, loosen it to a flowing consistency with more stock; heat to a bubbling simmer, and cook for another 15 minutes. Add salt and freshly ground black pepper to taste. Let the sauce cool again, or use some or all of it to dress the pappardelle now.

To dress 1 pound of pappardelle, put half the sauce in a wide skillet (or the same pan you cooked it in, if you are using it right away); use all the sauce if cooking 2 pounds pappardelle. Have the sauce at a simmer when you drop the pasta into the cooking water. If it is concentrated, moisten it with stock or hot pasta water.

Cook the pappardelle in at least 6 quarts of salted water (8 quarts or more for 2 pounds), at a rolling boil, just until *al dente*, about 2 or 3 minutes. With a spider, lift the strands from the pot, briefly drain, and lower them into the sauce. Toss the pappardelle over and over to dress them thoroughly—if the sauce is too thick, loosen it with spoonfuls of pasta-cooking water; if the sauce is soupy, cook rapidly, tossing the pasta, until it thickens.

Turn off the heat, and toss the pasta with half of the grated cheese; drizzle over it a final flourish of olive oil. Serve from the skillet, or pile the pappardelle in a large warm serving bowl. Pass more cheese at the table.

Fresh Pasta for Pappardelle (and Tortelli Maremmani)

2 cups all-purpose flour

1 large egg

2 egg yolks

4 tablespoons extra-virgin olive oil

Ice water as needed

Recommended Equipment
A food processor fitted with steel blade

A pasta-rolling machine

Put the flour in the bowl of the food processor and process for a few seconds to aerate. Mix the egg, egg yolks, and olive oil in a measuring cup or other spouted container.

With the machine running, pour the liquids quickly through the feed tube on top of the flour. After 20 seconds, most of the dough should clump up on the blade. Process for another 15 seconds or so—no more than 40 seconds total. (If the dough does *not* gather on the blade and process easily, it is too wet or too dry. Feel the dough, then work in either more flour or some ice water, in small amounts, using the machine or kneading by hand.)

Turn the dough out on a lightly floured surface and knead it by hand for a minute, until it's smooth, soft, and stretchy. Press it into a disk, wrap well in plastic wrap, and let it rest at room temperature for ½ hour.

To roll out the dough in a pasta machine, cut the pound of dough into four equal pieces. Work with one at a time, keeping the others covered. Run the first piece of dough through the rollers at the widest setting several times, to develop strength and smoothness. Repeat with all the pieces. Reset the machine to a narrower setting, and run the first piece through, extending it into a rectangular strip. Let the rollers move the dough, and catch it in your hand as it comes out. Roll it again, to stretch and widen it. Lightly flour and cover the strip, then stretch the other pieces.

Roll and stretch all the pieces at progressively narrower settings, until they spread as wide as the rollers (usually about 5 inches) and stretch to 20 inches or longer. Cut the four long pasta strips in half crosswise, giving you eight sheets, each about a foot long and 5 inches wide. Lay these flat on the trays in layers, lightly floured, separated, and covered by towels.

Lay out a rolled sheet on the floured board; dust the top with flour. Starting at one of the short ends, fold the sheet over on itself in thirds or quarters, creating a small rectangle with three or four layers of pasta.

With a sharp knife, cut cleanly through the folded dough *crosswise*, in 2-inch-wide strips. Separate and unfold the strips, shaking them into long noodles. Sprinkle them liberally with flour so they don't stick together. Fold, cut, and unfurl all the rolled pasta sheets this way, and spread them out on a floured tray. Leave them uncovered, to air-dry at room temperature, until ready to cook.

Two Long-Cooked Sauces for Pasta

Because of the strong hunting tradition in the Maremma, many delicious preparations for wild fowl and game abound in the region. I've chosen two braises, one for duck (page 183) and one for rabbit, to give you a taste of game as it would be enjoyed in Maremma, slowly cooked into a *sugo*—a deeply flavored sauce, full of succulent morsels of meat—here tossed with fresh homemade pappardelle. It is also excellent when served with gnocchi, polenta, or most fresh and dried pastas.

You will find similarities in the recipes. Both employ important techniques that I use often in meat cookery: first developing a flavor base with a finely chopped *pestata* of aromatic vegetables and herbs, then creating an exchange of flavor between the meat and the braising liquid during long cooking.

Do make both recipes, though, and appreciate the differences. Notice how the particular *pestata* seasonings give each sauce a distinctive savor and complexity. Most of all, relish the special flavors of duck and rabbit, the latter a delicious meat that Americans should appreciate and enjoy more often.

Pappardelle with Long-Cooked Rabbit Sugo

PAPPARDELLE AL SUGO DI CONIGLIO

As with the preceding duck recipe, either a whole rabbit or rabbit pieces can be used for this sauce. If you're getting a whole rabbit, ask the butcher to cut it into eight or ten pieces, or do it yourself, just cutting between the joints. (If you have my book *Lidia's Family Table*, look at the photos on page 321 to see how to cut up a rabbit.) If you can find rabbit legs, hind and/or front, they would be even better for this recipe. As with the duck, the legs have more meat, are easier to handle, and cost less.

Serve this sauce with pappardelle, following the procedures in the duck recipe, or with gnocchi, polenta, or dry pasta.

Makes sauce for 1 pound of fresh pasta (or gnocchi or polenta), serving 4 to 6

1 rabbit, about 3½ pounds, cut up (or 6 rabbit legs)

1 small onion, chopped (1 cup)

1 cup celery cut in 1-inch chunks

½ cup carrot cut in ½-inch pieces

3 garlic cloves, peeled

10 big fresh basil leaves (¼ cup, packed to measure)

1 teaspoon coarse sea salt or kosher salt, or to taste

6 tablespoons extra-virgin olive oil

½ teaspoon peperoncino flakes, or to taste

6 cups poultry or vegetable stock, or as needed, heated

Freshly ground black pepper to taste

Trim the rabbit pieces of any fat, rinse them well, and pat dry.

Using the food processor, mince the onion, celery, carrot, garlic, and basil for 15 to 20 seconds, to a paste.

Season the rabbit pieces all over with ½ teaspoon salt. Pour the olive oil into the saucepan, and set over medium heat. Lay all the meat in the pan, and let the pieces caramelize gradually, turning them every couple of minutes, until lightly browned on all sides, 6 to 8 minutes.

Scrape in the *pestata*, and stir it around the pan, tumbling the rabbit pieces over to coat them with the paste. Sprinkle in the peperoncino and keep stirring, scraping up the browned bits on the pan bottom and sides, as the *pestata* steams and sizzles.

When the *pestata* is dry and starting to stick in the pan, pour in 2 cups or so of hot stock, almost to cover the meat. Sprinkle in ½ teaspoon of salt. Bring the liquid to a boil, adjust the heat to keep it perking gently, and cook partially covered, occasionally turning the rabbit pieces and stirring up the seasonings. As the liquid reduces, stir in another cup of hot stock every 20 minutes or so. Cook 1½ hours or more, until the rabbit meat is quite tender; then turn off the heat, cover the pan, and let the *sugo* cool completely.

Remove the rabbit pieces from the braising juices, and pull all the meat off the bones. Discard bones and cartilage; shred the meat in bite-sized morsels, and stir it back in the juices. Add more stock

Recommended Equipment
A food processor

A large, heavy-bottomed sauté pan, wide enough to hold the rabbit pieces in 1 layer, with a cover

so the sauce has a flowing consistency, heat to a simmer, and cook for another 15 minutes or longer, until the meat is moist and melded with the sauce. Season to taste with salt and freshly ground black pepper.

While the sauce is hot, toss in pappardelle (as detailed in the preceding recipe), other pasta, or gnocchi. Or cool the sauce to use later; thin it with stock when reheating.

Chicken with Artichokes (see recipe page 214)

Hunter's-Style Chicken with Rosemary

POLLO ALLA CACCIATORA

Pollo alla cacciatora is served in many regions of Italy, but when you see lots of fresh rosemary and tomatoes it is a dead giveaway—you know it is from Tuscany. And in this case the dish is typical of Maremma, straightforward and elementary, with nothing more than good chicken, good tomatoes, and fresh rosemary to make it delicious.

This dish ought to be done in advance, as it gets better as it sits. Though it is delicious served as is with just some crusty bread, I especially love it with polenta. And when it is too hot to cook polenta, some tubular pasta, like rigatoni, will do just fine.

If you have some left over, just pluck the meat off the bones and save it for another meal, to dress pasta or make a risotto with it.

Serves 6

4-pound chicken (organic or naturally raised), cut in 8 or 10 pieces

1½ teaspoons coarse sea salt or kosher salt, or to taste

½ cup extra-virgin olive oil

8 garlic cloves, peeled and sliced in half

2 short branches fresh rosemary with lots of needles

½ teaspoon peperoncino flakes, or to taste

4 cups (or a 35-ounce can) canned Italian plum tomatoes, preferably San Marzano, crushed by hand

Recommended Equipment
A heavy-bottomed sauté pan, 12-inch diameter or wider, with a cover

Rinse the chicken, and pat the pieces dry. Season all over with 1 teaspoon salt.

Pour the olive oil in the pan, and set over medium-high heat. Lay chicken pieces in the pan, skin side down, to brown for 2 to 3 minutes. Turn them over and brown another 2 to 3 minutes. Scatter the sliced garlic into the hot fat, in between the chicken pieces, then drop in the rosemary stems, and sprinkle the peperoncino over.

Keep turning the chicken pieces until they're nicely browned all over, 10 minutes or so, then pour in the tomatoes. Slosh the tomato can with a cup of water, and pour that in too. Sprinkle over it another ½ teaspoon salt, raise the heat, and turn and stir the chicken in the tomato juices as they come to a boil.

Cover the pan, leaving it a crack ajar, and adjust the heat to maintain a steady bubbling in the pan; cook for about 20 minutes, stirring occasionally and turning the chicken. Remove the cover and cook another 20 minutes or more, until the chicken is tender and cooked through and the tomato sauce is slightly reduced but still loose.

You can serve right away, but I prefer to let the chicken cool in the sauce and reheat later.

Spicy Braised Pork

MAIALE ALL'ARRABBIATA

Like *Antico Peposo*, page 195, this is a rugged, spicy, Maremma-style meat stew—chunks of pork marinated in wine, then browned and braised with ground fennel, peperoncino, and black olives. Traditionally, secondary cuts of pork were used for this dish, but if you prefer, pork chops can be substituted for the pork shoulder. Just keep in mind not to overcook them—use less stock, and cook for a shorter time.

Serve with Braised Swiss Chard and Cannellini Beans, page 175, or polenta.

Serves 6

2½ pounds boneless pork butt (shoulder roast)

For marinating the meat
1 tablespoon coarse sea salt or kosher salt

2 cups red wine, or as needed

For cooking the meat
1 teaspoon coarse sea salt or kosher salt

¼ cup extra-virgin olive oil

6 plump garlic cloves, crushed and peeled

½ teaspoon peperoncino flakes, or more to taste

1 tablespoon fennel seeds, finely ground

2 cups light stock (chicken, turkey, or vegetable broth), very hot, plus more if needed

½ cup oil-cured black olives, pitted

Trim the pork roast of fat and gristle, and cut it into 1½-inch cubes. Put the meat chunks in a bowl, toss with the tablespoon of coarse salt, and pour in enough wine to cover. Let the meat marinate for at least 8 hours or overnight, refrigerated.

Drain the pork chunks and pat them dry on paper towels; season them all over with 1 teaspoon salt. Film the pan with the olive oil, and set over medium-high heat. Scatter the pork pieces, and let them brown for a couple of minutes, without moving, then turn them to caramelize another side. Now drop the garlic cloves into hot spots in the pan; sprinkle the peperoncino and ground fennel over all the chunks. Keep turning the chunks (and the garlic), so the spices toast and coat the meat as it browns.

When the meat is nicely colored and crusted on all sides, in about 6 minutes, pour a cup or so of hot stock into the pan, to a depth of at least ¼ inch. Bring it to a boil, scraping and deglazing the pan bottom, then cover the pan, and adjust the heat to keep the liquid simmering steadily.

Cook the pork covered for about an hour, turning the chunks in the sauce and stirring things around every 15 or 20 minutes. Add hot stock as needed to keep the liquid level up. After 45 minutes, scatter the olives, and stir them into the sauce (with more stock if necessary). Cook meat and olives together for about 15 minutes, covered, until the pork chunks are tender all the way through—they'll be firm but readily pierced with a fork.

Recommended Equipment
A heavy-bottomed, high-sided sauté pan, 11 inches in diameter or larger, with a cover

If you are going to serve the stew right away, uncover the pan and cook it for a few more minutes over medium heat, until the sauce thickens and coats the pork chunks, with no soupiness in the pan. Serve hot.

To serve the *maiale all'arrabbiata* later, remove the pan from the heat while the sauce is still loose, and let the meat cool in it. The sauce will thicken on standing; if necessary, loosen it with a bit of stock or water when reheating. Store up to 2 days refrigerated; freeze for longer keeping.

Filet of Wild Boar with Prune and Apple Sauce

CINGHIALE CON LE PRUGNE

The foothills of the Apennines line the eastern part of the Maremma and provide a congenial habitat for many species of wildlife, notably wild boar. As they range the hills, foraging at different altitudes, their diet varies, from rough vegetation to earthy treasures like acorns, chestnuts, and hazelnuts. Boar is prepared in infinite ways, from curing it and making sausages, prosciutto, and salami, to braising and roasting it. As with domestic pigs, the flavor of boar meat varies according to what the animal has consumed. Part of the luck of the hunt is bagging a boar that has feasted on acorns or chestnuts rather than meager plant foods—you can taste the difference.

Here in the States, boar are domestically raised, though often allowed free range like true wild boar. The meat is generally excellent, complex in flavor and surprisingly tender. It is also easily purchased, over the Internet, right from the producers or through specialty-food merchants (see Sources, page 340) but it is expensive and you can use pork tenderloins instead in this recipe (but marinate them for only half the time).

If you've not tried boar, this recipe for tenderloins will be a tasty and easy introduction. After marinating for several hours in wine and aromatics, the filets need only brief cooking on the stovetop. Most of the work here is transforming the marinade into a beautiful, savory-sweet condiment with plump apple wedges and prunes. It is a memorable special-occasion dish.

Serves 4 to 6

For the marinade
3 cups red wine (one 750-milliliter bottle)

1 cup chopped onion

1 cup chopped celery

1 cup chopped carrot

2 plump garlic cloves, crushed and peeled

2 branches fresh rosemary

4 large fresh sage leaves

Pour the wine into a deep stainless-steel or glass bowl, then mix in all the chopped vegetables, herbs, and spices. Trim the tenderloins of any fat or loose bits of meat, and submerge in the marinade. Cover, and marinate the meat in the refrigerator for at least 6 hours or up to 1 day.

A couple of hours before cooking the meat (or earlier if you prefer), remove the tenderloins from the bowl and scrape them clean, saving all the bits and liquid of the marinade. Wrap the meat pieces, and set them aside (or refrigerate) while you prepare the sauce.

Scrape the entire marinade into the wide saucepan, and pour in 8 cups water, stirring up the solids. Cut one of the apples into chunks (remove the core but leave the peel on), and add to the pan along with 1 cup of the prunes.

4 whole cloves

½ teaspoon whole black peppercorns

3-inch piece stick cinnamon

3 pounds wild boar or pork tenderloins (2 to 4 pieces, depending on size)

For the sauce
6 Granny Smith or other firm apples (about 2 pounds)

¾ pound pitted prunes (about 3 cups)

½ teaspoon coarse sea salt or kosher salt

For cooking the meat
2 teaspoons coarse sea salt or kosher salt

4 tablespoons extra-virgin olive oil

3 small branches fresh rosemary

Recommended Equipment
A heavy-bottomed, deep sauté pan or a wide, shallow saucepan, 5- or 6-quart capacity, with a cover, for cooking the sauce

A heavy, high-sided skillet or sauté pan, 13-inch diameter or larger, with a cover, for cooking the meat

Cover, and bring the liquid to the boil. Set the cover slightly ajar, and cook at a steady boil until all the vegetables are very soft and have released their flavor, 40 minutes or more. Uncover the pan, and continue cooking to reduce the sauce more rapidly, stirring often, until there are only 3 cups of liquid left.

Pour the cooked marinade through a sturdy sieve or colander set over a bowl, and press on the solids to release all the juices. Return the strained liquid to the saucepan, and drop in the rest of the prunes. Peel the remaining apples, remove the cores, cut into thick wedges (at least 2 inches wide, so they will not fall apart), and drop them into the pan. Sprinkle over everything the ½ teaspoon salt.

Bring the sauce back to the boil slowly, turning the fruit pieces so they're coated in liquid. Poach the fruit at a gentle boil for 15 to 20 minutes, until the prunes are plump and soft, the apple wedges are tender but not mushy, and the juices are syrupy. Turn off the heat, and keep the fruit sauce warm while you cook the tenderloins.

Bring the tenderloins to room temperature if chilled. Pat the meat dry, and season on all surfaces with the 2 teaspoons salt. Pour the olive oil into the wide skillet, and set over medium heat. Lay the tenderloins in the pan, side by side, and rest the rosemary branches on top. After a minute or more, when the meat is sizzling on the underside, turn the tenderloins to brown another surface, and put the rosemary back on top. Cook for another minute, rotate the tenderloins again, and reposition the rosemary.

Now cover the pan tightly, lower the heat a bit, and cook covered, turning the tenderloins and shifting their position in the pan every couple of minutes. Keep the rosemary on top of the tenderloins, so its flavor permeates the meat.

After 8 to 10 minutes of slow cooking, uncover the pan, raise the heat, and cook rapidly for 4 to 5 minutes, turning and shifting the tenderloins in the sizzling juices until they're nicely caramelized all over. (Let the rosemary brown briefly in the pan, but discard before it burns.)

Remove the tenderloins to a warm platter, to rest for 5 minutes or so. When ready to serve, cut them into inch-thick slices. Serve with warm prune-apple sauce on the side.

Beef Braised with Black Peppercorns

ANTICO PEPOSO

Antico peposo, a very old recipe for cubed beef, is cooked with lots of pepper and no other condiment—not even a drop of oil or any other fat—and it becomes a delightfully savory and peppery dish. The dish probably dates back to medieval times, when there was no refrigeration and meat was preserved with salt or lots of pepper and herbs. Once the meat was embedded with the pepper, it was cooked just as it was. Or with a little wine and garlic.

My *peposo* uses only a fraction of the amount of black peppercorns that are in traditional recipes, but it will still please even the most fanatic pepper-lover: this is peppery!

To balance the spiciness of the meat and mop up the sauce, you need some starch. I like to serve the *peposo* with one of the following: polenta, boiled or mashed potatoes, gnocchi, or just beans cooked with olive oil.

Serves 6

2 pounds beef chuck or round, trimmed, in 2-inch chunks

4 cups red wine

1 teaspoon coarse sea salt

2 to 4 tablespoons whole black peppercorns

½ cup garlic cloves, peeled

Recommended Equipment
A mortar and pestle or spice grinder

A heavy-bottomed saucepan with a cover, such as an enameled cast-iron French oven, 5-quart capacity

Put the meat chunks, wine, and salt in the heavy saucepan. Crack 2 tablespoons or more of peppercorns into coarse bits in a mortar or spice grinder, and dump them into the pan. Mince the garlic into fine bits, and scrape into the wine.

Bring the wine to a boil, cover the pan tightly, and reduce the heat to a steady simmer. Cook for 4 to 5 hours, until the meat is very tender and the wine has thickened and reduced to barely cover the meat chunks.

Serve hot.

Beefsteak Maremma Style

BISTECCA CHIANINA ALLA MAREMMANA

Bistecca fiorentina is what everyone eats when traveling to Tuscany, but since I have taken you to Maremma, I want to share with you the way they cook and eat *bistecche* in Maremma. One would expect that in this cattle-grazing region, the *bistecca* would be from the longhorns that roam the hills and pastures there, and traditionally it was. But the Maremma is not known for tender meat, and today on the grills of the best places and homes in Maremma you will find beef from Chianina. Still, although the meat may be Chianina, the preparation still reflects Maremma.

The cut of the meat is a porterhouse steak, which is similar to a T-bone steak but with a larger cross-section of the tenderloin (filet mignon) along one side of the "T." The loin of the Chianina is enormous; hence the big pieces of meat that surround the T-bone. Choose a prime or "top choice" steak that has been aged properly for 2 to 3 weeks.

Serves 6 or more

1 tablespoon fresh rosemary needles

2 teaspoons coarse sea salt

2 tablespoons extra-virgin olive oil, plus more for serving

1 porterhouse steak, 2½ to 3 inches thick, about 3 pounds, at room temperature

Recommended Equipment
A mortar and pestle

A gas or charcoal grill

Chop the rosemary needles finely with a chef's knife, and place in the mortar with the salt. With a pestle, crush and grind it all together into a coarse rub.

Continue grinding with the pestle as you drizzle in the olive oil, until the mixture has thinned to spreading consistency. Cover and set aside.

Heat the grill thoroughly over a high gas flame or a deep, glowing bed of charcoal. Lay the steak on it, and grill the first side for 8 to 10 minutes, until the meat is well browned and marked. Turn onto the other side, and cook for another 8 to 10 minutes, to brown and mark it. Prop the steak up, and holding it with tongs, grill the edges until browned. Grill the sides again for equal lengths of time, to cook the steak to doneness.

The steak may need anywhere from a total of 25 to 35 minutes to cook to rare, depending on thickness and the heat of your grill. It should feel springy to the touch. If you have an instant-read meat thermometer, it should read about 120° when inserted a couple of inches into the side of the steak (but register cooler temperatures nearer the bone).

When done, set the steak on a platter or carving board and immediately brush it with the rosemary paste, coating it lightly on all surfaces. Let the steak rest for 10 minutes, allowing the natural juices and the seasoning to permeate the entire cut.

First cut the large loin and tenderloin sections away from either side of the T-bone. Slice each piece on a slight angle into ½-inch-thick strips, and reassemble them next to the bone (see photo). Pour over the meat any juices released in carving, and drizzle with a bit of extra-virgin olive oil.

Poached Fresh Figs

FICHI AL GALOPPO

Literally *fichi al galoppo* means "galloping figs," an intriguing name for such a simple dish. As the figs poach slowly in bubbling syrup, it sounds like galloping horses. The trick here is to cook them with enough sugar so the fruit will absorb the syrup, rather than release its own juices. When this balance is reached, the silky figs remain whole and deliciously impregnated with the syrup.

Serves 10 to 12

1 cup sugar

½ cup water

3 tablespoons freshly squeezed lemon juice

2 pounds ripe but firm fresh figs

Zest of 1 lemon, peeled in strips about ½ inch wide

2 bay leaves, preferably fresh

Recommended Equipment
A heavy-bottomed 9-inch sauté pan, 3 inches deep

Spread the sugar in the bottom of the pan, and pour in ½ cup water and the lemon juice. Set the figs in the pan, stem up, in one layer. Nestle the strips of lemon zest and the bay leaves in between the figs.

Set the pan over low heat, and cook slowly until the sugar melts and the figs release their juices. As the juices rise in the pan, gradually raise the heat to keep them bubbling (and "galloping"). When the figs are soft and the liquid level comes halfway up their sides, in 30 minutes or more, turn off the heat, and let the figs rest in the pan for an hour or longer, to reabsorb some of the juices.

Slowly heat the figs and juices until they're bubbling again, and cook for 30 minutes or so, until the figs are very soft (but still intact) and the juices have become thick and syrupy.

Let the figs cool before serving. Arrange them in a serving dish if you like, with the syrup all around. Enjoy the fruit and syrup on their own, or atop vanilla ice cream, or with a soft, creamy cheese such as Taleggio or Robiola.

Roasted Chestnuts with Red Wine
CASTAGNE AL VINO

Castagne al vino are a delightful reminder from Maremma that the simple pleasures of rustic life are truly irreplaceable. Roast some chestnuts, and while they are still hot, wrap them in a wine-soaked cloth . . . wait a few minutes . . . then peel and enjoy them with a glass of wine. The question is: red or white wine? The *maremmani* enjoy, as I do, red wine, a good Morellino. But white wine is also delicious.

Serves 6

1 pound plump fresh chestnuts, in the shell

1 cup or so good red or white wine

First pan-roast the chestnuts. Cut a short slit or cross in the shell of each chestnut, and scatter them all in a heavy skillet, one that has a good cover and is big enough for the nuts to roll around in one layer. Pour in a cup of water, cover the pan, turn the flame on high, and cook for 5 minutes or more, shaking the pan frequently, until all the water is evaporated. Check whether the shells have started to peel open; if they haven't, add more water and steam a bit longer.

Next lower the heat and slowly roast the chestnuts in the dry pan, with the cover still on, for 15 to 20 minutes. Shake the pan every minute or two so the nuts roll around and don't burn. When the shells are toasted and the nut meats are tender, turn off the heat and douse with half the wine.

Meanwhile, put a clean absorbent cloth (like an old table napkin) in a wide, shallow bowl or baking dish. Dump the chestnuts into the towel and drizzle with the remaining wine. Cover the chestnuts with the wet cloth while they're still hot. Let the chestnuts absorb the wine for about 10 to 15 minutes before peeling and devouring them!

Sage Pudding

BUDINO ALLA SALVIA

It was on a visit to La Mozza that I discovered this simple but elegant dessert, *budino alla salvia*—sweet sage pudding. Fresh sage has always been one of my favorite herbs. We grow it in the garden all summer, and pot the plants and keep them in the sunroom in winter. I use *salvia* leaves in all kinds of savory dishes, from pasta sauces to roasts—and now I use them in desserts too. To keep its assertive flavor in check, I infuse the custard with sage, then strain out the leaves.

Serve the pudding chilled—plain, or topped with a dollop of whipped cream or crème fraîche, or with a biscotto or cookie (such as *Fregolotta*, page 122).

Makes 6 small puddings (about 3 cups total)

20 small, tender sage leaves (enough to almost fill a table-spoon, firmly packed)

1 quart milk

4-inch piece vanilla bean

½ cup plus 2 tablespoons sugar

4 tablespoons cornstarch

A large pinch of salt

6 large egg yolks

Recommended Equipment
A heavy-bottomed saucepan, 3-quart capacity

A sturdy wire whisk

Ramekins, small soufflé molds, or your favorite serving cups or glasses

Stack up the sage leaves and, with a sharp paring knife, slice crosswise into fine threads.

Pour 3¾ cups of the milk into the saucepan, and drop in the shredded sage leaves. Slit the vanilla bean open lengthwise, scrape the tiny seeds into the milk, and drop in the pod pieces too. Set the pan over medium heat, and bring the milk nearly to the boil, stirring frequently. Turn off the heat, cover the pan, and let the vanilla and sage steep and flavor the milk for ½ hour or so.

Meanwhile, stir or sift together the sugar, cornstarch, and pinch of salt in a small heat-proof bowl. With a fork, beat the reserved ¼ cup of unheated milk into the dry ingredients, making a smooth, lump-free paste. In another heat-proof bowl (at least 4-cup capacity), drop all the egg yolks and break them up a bit with a fork.

Remove the vanilla pod from the steeped milk, and whisk a cup of the milk into the sugar-starch paste. Scrape all of the warmed paste into the saucepan of milk, put it back over medium heat, and, stirring steadily, bring to a slowly bubbling boil. Cook for 3 to 4 minutes, whisking constantly and scraping all over the bottom and sides of the pan, as the milk thickens and the starch cooks.

Turn off the heat, and pour or ladle small amounts of the thickened milk into the egg yolks, whisking rapidly, to heat the yolks without curdling (a process called "tempering"). Gradually whisk in about 2 cups of hot milk, then scrape the tempered yolks into the saucepan (with the rest of the milk), and set it over medium-low heat.

Whisking all the time, heat the custard just to the boiling point, when bubbles break slowly on the surface. Turn the heat to low, and cook, still whisking and scraping the bottom and sides of the pan (to avoid scrambled eggs!), for 3 minutes or so, until the custard is fully cooked and thickened.

Immediately pour it through a sturdy sieve set over a bowl or large measuring cup, to strain out the herb shreds and any lumps, then fill each ramekin or serving glass with ½ cup pudding (or more if you like). To prevent a skin from forming, lay a piece of plastic wrap right on top of each hot pudding. Let them cool at room temperature for a few minutes, then refrigerate for at least 4 hours, until thoroughly chilled and set.

Tanya's Tour

MAREMMA

PARCO NATURALE DELLA MAREMMA: Hikes, History, Coastline, and Cowboys
Location: In southwestern Tuscany, extending inland and along the coast from Principina a Mare and Albarese to Talamone

Whereas visitors crowd Florence and Siena to view art and architecture, what draws people to Maremma is its natural beauty. And to appreciate the landscape in all its aspects, there's no better place than the region's major park, Parco Naturale della Maremma. A short drive west of La Mozza and Scansano (and my family's vineyard), the park encompasses fifty square miles, ranging from the Uccellina mountain chain, along the Ombrone River, through marshland, to the sandy coast.

One can explore different parts of the park along marked trails and walkways; or organized walks can be scheduled with a guide. In the marshlands and on the shores of the Ombrone is some of the best bird-watching in Italy. A spectacular hike leads to a series of mountaintop towers, built in the Middle Ages by the Knights of Malta and Cosimo de' Medici, so they could watch for invading Saracens. Today the lookouts afford serene vistas over the coast and out to sea. A great treat for me, on walks through the park, is an encounter with the *butteri*, the dashing cowboys of the Maremma, herding their cattle on horseback. I love seeing the longhorn *maremmani* cattle too—from afar, of course.

SAN GALGANO: A Ghost of Grandeur
Location: In the province of Siena, between the medieval villages
of Chiusdino and Monticiano

When I drive from Siena to Maremma, I always make a detour to an isolated Cistercian abbey, nearly hidden in greenery and largely in ruins. But though the Abbey of San Galgano lies off the beaten tourist path, it is one of the most special places you will ever visit.

The abbey was founded in the twelfth century by Galgano Guidotti, a onetime playboy who experienced a religious conversion and retreated to a small hermitage. During his short life of devotion, he managed to drive his sword into a stone, forming the shape of a cross—a miracle that led to his beatification as San Galgano, after his death at age thirty-three. (You can see the sword, still in the stone, on display in a circular oratory.)

In 1218, his followers at the abbey began construction of an immense Gothic structure. These Cistercian monks, despite their vows of poverty, had accumulated great wealth, and the abbey's grandeur reflected the order's power and prestige. It was decorated in frescoes by one of the leading Sienese painters of the time, Ambrogio Lorenzetti. Eventually, though, the corruption of the order led to the sacking of the abbey by the mercenary soldier John Hawkwood in the late fourteenth century.

Today San Galgano is completely hollow: only the outer walls of the magnificent structure are still standing. Bare traces of Lorenzetti's frescoes can be seen on the walls, now exposed to the blue Tuscan sky. Yet even now—perhaps more than ever—this is truly a spiritual place and, in its ruin, awe-inspiring.

PITIGLIANO: Meander Back Through Time
Location: In the province of Grosseto, to the west of Manciano

In the eastern reaches of the Maremma, Pitigliano is a medieval town perched high up on a rocky hill. It is wonderful just to wander through the tiny streets and leave the twenty-first century behind. Look for relics of the Jewish ghetto, dating from the seventeenth century, when Jews fleeing persecution by the Catholic Church built a ghetto in Pitigliano. Find the *palazzo* of the famous Orisini family, who once ruled the town, and the private aqueduct that brought water to the palace.

MONTE ARGENTARIO: For Those Who Love the Sea
Location: Off the coast of southern Tuscany, accessible by passing through Orbetello

The Monte Argentario is a promontory jutting from the coastline of the Maremma, and a fantastic getaway place. Originally an island mountain (but now connected to the mainland), its slopes drop down to the sea dramatically, and in the coves and bays are nestled many adorable vacation towns. Porto Ercole and Porto Santo Stefano are two that have become favorite vacation spots for wealthy Italians during the summer months.

ROME

Chapter 7

Artichokes Braised in Tomato Sauce
BRASATO DI CARCIOFI AL POMODORO

Braised Artichokes with Pecorino
CARCIOFI AL TEGAME

Roasted Potatoes and Artichokes
PATATE E CARCIOFI AL FORNO CON ORIGANO

Chicken with Artichokes
POLLO AI CARCIOFI

Monkfish in Brodetto with Artichokes
RANA PESCATRICE IN BRODETTO CON CARCIOFI

Fennel and Orange Salad
INSALATA DI FINOCCHI ED AGRUMI

Sausages with Fennel and Olives
SALSICCE CON FINOCCHI E OLIVE

Skillet Fennel with Capers
FINOCCHI AL TEGAME CON CAPPERI

Baked Fennel with Prosciutto
FINOCCHI ALLA PARMIGIANA CON PROSCIUTTO

Fresh Pasta for Fettuccine

**Spaghetti with Crushed Black Pepper
and Pecorino Cheese**
SPAGHETTI CACIO E PEPE

Bucatini with Onion, Bacon, and Tomato
BUCATINI ALL'AMATRICIANA

Fettuccine with Tomato and Chicken Liver Sauce
FETTUCCINE ALLA ROMANA

Roman-Style Semolina Gnocchi
GNOCCHI DI SEMOLINO

Ricotta Cake with Almonds
TORTA DI MANDORLE E RICOTTA

For me, one of the most magical places in Rome is the local market in Piazza Campo dei Fiori. Campo dei Fiori is an open square about one-third the size of a football field. It is nestled in the middle of Rome, between Il Tevere—the Tiber River—and Piazza Navona. A trip to this market—for that matter, to any market in Italy—will give you a good indication of the season, of the local flavors, and of what most of the Roman families will be having for dinner that evening.

The cuisine of Rome is rooted in its local history and products: it is one of Italy's regional cuisines least affected by outside influences. The cooking is straightforward, accented with gutsy flavors like peperoncino, anchovies, garlic, and pecorino. Among the prized meat dishes are *l'abbacchio,* a sixteen-pound (or less) milk-fed lamb, and *porchetta,* whole boneless pig with generous amounts of herb *pestata* and seasonings spread on the meat, which is then rolled into a cylinder, tied, and roasted slowly for hours.

Veal, birds, and game are also part of the Roman cuisine but seem to play a lesser role, most likely because they have become too expensive over the years. So it's the *frattaglie,* the innards, that are cooked most in Roman cuisine: tripe, *coda alla vaccinara* (braised ox tail), *coratelle di abbacchio con carciofi* (lamb lungs and liver with artichokes), *milza di bue* (beef spleen), *pagliata con rigatoni* (the intestines of suckling veal, still with its milk, which, when cooked in a tomato sauce, curdles like ricotta). But don't let this put you off. In Rome you'll also find some of the best lamb chops *scottadito; saltimbocca alla romana,* thin slices of tender veal topped with savory prosciutto and flavored with fresh sage; and *spaghetti alla carbonara.* And vegetables—artichokes, fennel, chicory—abound in the Roman kitchen, as is evident in the recipes I share with you.

Romans love their *tavolata,* their table full of people and food. As one travels through Rome, more than any other city in Italy, one is bound to see, especially on Sundays, big tables filled with people enjoying, eating, living life to the full.

Artichokes

If you are in Rome in spring, somewhere between late April and May, you are bound to eat the best artichokes of your life. There are stands towering with artichokes in the marketplace; they are served in every restaurant, expensive or popular, cooked in every home, and sold at every store and stand. They are even sold on the *autostrada* (highway) stops. There is an unannounced artichoke festival all over Rome, put on when the artichoke is meaty and large enough, just before the tough choke inside has formed. At this point it is at its most flavorful, most tender and sweet, and the whole artichoke can be eaten without reservation. But artichokes are delightful anytime and should be enjoyed throughout their season. An artichoke, no matter how large, should always be tight; it should have a stem—the longer the better—with small leaves, fresh and green, attached to it. The artichoke should be of a vibrant olive-green color, preferably with purple brushings. When pressed in the palm of the hand, it should gently squeak, almost whispering, "Cook me now." Here are some simple and delicious artichoke recipes that you can easily do at home to capture the flavor of Rome.

Artichokes Braised in Tomato Sauce

BRASATO DI CARCIOFI AL POMODORO

This dish accents the meatiness of the artichoke. Braised slowly with the tomatoes, it develops a harmonious flavor, sweet with a refreshing licorice finish.

Since this recipe calls for a lot of artichokes, I make it when they are plentiful. Serve with a piece of grilled meat or fish, or make some extra to spread on bread as an appetizer. Use as a dressing for pasta, or to make a risotto. These braised artichokes can be frozen, so make a big batch to pull out when unexpected guests come by.

Serves 6

3 pounds small artichokes (or more if using large ones; see Preparing Artichokes, page 213)

1 lemon for acidulated water

¼ cup extra-virgin olive oil, plus more for drizzling on the cooked artichokes

8 garlic cloves, peeled and crushed

½ teaspoon coarse sea salt or kosher salt, or to taste

½ teaspoon peperoncino flakes, or to taste

4 cups (or a 35-ounce can) canned Italian plum tomatoes, preferably San Marzano, crushed by hand

1 tablespoon fresh mint leaves, loosely packed

2 tablespoons chopped fresh Italian parsley

Recommended Equipment
A heavy-bottomed skillet or sauté pan, 12-inch diameter or larger, with a cover

Trim the artichokes, and cut them into wedges about 2 inches wide; keep them in acidulated water (see Preparing Artichokes, page 213).

Pour the olive oil into the skillet, drop in the garlic cloves, and set over medium-high heat. Cook 2 to 3 minutes, stirring occasionally.

When the garlic is just starting to color, lift the artichokes from the acidulated water and drop them into the skillet. Cover the pan immediately, and let the artichokes steam in the moisture for a minute or two.

Lower the heat a bit, stir the artichokes, and season them with ¼ teaspoon salt and the peperoncino. Cover the skillet again, and cook the artichokes for about 5 minutes, then pour in the crushed tomatoes, stir well, cover once more, and raise the heat to bring the liquid to a boil. Season with another ¼ teaspoon salt; scatter in the mint leaves and 1 tablespoon of the chopped parsley.

Lower the heat to keep the tomatoes bubbling gently, cover the skillet, and let the artichokes cook, stirring occasionally, until thoroughly softened—their thickest leaves should be flat and floppy—45 minutes or more. Remove the cover and cook rapidly, reducing the sauce to half the original volume, so it coats the artichokes thickly.

Just before serving—from the skillet, or a warm platter if you prefer—drizzle over the artichokes a spoonful or two of olive oil and sprinkle with the remaining chopped parsley.

Braised Artichokes with Pecorino

CARCIOFI AL TEGAME

Here is a quick and tasty way to cook young artichokes: thin-sliced, slowly braised in a skillet in their own juices, and served with a shower of soft pecorino. The method is simple, and will yield delicious results even with the larger, more mature artichokes you'll find in the supermarket.

This dish makes a great vegetarian sandwich, or, for a carnivore, a topping for a juicy hamburger. Artichokes prepared this way are also a great appetizer topped with a poached egg or a thin slice of prosciutto.

Serves 6

2 pounds small artichokes (or more if using large ones; see Preparing Artichokes, page 213)

1 lemon for acidulated water

¼ cup extra-virgin olive oil

4 garlic cloves, sliced

2 cups chopped onion

½ teaspoon coarse sea salt, or to taste

½ teaspoon peperoncino flakes, or to taste

1 cup shredded pecorino (6 to 8 months old) or mild Cheddar

Recommended Equipment
A heavy-bottomed skillet or sauté pan, 12-inch diameter or larger, with a tight-fitting cover

Trim the artichokes, slice very thinly, and soak the slices in acidulated water (see Preparing Artichokes, page 213).

Pour the olive oil into the skillet, and set it over medium heat. Scatter the garlic and onion in the pan. Cook for 4 minutes or so, stirring and tossing occasionally; season with the salt and peperoncino.

When the vegetables are sizzling and wilting, lift the artichoke slices from the acidulated water, drain briefly, and drop them into the skillet. Stir well, cover the pan tightly, and let everything cook slowly, giving the pan a shake now and then.

After 10 minutes, the artichoke slices should be softening—if they're hard and the pan is dry, add a couple spoonfuls of acidulated water and continue cooking, covered. Braise for 15 to 20 minutes total, until the artichokes are tender and lightly colored. Cook uncovered for more caramelization if you like.

Turn off the heat, and spread the artichokes out in the skillet bottom. Scatter the shredded cheese evenly on top, and cover the pan. Let it melt into the vegetables for several minutes before serving.

Roasted Potatoes and Artichokes

PATATE E CARCIOFI AL FORNO CON ORIGANO

Everyone loves roasted potatoes, and here they are tossed with slivered artichokes (already skillet-cooked with onion and garlic), lots of fresh oregano, and extra-virgin olive oil. It is a completely vegetarian dish full of flavor that will transport your table to the Seven Hills.

Serve with grilled fish or meat, especially grilled lamb chops. Or simply turn this dish into a crispy baked treat by adding some shredded young Pecorino Romano, spreading it over the potatoes and artichokes in the last 5 minutes of baking.

Serves 6

1½ pounds small artichokes (or more if using large ones; see Preparing Artichokes, page 213)

1 lemon for acidulated water

½ cup extra-virgin olive oil

4 plump garlic cloves, sliced

1½ cups sliced onion

1½ teaspoons salt, or to taste

¼ teaspoon peperoncino flakes, or to taste

2 pounds Yukon Gold or other good roasting potato

¼ cup fresh oregano leaves, or 1 teaspoon dried

Recommended Equipment
A heavy-bottomed skillet or sauté pan, 12-inch diameter or larger, with a tight-fitting cover

A large baking dish or shallow casserole, about 10 by 15 inches

Trim the artichokes and cook them *al tegame:*

Slice the artichokes lengthwise ¼ inch thick, and soak the slices in acidulated water (see Preparing Artichokes, opposite).

Pour 4 tablespoons of the olive oil into the skillet, stir in the garlic and onion, and set it over medium heat. Cook for 4 minutes or so, stirring occasionally, until the onion is wilting.

Drain the artichokes, and drop them into the skillet. Stir and season with ½ teaspoon salt and the peperoncino. Cover the pan, and cook for 8 to 10 minutes, stirring occasionally, until the artichokes are slightly wilted and can almost be pierced with a fork tip. (If the artichokes are still hard after 5 minutes or so, and the pan seems dry, add a couple tablespoons of acidulated water to steam the slices.) Scrape the softened artichokes, onion, garlic, and all the oil from the skillet into a large bowl.

Meanwhile, arrange a rack in the middle of the oven; preheat to 375°.

While the artichokes are cooling in the bowl, peel the potatoes and slice them into rounds, about ⅓ inch thick.

Toss the sliced potatoes with the artichokes in the bowl. Drizzle on 3 more tablespoons olive oil; scatter the oregano and 1 teaspoon salt on top, and toss again.

Brush the baking dish with the remaining tablespoon of oil, and fill it with the seasoned potatoes and artichokes, spread evenly. Cover the dish with a sheet of aluminum foil; tent the foil so it does not lie on the vegetables, and crimp it against the sides of the dish.

Bake the potatoes, covered, for about 25 minutes, then remove the dish from the oven and take off the foil. With a wide spatula, gently turn the potatoes over in the dish, without breaking them. Return the pan to the oven, and bake uncovered for another 15 minutes, or until the potatoes are cooked, crisped, and colored nicely—the way you like them.

Taste the potatoes and adjust the seasoning; serve them hot right from the baking dish.

Preparing Artichokes

The part of the artichoke that we cook and eat is the unopened bud of the *Cynara scolymus* plant. In its smaller and younger form, the artichoke can be eaten almost in its entirety—leaves, heart, and stem. Once the artichoke grows, it develops a choke, and the outer leaves take on a tougher texture.

There are many different varietals of artichokes, from small to medium to large, from fat and wide to elongated, having bracts (petals) from wide and short to long and thin, from meaty to skinny. There are color variations also, from pale green, to olive green, to green with purple brushings. The ones I enjoy in Rome are the medium-sized pudgy, meaty ones that have purple brushings on their outer bracts.

California artichokes are sold across the United States all year round. I occasionally find my preferred type of chokeless baby artichokes in New York City markets, but most often I make artichoke dishes with medium and large artichokes, which have chokes that must be scraped out.

- Fill a large bowl with a couple of quarts of cold water, and squeeze in the juice of a medium lemon (drop in the cut lemon halves too). This acidulated water bath will minimize the discoloration of peeled artichokes due to oxidation.

- Trim one artichoke at a time, first snapping off the thick outside leaves, until you reach the tender, pale inner leaves.

- Trim the tip of the stem, but leave most of it attached to the base of the artichoke.

- With a sharp paring knife or vegetable peeler, shave off the dark skin of the stem, exposing the tender core. Peel around the globe of the artichoke too, removing the dark-green spots where the tough leaves were attached.

- Cut across the leaf tips with a serrated knife, removing the top third of the artichoke. Slice the entire artichoke in half lengthwise, splitting the bulb and stem. Scrape out the choke (found in mature artichokes) with a paring knife or the edge of a teaspoon and discard. Drop the pieces into the acidulated water.

- For braising recipes, I like to cut artichokes into pieces no bigger than 2 inches. Baby artichokes just need to be split in two; bigger artichoke halves should be sliced lengthwise in quarters or sixths, in wedge shapes. Drop the wedges into acidulated water as you cut them.

- For salads or skillet cooking, lay each half cut side down (after scraping out the choke). Slice the bulb and stem lengthwise in thin slivers, and submerge in acidulated water.

Chicken with Artichokes

POLLO AI CARCIOFI

Chicken braised in tomato sauce is always good, but it's especially flavorful when chunks of fresh young artichokes are added to the cooking pot.

You can serve this with polenta, mashed potatoes, rice, or anything that will sop up the sauce. Some slices of grilled country bread are my favorite, particularly on a summer day. The dish tastes even better if it is cooked in advance and then allowed to cool and rest in the pot. Reheat just before serving.

If you have some left over, try pulling the remaining chicken off the bone and returning it to the sauce, and bringing it to the boil; after letting it all cook for a few minutes, you have a great dressing for pasta. I like rigatoni or shells with this.

Serves 6

1½ pounds small artichokes (or more if using large ones; see Preparing Artichokes, page 213)

1 lemon for acidulated water

1 whole chicken, about 4 pounds

1½ teaspoons coarse sea salt or kosher salt, or to taste

3 tablespoons extra-virgin olive oil

5 garlic cloves, peeled and crushed

¼ teaspoon peperoncino flakes, or to taste

1 cup dry white wine

3 cups (or a 28-ounce can) canned Italian plum tomatoes, preferably San Marzano, crushed by hand

1 tablespoon chopped fresh Italian parsley

Recommended Equipment

To prepare the artichokes, trim the artichokes and cut them into halves or wedges, about 1½ inches wide; soak them in acidulated water (see Preparing Artichokes, page 213).

Rinse the chicken, and pat it dry. Cut it up into 10 or 12 pieces (including the backbone), and season with ½ teaspoon salt.

Heat the olive oil in the big saucepan over medium-high heat, and lay the chicken pieces in it without crowding—cook them in batches if necessary. Brown the pieces for about 3 minutes on one side, turn, and cook another 3 minutes, until each is nicely colored on all sides. Remove the pieces to a platter or bowl.

When all the chicken is out of the pan, drop the crushed garlic into the hot fat and cook it for a minute or two, until sizzling. Lift the artichoke wedges out of the water, and drop them, still damp, into the saucepan. Stir well, and season them with ½ teaspoon salt and the peperoncino.

Cook the artichokes for 4 or 5 minutes, tossing them often and deglazing the browned bits on the pan bottom. When the artichokes are dry and starting to take on color, pour in the wine and cook over high heat, stirring, until it is nearly evaporated, about 3 minutes.

Pour in the tomatoes and 3 cups water; slosh the tomato containers with some of the water to rinse them into the pan. Cover the pan, and bring the liquid to a boil. Adjust the heat to maintain a steady bubbling, and cook the artichokes and sauce for about 15 minutes.

A large, heavy-bottomed saucepan with a cover, such as an enameled cast-iron French oven, 6-to-7-quart capacity, 12-inch diameter or larger

Return all the chicken pieces (and any accumulated juices on the platter) to the saucepan, submerging them in the sauce. Cover the pan, get the sauce perking again, and cook chicken and artichokes together for about 40 minutes. The chicken should be nearly done, the artichokes tender, and the sauce somewhat reduced. Set the cover ajar—or remove it altogether—and continue cooking 15 minutes or more, until the sauce has thickened and coats the chicken and artichoke pieces. Taste and adjust the seasoning.

Serve right away, or—for the best flavor—let the chicken cool in the pot and reheat later. If the sauce has thickened, stir in a bit of water. Serve hot from the pan, or from a big bowl if you prefer. Sprinkle the parsley over it just before serving.

Monkfish in Brodetto with Artichokes

RANA PESCATRICE IN BRODETTO CON CARCIOFI

Monkfish, meaty and firm, is well suited for the fast-cooking technique of browning and braising that I use in all my seafood *brodetti*. This one features fresh artichokes as a foil for the sweet fish—with other bright notes from capers, wine, and a healthy dose of peperoncino.

A fish dish that does not suffer from overcooking, it can be prepared even the day before. Just reheat, bringing it back to a boil.

If you have any leftovers, monkfish *brodetto* makes a wonderful risotto the next day.

Serve with some grilled country bread. I also like it with polenta.

Serves 6

1½ pounds small artichokes (or more if using large ones; see Preparing Artichokes, page 213)

1 lemon for acidulated water

2 pounds monkfish fillets

1 teaspoon coarse sea salt or kosher salt, or to taste

1 cup all-purpose flour for dredging

⅓ cup extra-virgin olive oil, plus more for serving

1 cup chopped onion

½ teaspoon peperoncino, or to taste

3 tablespoons tomato paste

1 cup dry white wine

3 tablespoons capers, drained

3 tablespoons chopped fresh Italian parsley

To prepare the artichokes, trim and cut them into wedges, about 1½ inches wide; soak them in acidulated water (see Preparing Artichokes, page 213).

To remove the monkfish's silver skin—the translucent membrane covering the outside of a fillet—pierce it with the tip of a sharp knife, run the blade under the skin, and peel it away in strips. Slice the fillets crosswise into chunks, 3 to 4 inches wide; season with ⅓ teaspoon of salt, and dredge them in the flour.

Pour the ⅓ cup olive oil into the big saucepan, and set it over high heat. Shake excess flour off the fish pieces, and lay them in the hot oil. Cook for a minute or more, until crisp and opaque on the underside; turn the pieces, and brown them for a minute or so on the other side. Remove them to a bowl.

Dump the onion into the pan and cook for a couple of minutes over medium-high heat, stirring and scraping the bits off the pan bottom. Drain the artichoke wedges, and scatter them in the pan. Season with another ⅓ teaspoon of salt and the peperoncino. Cook the onion and artichokes together for 6 or 7 minutes, stirring frequently, until everything is wilted, dry, and starting to color.

Drop the tomato paste into a hot spot in the pan, toast it for a minute, then stir it in with the vegetables. Pour in the wine, turn the heat to high, and cook, stirring and deglazing the pan bottom, until the wine is reduced and syrupy. Scatter the capers in the pan, stir and cook them for ½ minute, then pour in 3 cups of hot water. Sprinkle in the remaining salt, stir well, and bring the sauce to a

Recommended Equipment
A large, heavy-bottomed
saucepan 13-inch diameter
or larger, with a cover

boil. Adjust the heat to maintain a steady bubbling, cover the saucepan, and cook the sauce for 8 minutes or so, until the artichokes are fairly tender.

Nestle all the monkfish pieces in the sauce, and pour in any fish juices that accumulated in the bowl. Bring the sauce back to a boil, and continue cooking, covered, for 15 to 20 minutes, or until the artichokes and fish are both tender and easily pierced with a knife tip. Cook uncovered for a few minutes, if necessary, to thicken the sauce to a consistency you like. Taste and adjust the seasoning.

Just before serving, sprinkle over it the parsley, and drizzle with extra-virgin olive oil. Serve right from the pot, or from a big warm bowl.

Trimming and Cutting Fennel

▪ To trim a fennel bulb of any size, first slice off the tough base. Peel and break off the thick outer layers of the bulb and the attached hollow stalks. Then trim off any of the tender inner stalk attached to the bulb (and save these for soups, broths, and sauces).

▪ For fennel wedges (used in *Finocchi alla Parmigiana con Prosciutto*, page 223): Cut the trimmed bulb in half lengthwise, and then slice each half lengthwise into wedges, about 1½ inches thick. The leaf layers should remain attached to the core of each wedge so it stays intact during cooking.

▪ For fennel chunks (used in *Finocchi al Tegame con Capperi*, page 222, and *Salsicce con Finocchi e Olive*, page 221): Cut the trimmed bulb in half lengthwise, and then into 1-inch-thick wedges. Cut off the core of each wedge so the leaf layers can separate, then cut each wedge *crosswise* into chunks, about 1 inch wide or larger.

▪ For thin-sliced or shaved fennel (used in *Insalata di Finocchi ed Agrumi*, page 219): Cut the trimmed bulb in half lengthwise, cut out the core, then slice each half into very thin slices with a sharp knife. With a mandoline or vegetable slicer, slice the fennel into shavings. To keep the slices crisp, immerse them in ice water.

Fennel

I have many special memories of *tavolate* with my family and friends in Rome, and many vivid memories of my visits to the Campo dei Fiori to procure wonderful vegetables, fruits, fish, and meats for those meals. It was on one of those visits that my appreciation of fennel changed.

As I was heading for the fennel stall, where shoppers crowded like bees, I noticed the vendor standing there proudly. Obviously he was the farmer responsible for this prized collection. He was a small, pudgy man with worn, baggy brown tweed pants and a belt that hung like a tongue, and he wore a weathered cap over his gray hair. His fingers were short, stubby, and cracked, every crack marked by the color of the earth he worked. He was jovial and chatty, calling out to all who passed by, *"Signore, signore belle, finocchi freschi e croccanti"*—"Ladies, beautiful ladies, crunchy and fresh fennel here." Now and then he would break a piece from a bulb and munch

on it with delight, offering some to the nearest customer. As soon as there was a lull, I asked him what was the best way to cook fennel. He stopped for a moment, looked at me straight in the eyes, and said, *"Signora, finocchio cotto non vale un fico secco"*—"Madame, cooked fennel is not worth a dried fig"—and he proceeded to go on selling. I was startled for a moment, but then it was clear. Fennel is at its best when it crunches and crackles under your teeth, and the sweetness and the gentle essence of licorice permeate the mouth with an air of freshness, which lingers on.

I still cook and enjoy fennel in many ways, but since that day I must say that I have appreciated fennel best in its natural state, whether in a salad, *pinzimonio* (dipped in salt and oil), or just munched on as is. Next time you have a crispy bulb of fennel, try savoring it raw.

Fennel and Orange Salad

INSALATA DI FINOCCHI ED AGRUMI

The following is a simple recipe that will give you all the sensations of fresh fennel as the vendor would have it.

Serves 6

2 pounds fresh fennel, trimmed and sliced into thin shavings (see Trimming and Cutting Fennel, page 217)

4 large oranges

1 cup oil-cured black olives, pitted and sliced in half (or quarters, if large)

½ teaspoon coarse sea salt, or to taste

Freshly ground black pepper to taste

6 tablespoons extra-virgin olive oil, or to taste

2 tablespoons freshly squeezed lemon juice, or to taste

Shave the fennel as detailed on page 217, and drop the slices into ice water to crisp.

With a sharp thin-bladed knife, trim the orange and cut out the sections of pure fruit (called *supremes*) as follows.

First slice off the top (stem) and bottom ends of one orange; shave off the peel and *all* of the bitter white pith, so only the fruity flesh is showing.

Slice into the center of the orange, running the blade along each of the thin membranes that hold the fruit sections, so the slivered fruit is released—let these fall into a bowl. Peel and cut out the fruit section from all the oranges; you should have about 4 cups of segments. (After the fruit is removed, squeeze out the juice from the empty membranes and enjoy it!)

Drain the fennel slices, and pat dry on paper towels. Pile them in a large bowl with the orange segments and sliced olives, and toss together lightly.

Sprinkle ½ teaspoon salt on top, grind on some black pepper, and drizzle the olive oil all over; toss again. Spoon the lemon juice over, and toss. Taste; add more of any dressing component your salad needs, and give it another tossing.

Arrange portions of the salad in nice mounds on plates, and serve.

Sausages with Fennel and Olives

SALSICCE CON FINOCCHI E OLIVE

Fresh fennel is one of my favorite companions for good Italian sausage. Here meat and vegetables are skillet-cooked, separately and then together, until their flavors are merged and concentrated. It may seem that a lot of fennel is called for, but in cooking it diminishes greatly. Fennel prepared this way is also excellent with any grilled meats; it is even good with grilled fish.

Serves 6

4 tablespoons extra-virgin olive oil

12 sweet Italian sausages
(about 2 pounds)

1 cup dry white wine

6 plump garlic cloves, peeled
and crushed

¼ teaspoon peperoncino flakes,
or to taste

1 cup large green olives,
squashed to open and pit them

3 large fennel bulbs (3½ to
4 pounds), trimmed and cut into
1-inch chunks (see Trimming and
Cutting Fennel, page 217)

½ teaspoon coarse sea salt or
kosher salt

Recommended Equipment
A 13- or 14-inch heavy-bottomed
skillet or sauté pan, with a cover

Pour 2 tablespoons of the olive oil into the big skillet, and set over medium-high heat. Lay in all the sausages; cook them for 5 minutes or more, rolling them over occasionally, until they're nicely browned on all sides. Pour in the wine, and boil until it is reduced by half. Remove the sausages to a platter, and pour over them the wine remaining in the pan.

Add the remaining 2 tablespoons olive oil to the empty skillet, toss in the garlic cloves, and cook for a minute or so, over medium heat, until they're sizzling. Drop the peperoncino in a hot spot for a few seconds, then scatter the squashed olives in the pan; toss and cook for a couple of minutes.

Add the fennel chunks, and stir them in with the garlic and olives. Season the vegetables with ½ teaspoon salt, cover the skillet, and cook over medium-high heat for 20 minutes, tossing and stirring now and then, until the fennel softens, shrinks, and begins to color. Add a bit of water to the pan if the fennel remains hard and resistant to the bite.

When the fennel is cooked through, return the sausages and the wine to the skillet. Turn and tumble the meat and vegetables together, and cook uncovered another 5 minutes or so, until everything is deeply caramelized and glazed. Adjust the seasoning to taste; keep cooking and tumbling the sausages and fennel. Serve piping hot.

Skillet Fennel with Capers

FINOCCHI AL TEGAME CON CAPPERI

This is one of those simple recipes loaded with flavor that I am sure you will make part of your cooking repertoire. The fennel's sweetness and tinge of licorice are concentrated by the braising and balanced by the acidity and the saltiness of the capers. Almost all of the moisture needed in cooking comes from the fennel itself, rather than from other liquids, concentrating the vegetable's natural flavors.

Serves 6

⅓ cup extra-virgin olive oil

3 pounds fresh fennel, trimmed and cut into 1-inch chunks (see Trimming and Cutting Fennel, page 217)

2½ cups sliced onions

½ teaspoon coarse sea salt or kosher salt, or to taste

¼ cup small capers, drained

Freshly ground black pepper to taste

Recommended Equipment
A heavy-bottomed skillet or sauté pan, 12-inch diameter or larger, with a tight-fitting cover

Pour the olive oil into the skillet, and set it over medium heat. Dump in all the fennel and onions, season with the salt, and stir and toss well.

Cover the pan tightly, and let the vegetables cook and caramelize slowly, stirring occasionally. Adjust the heat as necessary so they're sizzling, softening, and cooking in their own moisture, but not burning or browning too fast.

After 15 minutes, stir in the capers; if the fennel pieces appear dry, add a few tablespoons of water too. Cook another 15 minutes, tightly covered, stirring now and then, until the fennel is tender and tinged golden brown. If they're pale, or you want deeper color, cook them uncovered for a few minutes.

Taste, and season with salt if you want; grind on pepper to taste just before serving, nice and hot.

Baked Fennel with Prosciutto

FINOCCHI ALLA PARMIGIANA CON PROSCIUTTO

This gratin of fennel wedges and strips of prosciutto drizzled with butter and topped with Grana Padano or Parmigiano-Reggiano, then baked until golden, is rich, aromatic, and irresistible. It's also quite convenient, since you can set up the baking dish hours ahead, keep it refrigerated, then pop it into the oven just before dinner. You can make this without prosciutto or substitute bacon, and it will be delicious, but it's even better with prosciutto.

Keep in mind that the cooking of prosciutto and cheese concentrates the saltiness, but the sweetness of the fennel brings it all into balance. Serve hot for best results.

Serves 6

2½ pounds fresh fennel, trimmed and cut into wedges (see Trimming and Cutting Fennel, page 217)

3 ounces thinly sliced Prosciutto (preferably di Parma or Prosciutto di San Daniele)

⅓ cup melted butter

½ teaspoon coarse sea salt or kosher salt

Freshly ground black pepper to taste

1 cup freshly grated Grana Padano or Parmigiano-Reggiano

Recommended Equipment
A 9-by-13-inch baking dish or shallow casserole

Bring about 4 quarts of water to the boil in a large pot. Drop in the fennel wedges, and cook them at a gentle boil for 10 to 15 minutes, just until you can pierce them easily with a sharp knife tip. Lift out the wedges and drain well.

Cut the prosciutto slices crosswise into strips, about ¼ inch wide. Set a rack in the middle of the oven; preheat to 350°.

Coat the bottom of the baking dish with a tablespoon or two of the melted butter. Lay the fennel wedges in one layer, filling the dish, and scatter the prosciutto strips over and in between the wedges. Add salt and pepper. Drizzle the remaining butter all over. Finally, sprinkle over it the grated cheese, covering the whole dish evenly.

Bake the dish for 25 minutes, or until the top is crusty and golden and the edges of the prosciutto and fennel are also colored and crisp.

Pasta

Here are some of the savory and gratifying pasta dishes for which Rome is famous: *Bucatini all'Amatriciana* (bucatini dressed with a sauce of tomato, cheek bacon, and peperoncino and topped with grated Pecorino Romano, page 228), *Spaghetti Cacio e Pepe* (spaghetti with grated Pecorino Romano and coarsely ground black pepper, page 226), *Fettuccine alla Romana* (fettuccine with fresh tomato, prosciutto, and chicken livers, page 230), *Gnocchi di Semolino* (delightful rounds of cooked durum wheat that are baked, then topped with Pecorino Romano, page 232). There's something for everyone in your family, and I am sure you will make these recipes often.

Fresh Pasta for Fettuccine

One would think that fresh pasta is a northern-Italian phenomenon, and in general northerners do eat more fresh pasta than dry, whereas southern Italians consume more dry. But the Roman tradition is to have freshly made tagliatelle as a Sunday treat. And in most cases it is served with *cibreo*—the giblets of a freshly killed chicken.

Makes 1½ pounds

3 cups all-purpose flour, plus more for working

3 large eggs

3 egg yolks from large eggs

3 tablespoons extra-virgin olive oil

¼ cup ice water, or more if needed

Put the flour in the bowl of the food processor and process for a few seconds to aerate. Mix together the whole eggs and the yolks, olive oil, and ¼ cup ice water in a measuring cup or other spouted container. Start the food processor running and pour in the liquids through the feed tube. Process for 30 to 40 seconds until a dough forms and gathers on the blade. If the dough does *not* gather on the blade or process easily, it is too wet or too dry. Feel the dough, then work in either more flour or ice water, in small amounts, using the machine or kneading by hand.

A food processor fitted with
steel blade

A pasta-rolling machine

Turn the dough out on a lightly floured surface and knead by
hand for a minute until it's smooth, soft, and stretchy. Press it into
a disk, wrap it well in plastic wrap, and let rest at room temperature
for ½ hour. (You can refrigerate the dough for up to a day or freeze
it for a month or more. Defrost in the refrigerator and return to
room temperature before rolling.)

To roll out the dough with a pasta machine, cut it in six equal
pieces. Keeping them lightly floured, roll each piece through the
machine at progressively narrower settings into sheets that are
5 inches wide (or as wide as your machine allows) and 20 inches to
24 inches long. Cut the long sheets in half crosswise, giving you
twelve strips, each about a foot long and 5 inches wide.

Cut the fettuccine by hand, one strip at a time. Lightly flour the
strip and, starting at one of the short ends, fold it over in thirds or
quarters, creating a small rectangle with three or four layers of
pasta. With a sharp knife, cut cleanly through the folded dough
crosswise, separating into ½-inch-wide pieces. Shake and unfurl the
cut pieces, opening them into long ribbons. Dust liberally with
flour and gather the fettuccine into a loose nest and set it on a
floured tray. Fold and cut all the pasta this way, piling the fettuccine in small floured nests. Leave uncovered to air-dry at room
temperature until ready to cook the pasta (or freeze the nests on
the tray until solid and pack in airtight ziplock bags).

Spaghetti with Crushed Black Pepper and Pecorino Cheese

SPAGHETTI CACIO E PEPE

Here is a classic pasta, as delicious as it is simple and fast. But because it is such a minimalist creation, every ingredient is of utmost importance. Use a very good authentic pecorino, one produced in Lazio (the Italian region where Rome is located), Tuscany, or Sardinia. The cheese is at its best when aged only 8 to 10 months. And grind the black peppercorns just before making the dish—I like to crush the black pepper by hand in a mortar, into coarse bits that explode with flavor as I enjoy the pasta.

Serves 6

Salt for the pasta water

2 tablespoons whole black peppercorns, or more to taste

1 pound spaghetti

1½ cups freshly grated Pecorino Romano, or more to taste

Bring a big pot of salted water to the boil.

Grind the peppercorns very coarsely, preferably crushing them in a mortar with a pestle or in a spice grinder.

Warm up a big bowl for mixing and serving the pasta—use some of the pasta water to heat the bowl, if you like.

Cook the spaghetti until *al dente*. Quickly lift it from the pot with tongs, let it drain for an instant, then drop it into the warm bowl.

Immediately scatter a cup of the grated cheese and most of the ground pepper on the pasta, and toss in quickly. As you mix, sprinkle over spoonfuls of hot water from the cooking pot to moisten and amalgamate the pasta and condiments—add more pepper or cheese to taste.

Serve right away, while the spaghetti is very hot.

Bucatini with Onion, Bacon, and Tomato (see recipe page 228)

Bucatini with Onion, Bacon, and Tomato

BUCATINI ALL'AMATRICIANA

This classic and delectable pasta dish originated in the region of Abruzzi, in the little town of Amatrice, northeast of Rome, where it was traditionally prepared without tomatoes. But it is the Roman version of pasta *all'amatriciana*, with tomatoes, that I share with you here—the version that is best known and deservedly popular.

Lots of onions; chips of *guanciale* (cured pork cheek, now available in the United States, see Sources, page 340), pancetta, or bacon; and San Marzano tomatoes are the essential elements of the sauce, Roma style. Note that the onions are first softened in water, before olive oil is added to the pan—a traditional but unusual step that is said to make the onions sweeter.

The standard pasta used is bucatini or perciatelli (spaghetti are only tolerated). The long, dry strands of perciatelli resemble very thick spaghetti but are hollow like a drinking straw. When cooked, they are wild and wiggly, so you might be tempted to cut them. Do not—once you've got them on your fork, they're delicious and fun to eat. It is quite all right to slurp them. Indeed, as kids we would suck them in so fast that the end of the noodle would whip us in the nose, splattering sauce all over our faces. What a wonderful memory!

Serves 6

One 28-ounce can Italian plum tomatoes, preferably San Marzano

½ teaspoon coarse sea salt or kosher salt, or to taste, plus 1 tablespoon for the pasta pot

4 cups ⅓-inch-thick onion slices (about ¾ pound)

4 tablespoons extra-virgin olive oil, plus more for serving

4 plump garlic cloves, peeled and crushed

6 ounces *guanciale,* pancetta, or bacon, cut in ½-inch pieces

Drain the canned tomatoes; save all the juices. Cut each tomato in quarters lengthwise; slice the quarters in strips, ½ inch wide.

Start heating 6 quarts of water with 1 tablespoon of salt in a large pot, to cook the bucatini.

Put ½ cup water in the wide skillet, and set it over medium-high heat. Dump in the sliced onions; spread them out and turn them over in the pan as the water starts to boil. Cook the onions, turning occasionally, for several minutes, until they're softened and the water is nearly evaporated.

Pour the olive oil over the onions, toss in the crushed garlic cloves, and sprinkle with ¼ teaspoon salt. Stir well to coat all the onion slices with oil; cook for a couple of minutes or more, until onions and garlic are sizzling.

Clear a space on one side of the skillet and scatter in the cured pork (*guanciale*, pancetta, or bacon). Heat and stir in the hot spot until they're rendering fat and sizzling, then stir in with the onions.

½ teaspoon peperoncino flakes

1 pound bucatini or perciatelli

1 cup grated Pecorino Romano cheese, plus more for passing

Recommended Equipment
A heavy-bottomed skillet or sauté pan, 13- or 14-inch diameter

Sprinkle the peperoncino in the pan, stir, and let everything cook for 4 or 5 minutes, until the onions and pork are caramelized and golden—adjust the heat so nothing burns.

Now spill all the sliced tomatoes and their juices into the skillet, and stir well. Rinse the tomato containers with a couple cups of "slosh" water, and stir that in too; season with salt lightly. Bring the sauce to a boil, stirring frequently, and then lower the heat to keep it simmering actively. Let the sauce cook and thicken for about 20 minutes, or until it has the consistency you like for pasta. (If you're pressed for time, concentrate the sauce at a boil, stirring frequently.)

When the tomatoes have been added and the sauce is simmering, you can start cooking the bucatini. (If you prefer, prepare the sauce ahead of time. Stop cooking when nearly thickened and let it cool. Return it to the simmer as your pasta cooks.)

With the water at a rolling boil, slide the bucatini into the pasta pot, letting the strands soften so they don't break, and fanning them out so they don't stick together. Stir well, cover the pot to bring the water back to the boil over high heat, then cook partially covered.

Stir the bucatini occasionally, and check doneness frequently. When the sauce has thickened, taste it and adjust seasoning—keep in mind that the Pecorino Romano will add salt.

When the bucatini are cooked through but still *al dente*, lift them from the cooking pot with tongs, drain for just a moment, then drop them right onto the simmering sauce. Toss together continuously, over moderate heat, for a couple of minutes, until the pasta is perfectly cooked and evenly coated with sauce. If the dish is dry, ladle in a bit of hot pasta water from the cooking pot. If the sauce is soupy, toss over higher heat to concentrate.

Turn off the heat, and toss in the grated cheese. Drizzle over it a final flourish of olive oil, and serve, either directly from the skillet or in a warm serving bowl, passing additional cheese at the table.

Fettuccine with Tomato and Chicken Liver Sauce

FETTUCCINE ALLA ROMANA

Here is a delicious pasta recipe, another example of the Roman affinity for offal. Whether tripe (*trippa*) or *paiata* (pasta sauce made with the stomach of a suckling lamb); or oxtails braised with tomatoes, celery and carrots (*coda alla vaccinara*), a true Roman meal is bound to include one of them. So what's a little chicken liver with pasta, as in this dish? The Romans love it and have been enjoying it for centuries, so why shouldn't you?

Serves 6

1½ pounds fresh fettuccine, page 224

For the sauce
½ cup dried porcini mushroom slices (about ½ ounce)

1½ cups hot chicken, vegetable, or other light stock

½ cup extra-virgin olive oil, plus more for finishing

1 cup chopped onion

2 plump garlic cloves, peeled and crushed

½ teaspoon coarse sea salt, or to taste, plus 2 tablespoons for cooking the pasta

2 ounces fatty prosciutto, preferably a thick slice, cut into ¼-inch-wide strips

½ pound chicken livers, cleaned and cut into ¼-inch pieces

½ cup dry white wine

2 cups canned Italian plum tomatoes, preferably San Marzano, with juices, crushed by hand

To prepare the sauce: Drop the dried porcini into the hot stock, and let it rehydrate for 30 minutes or longer. Before you start cooking, lift the soaked mushrooms from the stock and squeeze them dry—saving all the liquid, of course. Cut the mushrooms in bite-sized pieces, about ½ inch. Let the stock sit so any sediment settles to the bottom of the container.

Pour ⅓ cup olive oil in the skillet, and set it over medium-high heat. Stir in the onion and garlic, and salt lightly. Cook the onion for a couple of minutes, until it's wilting and sizzling.

Clear a space in the pan, and drop in the prosciutto strips. Toss these in the hot spot to caramelize for a minute, then stir them in with the onion.

Clear another hot spot for the chopped chicken livers; salt the pieces lightly, stir for a minute until they start to sizzle, then mix with everything else.

Introduce the porcini the same way: cook them for a minute in a hot spot, then stir in with other ingredients.

Pour in the wine, bring it to a boil, and let it bubble for a minute or so. Pour in the mushroom-soaking stock (but not the sediment in the container). Bring to a boil, and let cook rapidly to reduce slightly, about 2 minutes.

Pour the crushed tomatoes and their juices into the pan, and stir. Rinse the tomato container with a cup or so of "slosh" water, and stir in. Season lightly with salt.

Bring the sauce to a boil, then adjust the heat to keep it perking gently. Stir in another 2 tablespoons of olive oil; cook the sauce uncovered for about 20 minutes, to thicken it and develop the flavors.

1 cup freshly grated Pecorino
Romano

Recommended Equipment
A heavy-bottomed high-sided
skillet or sauté pan, 14-inch
diameter

As the sauce cooks, start heating a large pot of water for the fettuccine, if you will be serving it right away. You will need about 8 quarts of water with 2 tablespoons of coarse salt for this big batch of fresh fettuccine.

When the sauce is almost reduced to the consistency you like, start cooking the pasta. (If you will be cooking the pasta later, turn off the heat and let sauce cool; it will thicken as it sits.)

Have the pasta water at a full rolling boil. Just before adding the fettuccine, shake each small nest of noodles in a colander or sieve to remove excess flour.

Drop in the fettuccine nests at the same time; keep stirring and lifting with tongs to loosen the nests and separate the strands. Cover the pot, and bring the water back to the boil over high heat; stir once or twice to keep the fettuccine from sticking. (At this point, bring your sauce to a simmer if it has been turned off.)

When the water's at a rolling boil again, stir and cook the fettuccine for about 2 minutes, or until the strands are cooked *al dente*. Lift out the noodles in big bunches, using tongs and a spider, and lower them into the sauce; work quickly, so the noodles don't overcook.

Toss the fettuccine continuously in the simmering sauce until they're all coated. If the sauce is too thick, loosen it with spoonfuls of hot pasta-cooking water; if the sauce is soupy, cook rapidly over high heat for a few moments to thicken.

Turn off the heat, and toss the pasta with half of the grated cheese; drizzle over it a final flourish of olive oil.

Serve right away—from the skillet, or a large warm serving bowl if you prefer—passing more cheese at the table.

Roman-Style Semolina Gnocchi

GNOCCHI DI SEMOLINO

If you think all gnocchi are potato-based bite-sized dumplings (as do most Americans), you are in for a surprise—and a great treat. Roman-style *gnocchi di semolino* are much more like polenta, made from a cereal porridge that is cooked and cooled until firm, then cut into small pieces and baked with a rich topping of butter and cheese. Yellow semolina (ground durum-wheat flour) even looks a bit like polenta, but it gives the dish a flavor and texture that are quite distinct from cornmeal.

Gnocchi di semolino are usually served as a first course, instead of pasta, during a Sunday meal in a Roman household. It is a good dish when you have big crowds, since you can prepare it even the day before, leave it in the refrigerator covered with plastic wrap, and then just put on the butter and cheese and bake it in a hot oven where you might have a roast going. Because it holds its temperature for a while, you can set it on the table family style, with a serving spoon. Let people just take as much as they want.

Traditionally, these gnocchi are cut into 1-inch rounds with a cookie cutter, but often, to avoid any waste, they are cut into squares or diamonds, which is just as good.

Taleggio is a creamy cheese and I love it on this dish, but even just a Pecorino Romano will give you a nice flavorful crust.

Serves 8 or more

For the cooked semolina
5 cups milk

4 tablespoons butter

1 teaspoon salt

1½ cups coarse semolina flour

For saucing and baking the gnocchi
8 tablespoons butter

1½ cups freshly grated Grana Padano or Parmigiano-Reggiano

1 cup shredded Taleggio

Put the milk, 4 tablespoons butter, and salt in the saucepan. Set over medium heat, stir occasionally until the milk is hot and the butter melted, then gradually pour in the semolina, whisking steadily.

Cook the cereal slowly, over medium-low heat, for ½ hour or more, as the cereal thickens. Whisk frequently, scraping the bottom and sides of the pan too. Use a wooden spoon when the mixture stiffens, and cook until it is difficult to stir at all. If you want to cook it faster, raise the heat and stir constantly until done.

Scrape and pour the hot semolina in the middle of the baking sheet—it doesn't need to be greased or lined. Spread the cereal with a metal or rubber spatula to fill the pan in an even layer. Here's a tip: dip the spatula blade in water to keep it from sticking to the grain. Let the sheet of semolina cool to room temperature

Recommended Equipment

A heavy-bottomed 4- or 5-quart saucepan or deep sauté pan, about 10-inch diameter

A stiff wire whisk

A large, rimmed baking sheet, such as a jelly-roll pan (10 by 15 inches) or a half–sheet pan (12 by 18 inches)

A large baking dish or shallow casserole, such as a 4-quart Pyrex rectangular pan (10 by 15 inches)

A large ruler

and solidify. (If you want to bake it the next day, wrap and refrigerate the sheet.)

Set a rack in the middle of the oven, and heat it to 400°. Butter the insides of the baking dish, using about 2 of the 8 tablespoons of butter; melt the remainder, to drizzle on the gnocchi.

With a large ruler and a sharp knife, cut 2-inch rows, lengthwise and crosswise, in the sheet of firm semolina, dividing it into small squares. Lift out one square—it should come up easily with a spatula—and lay it down, oriented to appear diamond-shaped, in a corner of the baking dish. Lay a whole row of semolina diamonds, evenly overlapping each other, the length of the dish. Arrange another row right alongside the first, and so on, until the baking dish is completely filled with diamond shapes and the baking sheet is empty.

Drizzle the melted butter all over the rows of *gnocchi di semolino*. Toss the grated and shredded cheeses together, and sprinkle evenly over the dish.

Bake the gnocchi for 30 minutes, or until the butter is bubbling in the pan and the top is a beautiful golden brown. Let the dish sit for about 5 minutes; cut in squares and serve hot.

Ricotta Cake with Almonds

TORTA DI MANDORLE E RICOTTA

Of all the wonderful ricotta *torte* and *crostate* I have made, this one is so unpretentious and delightful that I urge you to put it in your dessert repertoire. The cake is moist and sweet, with a hint of orange and the crunch of toasted almond slices in each bite.

In Rome, this cake is made with sheep's-milk ricotta, giving it an additional layer of complexity, and if you do have access, by all means use sheep's-milk ricotta and follow the same procedures.

Top with a dollop of whipped cream, or, to make it fresher, fold into the whipped cream an equal amount of sour cream. Top all with berries in season, or some halved ripe figs when available.

Makes a 9-inch cheesecake, serving 8 or more

For lining the cake pan
6 ounces sweet tart dough, ⅓ of the recipe page 266, well chilled

1 tablespoon soft butter

⅓ cup fine dry bread crumbs

For the cake batter
3 large eggs

1 egg yolk

1 cup sugar

1 pound whole-milk ricotta (preferably fresh), drained overnight

Pinch of salt

1 tablespoon finely grated orange zest

1 cup heavy cream

1 cup sliced almonds, lightly toasted in the oven

Separate the springform side ring and bottom disk.

Roll the pastry dough into a round, about a foot in diameter. Lay the pan bottom on the dough, and cut around it to make a perfect 9-inch bottom crust. Butter the pan bottom, and place the dough round on top.

Butter the insides of the springform, and coat it with bread crumbs. Fit the ring around the dough-covered bottom disk and snap it closed.

Set the baking stone or tiles on the center rack of the oven, and preheat to 350°.

Put the eggs and egg yolk in the mixer bowl, and begin whisking at low speed. Add the sugar gradually, and whisk at high speed for 2 or 3 minutes.

Lower the speed, add the ricotta in several batches, then whip at high speed for 3 minutes or more, until the mixture is smooth and thick—scrape the bowl as needed. Drop in the pinch of salt and the orange zest, then pour in the cream gradually, whipping at high speed for several minutes (and scraping the bowl) so the batter is perfectly smooth and light.

Fold in the almonds by hand, and scrape all the batter into the prepared pan. Set the springform on a cookie or baking sheet, and place it on the baking stone. Bake for approximately an hour, until the cake top is golden brown and springs back when pressed, and the sides of the cake are starting to shrink from the pan.

Powdered sugar for dusting the baked cake

Garnishes: see suggestions in introduction to recipe or use heavy cream or ice cream

Recommended Equipment
A 9-inch springform cake pan

A baking stone or baking tiles

A heavy-duty electric mixer fitted with the whisk

Cool on a wire rack, and remove from the springform. Invert the cake to separate the metal bottom from the pastry crust, and place the cake on a platter.

When completely cool, dust the top of the *torta* with powdered sugar. Cut it in wedges to serve, as suggested above.

Dessert

Dessert is not a big event in Rome. An assortment of fresh fruit in season, ice cream, or a piece of cheese will do. But one of the sweet local specialties is cheesecake, always made with sheep's-milk ricotta in Rome.

Tanya's Tour

ROME

When you've feasted long enough on the Campo dei Fiori market's wonderful food, stroll around the square and into the neighboring quarters of Rome to discover these treasures of art and architecture that many tourists miss. Most are within a fifteen-minute walk from Campo dei Fiori, and it is not unusual for my mother and me to visit nearly all of them on the same day.

IN THE CAMPO DEI FIORI: Markers of a Long History

As its name indicates, Campo dei Fiori was once filled with grass and flowers, an open field facing the Theater of Pompey in ancient Rome. You'll find the site of the Teatro di Pompeo at the eastern end of the market, where fish is sold. Walk toward the Via dei Giubbonari, and look on the left for the Palazzo Pio-Righetti. Built on the remnants of the theater during the seventeenth century, the palace follows the curve of the original construction.

During the Renaissance, pilgrims coming from all over to visit St. Peter's tomb stayed at the many hostels around the piazza. Today, on the northwest corner of

Campo dei Fiori, where the Via del Pellegrino (Road of the Pilgrim) enters the piazza, you'll find a shield with the coat of arms of Vannozza Cattanei, a noble-woman who owned many of the hostels. Vannozza was the mistress of Pope Alexander VI, a Borgia (yes, the Pope)—note that the shield displays the Borgia symbols (*and* her husband's).

The statue in the center of Piazza Campo dei Fiori marks a darker episode in its history, depicting Giordano Bruno, a noted scholar and philosopher whose heretical views—that the earth moved around the sun—got him burned at the stake in the piazza.

Campo dei Fiori has been a marketplace since medieval times, although then it was more rustic, with no pavement in the center. Otherwise, the vibrant atmo-sphere is today much as it was when the servants of popes and noblemen did their shopping there. As you walk around, or away from the piazza, note that many streets are named for the crafts whose practitioners set up shop along these routes, such as Via dei Baullari (trunk-makers), Via dei Cappellari (hatmakers), and Via dei Giubbonari (jacket-makers).

PALAZZO SPADA: A Trick from the Sixteenth Century
Location: At the Piazza Capo di Ferro, about 5 minutes
from Campo dei Fiori. Start walking with the Palazzo Pio-Righetti (above)
on your left, and head south, toward the Tiber.

Inside its rich façade, this sixteenth-century palace houses the Italian Supreme Court and a superb collection of paintings by Titian, Rubens, and Caravaggio. The gallery is unusually serene for Rome, and from its windows you can view the elaborate stucco decoration in the courtyard. A particular delight is the trompe-l'oeil perspective (designed by Borromini) in the lower courtyard: there appears to be a long colonnade extending toward an imposing statue at the end of the court-yard, but in reality the colonnade is a fraction of its apparent length—and the statue is actually rather small.

VIA GIULIA: A Walk into the Past

Location: To the southwest of Campo dei Fiori, about 8 minutes' walk. Go past the Palazzo Spada (above) along Via dei Balestrari to meet the Via Giulia at the end of the block. Turn right onto Via Giulia; the street extends for almost 1 mile to the northwest.

Via Giulia is an extremely picturesque thoroughfare, lined with beautiful Renaissance palaces and squares, quaint courtyards, churches with priceless artworks, and fantastic fountains with zoomorphic masks. The street itself is a design masterpiece, laid out by the famous architect Bramante for Pope Julius II (who also commissioned Michelangelo to paint the ceiling of the Sistine Chapel) as a splendid corridor to the Vatican, cutting straight through the jumble of medieval roads that crisscrossed the area. Walk its length after visiting the marketplace, to take in the sights listed here and to browse in the many antique shops. I love to stroll Via Giulia at twilight too: it's wonderfully romantic when oil lamps light the street, and you'll feel as if you have returned to the Rome of five hundred years ago.

Here are some of my favorite spots along Via Giulia, from the end nearest Campo dei Fiori:

One block after you've turned onto the street, you'll pass under a bridge conceived by Michelangelo, strewn with hanging vegetation. Originally, it connected the huge Palazzo Farnese, up the street to the right, to its gardens by the Tiber.

After a very long block, look for Sant'Eligio degli Orefici, a small Renaissance church with a square plan (Greek cross) and dome created by Raphael. Inside are many wonderful Renaissance paintings: on the right altar is the *Adoration of the Magi* by Giovanni Francesco Romanelli (1639), and on the left altar the *Adoration of the Shepherds* by Giovanni de Vecchi (1574). By the high altar are frescoes of the Madonna and Child with saints by Matteo da Lecce and Taddeo Zuccaro.

After another block and a bit to the right, don't miss the frescoed façade of Palazzo Ricci, executed by a follower of Raphael, Polidoro da Caravaggio. Though they are faded, you can still discern the elements of classical tales. This must have been a much-discussed exterior in Renaissance Rome, where it was customary to use frescoes of narrative scenes only as interior decoration.

Look now for the foundation blocks of a building that was never completed: these are well known as the sofas of Via Giulia, since they look as though someone put sofas along the street.

You'll pass many beautiful palaces and churches you may want to visit, such as the seventeenth-century Santa Maria del Suffragio and the Palazzo Donarelli.

Be sure to stop, though, at the magnificent Palazzo Sacchetti to see its Renaissance Madonna and a gorgeous ancient Roman relief in the loggia. I always find these works empowering and moving.

The final stretch of Via Giulia, before it ends at the bend in the Tiber, was home to many Florentines in the Renaissance. Citizens of another state, they had their own church, San Giovanni dei Fiorentini. (Many nationalities had their own churches at the time, as did professions, such as the goldsmiths' Sant'Eligio degli Orefici, which you passed earlier.) Inside San Giovanni, see the marble bust of Bernini and the panel painting of St. Jerome by Santi di Tito, among a trove of masterpieces.

VILLA FARNESINA: Frescoes and Feasts

Location: Across the Tiber from the Campo dei Fiori neighborhood, nestled between Via della Lungara and the river. A 15-minute walk from the marketplace; cross the Ponte Sisto by foot and turn right to reach the villa.

Worth a walk across the river, this magnificent villa at the foot of the Janiculum Hill has art treasures not seen by most tourists and offers a bit of tranquillity in the midst of the city. In the early sixteenth century, the villa was the resplendent home of Agostino Chigi, a wealthy Sienese banker, and the decorative art by Raphael, architect Baldassare Peruzzi, and Sebastiano del Piombo took ten years to complete. Inside, Villa Farnesina is chock-full of grand mythological frescoes, most notably Raphael's *Triumph of Galatea*, an explosion of rich hues and energy. This fresco makes you almost feel the breeze blowing through the room, tossing Galatea's hair. Be sure to visit the Salon of the Perspectives, with its views of sixteenth-century Rome through an illusionistic loggia. Mythological representations abound outdoors too. Along the loggia, which leads to the gardens, frescoes tell the tale of Cupid and Psyche, accentuated by luscious garlands of every kind of flora and fauna imaginable. The Three Graces float amid the garlands, their long, sinuous legs perched on soft cloud; one of them is of Chigi's mistress, Imperia.

In the gardens, Chigi entertained princes and popes. From a loggia that once stood close to the river, legend has it that his servants would throw silver goblets and platters into the Tiber after each course, as a sign of his immense wealth. But (we are told) a net had been submerged in the river, and after dinner all the silver was fished out.

SAN LUIGI DEI FRANCESI: A Painting to Contemplate
Location: Just east of Piazza Navona, on the corner of Via di Salvatore
and Via della Scrofa; a 15-minute walk from the Campo dei Fiori

Inside the Church of San Luigi dei Francesi is a chapel that my mother and I cherish as one of our favorite spots in Rome—a place we love to visit together. It's the farthest chapel on the left, after you enter the church. Let your eyes adjust to the darkness, and if there's a large group in front of you, wait until they're gone. Then you can contemplate without distraction the three canvases of Caravaggio's *Life of St. Matthew*. Painted between 1597 and 1602, they display the richness of hue and the mastery of light and dark—*chiaroscuro*—characteristic of this great artist. His skillful attention to detail allows the story to unfold. Every time we view these paintings, we are drawn to new discoveries: window shutters, gold coins, small objects hidden in the shadows, the perspective created by the saint's dangling feet. And we're always awed by the emotional intensity of the works. You certainly don't need to be Catholic to feel the power of the moment when Matthew is inspired by the angel, or his surprise when he is called by Jesus.

In the nearby Piazza Navona you will also find the famous Four Rivers Fountain by Bernini, and Borromini's Sant'Agnese in Agone. And it's a wonderful place to stop and enjoy an ice cream.

SANT'IVO ALLA SAPIENZA: A Hidden Jewel
Location: A 15-minute walk from Campo dei Fiori, just off Piazza Navona,
on the corner of Via degli Staderari and Via della Scrofa. Check ahead of time,
as visiting hours are extremely limited.

This tiny church is one of the most beautiful buildings in Rome, yet it is almost unknown to tourists. Built in the mid-seventeenth century by Borromini, it encompasses both a triangle and a star shape. You will sense its masterful design as you approach the church through the courtyard and the concave lower level of façade welcomes you, like the colonnade at St. Peter's Basilica, whereas the upper level is convex. Once inside, the dynamics of the three concave walls, counteracted by three convex walls—and the rich decoration—creates a floating feeling. Indeed, the whole building appears to be in movement—undulating, swaying, and spiraling upward, to the lantern on top of the dome and beyond, as a visitor here can truly feel swept up to God.

PALAZZO DORIA PAMPHILJ: A Home of Great Paintings

Location: Right off Piazza Venezia on the Via del Corso, about a
20-minute walk from Campo dei Fiori

The Palace of Doria Pamphilj houses one of the great private painting collections
in Europe, with important works by Caravaggio, Brueghel, Velázquez, Titian,
Lorenzo Lotto, Bernini, Bellini, Guido Reni, Annibale Carracci, Guercino, and
Claude Lorrain. If you love great paintings, don't miss it (especially the portrait of
Pope Innocent X by Velázquez, a favorite of mine). Not only is the art magnifi-
cent, but a walk through the palace gives a feeling for the life of Roman nobility.
The furnishings remain in place, and the paintings are hung as a family would
have enjoyed them, intermingled with antiquities and tapestries.

NAPLES

Chapter 8

Little Turnovers Stuffed with Escarole and Sausage
PIZZELLE RIPIENE CON SCAROLA E SALSICCIA

Nonna Lisa's Stuffed Tiella
TIELLA

Nonna Lisa's Tiella Filling of Escarole, Olives, and Capers
TIELLA RIPIENA DI SCAROLA, OLIVE, E CAPPERI

Nonna Lisa's Tiella Filling of Octopus, Garlic, and Oil
TIELLA RIPIENA DI POLIPO, AGLIO,
ED OLIO EXTRA VERGINE DI OLIVA

Dry Fettuccine with Squash and Cauliflower
BAVETTE CON ZUCCA E CAVOLO

Maltagliati with Onion-Tomato Sauce
MALTAGLIATI ALLA SALSA DI CIPOLLA

Spaghetti with Quick Garlic-Tomato Sauce
SPAGHETTI ALLA SALSETTA D'AGLIO

Bucatini Mock Amatriciana
BUCATINI ALLA FINTA AMATRICIANA

Vermicelli with Clam Sauce
VERMICELLI CON LE VONGOLE

Ditalini with Potatoes and Provola
PASTA, PATATE, E PROVOLA

Stuffed Escarole
SCAROLELLE IMBOTTITE

Sausages with Potatoes and Hot Peppers
SALSICCE CON PATATE E PEPERONCINO

Savory Potato Cake
GATTÒ DI PATATE

Icy Espresso Frappe
FRAPPÈ DI CAFFÈ

Fried Cream
CREMA FRITTA

Poached Pear Tart
CROSTATA DI PERE MASTANTUONE

Babas Infused with Limoncello
BABÀ AL LIMONCELLO

Naples is a very special city where life is palpable. You sense it the moment you get there. You are caught up in this energy and you become part of the life there, especially when walking the winding cobblestone street of the Centro Storico. The moment is now, and although there are three thousand years of rich history in Naples, life is very much in the present tense. In the streets, children play hide-and-seek and chase stray cats; laundry lines full of clothes hang from one window to another like festive banners. Music belches forth from open windows, modern rock and traditional *stornelli,* folk songs, clashing in the air. There is the wafting aroma of the ragù perking behind some open windows, the inviting smells of *fritto misto* floating from others; laughter, discussions, and arguments all spill onto the streets, and are part of the Neapolitan way of life.

I first came to Naples on my honeymoon in 1966, and we visited the surrounding Mount Vesuvio, Pompeii, and Paestum, which has one of the largest and best-preserved Greek temples in Italy. But on that distant first trip, what I truly fell in love with was the Neapolitans. Not just any Neapolitans—Gods knows there are thousands upon thousands around the world. I fell in love with the Neapolitans in Naples. I fell in love with their zest for life, the communal beat of the city where everyone is included. And I fell in love with their food.

Little Turnovers Stuffed with Escarole and Sausage

PIZZELLE RIPIENE CON SCAROLA E SALSICCIA

You must be familiar with *timballo* from the film *Big Night*—*maccheroni* dressed with a wonderful sweet tomato sauce set in a big round form of *pâte brisée* to bake. A sweet crust with savory pasta might seem an unlikely combination, but the *timballo* is delicious and represents much of what is left of the Neapolitan kitchen from its aristocratic days under French-Spanish rule.

These delightful *pizzelle*—small half-moon turnovers of raised sweet dough, stuffed with braised escarole, garlic, and sausage—are a wonderful and much simpler rendition of the *timballo*. The bitterness of the escarole and savory flavor of the meat, enveloped in the sweet crust, reach a perfect balance.

These *pizzelle* make a great hors d'oeuvre, passed around still warm from the oven. They will win you much praise, and you do not need to labor over them at the last minute. You can make the dough and filling a day before. Moreover, the assembled *pizzelle* can be frozen and then baked when needed.

Makes about 30 *pizzelle*, serving 8 or more

For the pizzelle dough
1 tablespoon sugar

1 packet (2 teaspoons) dry yeast

3 cups all-purpose flour, plus more for kneading and rolling

¾ cup lukewarm milk

¼ teaspoon salt

2 large eggs, lightly beaten

10 tablespoons (5 ounces) soft butter, in pieces, plus more for the bowl

For the filling
1½ pounds escarole

3 tablespoons extra-virgin olive oil

3 garlic cloves, peeled and sliced

Make a sponge, or starter dough: Mix ¼ cup warm water with 1 teaspoon of the sugar in a large bowl, and sprinkle the yeast on top. Let the yeast dissolve and start to bubble, then stir in 1 cup of the flour and the warm milk. Cover the bowl, and set in a warm place to rise until light and bubbly, an hour or so.

To mix the flour in a food processor, scrape all of the sponge into the work bowl. Drop in the remaining 2 cups of flour, remaining sugar, salt, beaten eggs, and butter pieces. Pulse several times to mix, then process continuously for about 30 seconds. You should have soft and somewhat sticky dough that has come away from the sides of the bowl. If the sides are not clear, incorporate more flour, a tablespoon at a time, to stiffen the dough. (You can also use a heavy-duty electric mixer to form the dough, or do it by hand.)

Scrape all the dough onto a floured surface, and knead by hand briefly to form a smooth, soft ball. Work in more flour if necessary, but it is OK if the dough is still a bit sticky. Butter the insides of a bowl lightly, drop in the dough, and seal the bowl with plastic wrap. Let the dough rise in a warm place until doubled in volume, about an hour.

Meanwhile, make the *pizzelle* filling. Trim off the tough bottom of the escarole head, separate and rinse the leaves, then chop them

3 sweet Italian sausages, casing removed, meat crumbled (about 1½ cups)

½ teaspoon peperoncino flakes, or to taste

½ teaspoon coarse sea salt or kosher salt, or to taste

1 egg for brushing the *pizzelle*

Soft butter for serving

Recommended Equipment
A food processor fitted with the metal blade

A heavy skillet or sauté pan, 12-inch or wider

One or more large baking sheets, covered with parchment or buttered

crosswise into 2-inch-wide strips. Pour the olive oil into the skillet, and set it over medium-high heat. Scatter the sliced garlic in the pan, and cook for a minute or two, until sizzling. Add the sausage, breaking up the meat and spreading it in the pan. Push aside the sausage, and sprinkle the peperoncino in a cleared hot spot to toast it, then sprinkle the salt over. Stir together with the sausage, and cook for 2 to 3 minutes, until all the meat is browned.

With the heat on high, pile all the chopped escarole in the pan, and toss the strips over and over, to heat and start cooking (tongs are useful for this). Pour a cup or so of water into the skillet, and continue turning the escarole, as it steams and wilts, until all the water has evaporated. Lower the heat, and cook, stirring frequently, until the escarole is very soft and almost dry, about 10 minutes. Adjust the seasoning, and let the filling cool. Turn onto a board and chop it up in small bits with the sausage.

When you are ready to form the *pizzelle*, deflate the risen dough, remove it from the bowl, and gently knead it into a smooth round. If you will be baking some or all of the *pizzelle* right away, heat the oven to 375° and arrange racks for one or more baking sheets.

Cut the dough in thirds. On a lightly floured surface, roll out one piece into an oblong approximately 20 inches by 12 inches. With a ring-shaped cutter or the rim of a can or plastic container, cut circles in the sheet of dough, 4 inches in diameter (or larger or smaller if you prefer).

Gather the dough scraps from between the cut rounds, and mound a tablespoon of filling on each round. Moisten the outside edge of each circle with water (use your finger or a small brush), then fold the dough over the filling. Line up the edges and pinch them together, forming a neat half-moon-shaped turnover. Press the tines of a fork around the edges to seal the dough. Roll out the remaining dough pieces (incorporating any scraps), and form all the *pizzelle* this way.

Arrange the *pizzelle* on the parchment-lined (or buttered) sheet at least 1 inch apart. Beat the egg well with a little water, and brush the tops of the *pizzelle* with the wash. Set the sheet (or sheets, if you fill several) in the oven, and bake for about 30 minutes, or until the *pizzelle* are crusty and golden, shifting the position of the sheets as needed for even baking.

Serve them warm, lightly buttered.

Nonna Lisa's Tiella

TIELLA

Driving north from Naples to Rome, you are bound to come to Gaeta, and you should make a point of sampling some *tiella* there. Every time I am in that vicinity, I stop by and enjoy some *tiella* with Nonna Lisa Corrado, my son-in-law's maternal grandmother. According to him, she makes the best *tiella* in all of Italy.

Tiella is made in Naples and throughout Italy, but it is a specialty in Gaeta, a beautiful seaside town on the border of Campania (Naples) and Lazio (Rome) regions.

So what is *tiella*? It is a thin-crusted deep-dish pizza, stuffed with different combinations of vegetables and fish—escarole, broccoli rabe, octopus, olives, ricotta and Swiss chard, artichokes, and any other vegetable that is in season. It is topped and sealed with the same dough and baked until golden.

Every time I stop for a piece of *tiella*, Nonna Lisa teaches me another filling. I take notes, and then I enjoy. I now make them at the restaurants and at home in New York, for my son-in-law. He enjoys them with a touch of nostalgia and following are two for you to enjoy.

Makes 1 large *tiella,* serving 8 or more

For the tiella dough
1 package (2 teaspoons) dry yeast

¼ cup warm water

1½ cups all-purpose flour, plus more for handling the dough

1½ cups semolina flour

1 teaspoon coarse sea salt or kosher salt

1½ teaspoons sugar

¾ cup cool water plus more if needed

5 tablespoons extra-virgin olive oil, plus more for the bowl

To make the dough, dissolve the yeast in ¼ cup warm water, and let it sit for several minutes.

Put the flours, salt, and sugar in the bowl of the food processor, and run the machine for a few seconds to blend the dry ingredients.

Stir the active yeast together with the cool water and 3 tablespoons of the olive oil in a spouted measuring cup. With the food processor running, pour all the liquid into the flours, and continue processing for 30 seconds or so. A soft dough should gather on the blade and clean the sides of the bowl. If the sides are not clear, incorporate more flour, a tablespoon at a time, to stiffen the dough. If the dough is very stiff, work in more cool water in small amounts. (You can also use a heavy-duty electric mixer to form the dough, or do it by hand.)

Turn the dough out onto a floured surface, and knead by hand briefly to form a smooth round. Place the dough in a lightly oiled bowl, and cover with plastic wrap. Let the dough rise in a warm place until doubled, about an hour. Deflate the dough when

Nonna Lisa's Tiella (continued)

1 recipe Escarole, Olives, and
Caper Filling or 1 recipe
Octopus Filling (recipes follow)

Recommended Equipment
A food processor fitted with the
metal blade

A heavy ovenproof skillet with
rounded sides, 12 inches across
the top, or a deep-dish pie pan,
12 inches or wider (or an authentic
12-inch *tiella* pan!)

A baking stone or pizza stone,
if you have one

doubled, knead it briefly, and return to the bowl for a second rise. If you like, refrigerate the dough, sealed airtight, for up to a day (deflate and knead it whenever it doubles).

When your filling is prepared and you are ready to bake the *tiella*, heat the oven to 375°. Arrange a rack in the center of the oven and put the baking stone on it, if using. Brush the bottom and sides of the skillet or baking pan lightly with olive oil.

Deflate the dough, knead it briefly to form a round again, and cut off a third of the dough for the top crust of the *tiella*. The larger, two-thirds piece will be the bottom crust. Let the dough relax (especially if it has been chilled) before rolling.

On a floured surface, roll out the big piece of dough to a 14-inch round. Transfer the round to the skillet or baking pan, centered and lying flat on the bottom and sides. Trim the top edge of the dough neatly so it is an even height, about 1½ inches, up the sides all around.

Scrape the cooled escarole or octopus filling into the bottom crust, and spread it in an even layer, slightly compressed. The escarole filling makes a thinner layer than the octopus, but with either, the bottom crust should extend at least ½ inch above the filling all around.

Roll out the smaller piece of dough to a 12-inch round and trim it into a neat circle that is a bit larger than the layer of filling—use a ruler to get the right dimensions. Center the circle, and lay it on top of the filling. Pinch together the overlapping edges of the bottom and top crusts all around. Fold this wide flap of dough inward, and press it down and against the pan sides all around. Make uniform indentations with your fingertips, to seal the *tiella* tightly and create a decorative rim of dough at the same time.

With the tip of a sharp knife, pierce the top crust all over with a dozen or so small slits. Finally, brush the remaining extra-virgin olive oil all over the *tiella*, including the border of crust.

Bake the *tiella*, on the heated stone if you have one, for about 45 minutes, or until the crust is a deep golden brown. Cool it on a rack for at least an hour in the skillet. Invert and remove the *tiella* if you want, or leave it in the pan for serving. Cut wedges, and serve slightly warm or at room temperature.

Nonna Lisa's Tiella Filling of Escarole, Olives, and Capers

TIELLA RIPIENA DI SCAROLA, OLIVE, E CAPPERI

2 pounds or more escarole

6 tablespoons extra-virgin olive oil

1½ tablespoons chopped garlic

⅓ cup small capers, drained

⅓ cup Gaeta olives, pitted

½ teaspoon coarse sea salt or kosher salt

½ teaspoon peperoncino flakes, or to taste

Recommended Equipment
A heavy-bottomed, high-sided skillet or sauté pan, 12 inches in diameter or larger, with a cover

Trim off the base of the escarole, separate the leaves, and discard any that are wilted or blemished. Rinse and drain the leaves, and chop them into shreds about an inch wide.

Pour ¼ cup of the olive oil in the big skillet, set it over medium-high heat, and stir in the garlic. Cook for a minute or so, until sizzling, then pile in all the escarole, and tumble the shreds over and over with tongs, over high heat. Scatter the capers and olives on top, season with the salt and peperoncino, and toss. Pour ½ cup water into the pan, and cover tightly.

Steam the escarole for about 5 minutes. Uncover the pan, and continue cooking over medium heat, stirring frequently, until all the moisture has been cooked off and the filling is condensed and fairly dry, about 20 minutes more. Near the end of cooking, drizzle over it the remaining 2 tablespoons olive oil and toss.

Cool the filling before assembling the *tiella*.

Pizza: The Pride of Napoli

Ristorante L'Europeo has the best pizza in Naples, I was told, hence the world. Although I am not giving you the recipe for pizza in this book (see *Lidia's Italian-American Kitchen,* page 201), I want to share with you the characteristics of a true Neapolitan pizza. The pizza in Naples, according to my good friend Bruno di Rosa, a born Neapolitan, should have a puffy, almost blistered cornice and a very thin center. The puffy cornice should be well toasted and should have the taste of the wood oven. The mozzarella should be made from the milk of water buffalo and should be *staccato,* in distinctive pieces—not one big oozing, stringy mess. The tomato sauce should be the uncooked pulp of the San Marzano tomatoes, passed through a mill, and there should not be too much of it on the pizza.

When you cut into a pizza in Naples, it should be fairly contained and not ooze all over the plate. A few pieces of fresh basil scattered on top, and that is it. A minimalist approach to pizza-making. What is paramount to a Neapolitan in eating his pizza is the nuances of flavor in the dough. It was all of that and more at L'Europeo.

Nonna Lisa's Tiella Filling of Octopus, Garlic, and Oil

TIELLA RIPIENA DI POLIPO, AGLIO, ED OLIO EXTRA VERGINE DI OLIVA

The Golfo di Gaeta teems with octopus, and Nonna Lisa can buy them fresh all year round to make this delicious *tiella* filling. With rare exceptions, however, octopus sold in the United States has been frozen (and usually cleaned) before coming to market. And while I almost always prefer fresh seafood, properly frozen octopus is easy to handle and tastes excellent—some claim that freezing helps to tenderize the flesh. Buy octopus still frozen (not thawed) from a reliable fishmonger or online merchant.

Makes about 4 cups of filling, for a 12-inch *tiella*

4 pounds frozen, cleaned octopus (tentacles about ½ inch wide at thickest part)

2 bay leaves

1 pound ripe plum tomatoes (4 tomatoes)

4 tablespoons extra-virgin olive oil

1½ tablespoons sliced garlic

⅔ cup Gaeta olives, pitted and cut in half

¼ teaspoon peperoncino flakes

½ teaspoon coarse sea salt or kosher salt

2 tablespoons chopped fresh Italian parsley

Recommended Equipment
A large pot for cooking the octopus

A heavy-bottomed skillet or sauté pan, 12-inch diameter or larger

Defrost the octopus, and put it in a big pot with several inches of water to cover. Add the bay leaves. Bring to a boil, and cook at a bubbling simmer for about 35 minutes, or until the octopus is tender but *al dente*. You should be able to pierce the flesh with a big meat-fork but still feel a bit of resistance when you withdraw it. The skin of the octopus should still be largely intact—not broken and peeling off, which indicates overcooking. Let it cool in the cooking water, then drain well and cut it up into ¾-inch pieces.

Rinse, core, and seed the plum tomatoes, and cut into ⅓-inch dice.

Pour the olive oil into the big skillet, set it over medium heat, and stir in the garlic. Cook for a minute, until sizzling, then add the octopus pieces and toss them in the oil. Scatter the olives in the pan, and cook for a couple of minutes, stirring and tossing; sprinkle in the peperoncino. When the octopus is sizzling, toss in the diced tomatoes, and season with the salt.

Cook at the simmer, stirring frequently, for another 10 minutes or so, until the filling is dense and glistening, with no liquid left in the pan. Toss in the parsley, and cool the filling before assembling the *tiella*.

Spaghetti with Quick Garlic-Tomato Sauce

SPAGHETTI ALLA SALSETTA D'AGLIO

Serves 6

1 teaspoon coarse sea salt or kosher salt, plus 1 tablespoon for the pasta pot

½ cup extra-virgin olive oil

⅓ cup sliced garlic

4 cups (or a 35-ounce can) canned Italian plum tomatoes, preferably San Marzano, crushed by hand

1 pound spaghetti

¼ cup shredded fresh basil leaves (10 large leaves)

Recommended Equipment
A heavy-bottomed skillet or sauté pan, 12-inch diameter or larger

A large pot, 8-quart capacity or larger, with a cover, for cooking the pasta

Before starting the sauce, heat the pasta-cooking water—at least 6 quarts water and 1 tablespoon salt—to a boil.

Pour ⅓ cup of the olive oil into the big skillet, and set over medium-high heat. Scatter in the sliced garlic and cook 2 minutes, until lightly colored. Pour in the crushed tomatoes; rinse the tomato containers with a bit of water and pour that in. Sprinkle on the salt, stir well, and bring to a boil. Cook, stirring occasionally, maintaining a steady boil.

Drop the spaghetti into the cooking water when the tomatoes are perking along. Cook until quite *al dente*, lift the pasta from the pot, drain briefly, and drop it onto the sauce. Toss the spaghetti and tomatoes for a minute or two, until the pasta is perfectly cooked and dressed.

Turn off the heat, scatter the basil over the pasta, and drizzle on the remaining olive oil. Toss well, and serve immediately.

Neapolitan Pastas

Pasta in Naples defines the term "cooked *al dente*." No city in Italy is more in tune with the texture of cooked pasta. One can experience it at Da Dora, a fabulous fish restaurant in the ritzy Chiaia part of town, hidden along one of the cobblestone streets. There one can have perfect *Spaghetti alla Salsetta d'Aglio* (page 254), *Vermicelli con le Vongole* (page 256), *Bucatini alla Finta Amatriciana* (page 255), and a host of others.

Many Neapolitan pastas highlight the fresh flavor of San Marzano tomatoes, the prized variety grown in a farming region outside the city. Whether fresh or canned, the tomatoes cook only for a short time over high heat, just to bring out the flavor and thicken the consistency. In these fast pastas, it is best to make the sauce in a large skillet over a hot fire, at the same time as the pasta cooks *al dente*.

Bucatini Mock Amatriciana

BUCATINI ALLA FINTA AMATRICIANA

Serves 6

2 onions, sliced ⅓ inch thick
(at least 3 cups)

½ cup extra-virgin olive oil

1 teaspoon coarse sea salt or
kosher salt, plus 1 tablespoon
for the pasta pot

½ teaspoon peperoncino flakes,
or to taste

4 cups (or a 35-ounce can)
canned Italian plum tomatoes,
preferably San Marzano,
crushed by hand

1 pound bucatini

2 cups freshly grated pecorino

Recommended Equipment
A heavy-bottomed skillet or
sauté pan, 12-inch diameter
or larger

A large pot, 8-quart capacity or
larger, with a cover, for cooking
the pasta

Scatter the sliced onions in the big skillet, and pour in a cup of water. Bring the water to a boil, and simmer over moderate heat, softening the onions, until the water has almost totally evaporated.

Pour in ⅓ cup of the olive oil, and stir to coat the onions. Raise the heat a bit, season with the salt and peperoncino, and cook, stirring frequently, until the onions are lightly colored, 4 to 5 minutes. Pour in the crushed tomatoes, stir well, and bring to a boil. Cook the sauce at a good bubbling pace for 10 minutes or so, until slightly thickened.

Meanwhile, heat 6 quarts of water, with a tablespoon salt, to the boil in the large pot. When the tomatoes have been perking for a few minutes, drop in the bucatini and cook until quite *al dente*. Lift the pasta from the pot with tongs, drain briefly, and drop it onto the simmering sauce. Toss together for a minute or two, until the pasta is fully cooked and coated with sauce. If necessary, boil rapidly until any soupiness in the skillet has been cooked down.

Turn off the heat, drizzle over the remaining olive oil, and toss with half of the grated pecorino. Serve immediately, passing more cheese at the table.

Vermicelli with Clam Sauce

VERMICELLI CON LE VONGOLE

With thin vermicelli and tender small clams, this is a very quick-cooking (and very delicious) pasta. To yield their most intense flavor, though, the clams should be freshly shucked and totally raw when they go into the sauce, rather than being steamed in the shell. The method given here—freezing the clams briefly before shucking—makes this task easier than you can imagine, even if you are not a skilled shellfish shucker.

Serves 6

3½ pounds littleneck clams

½ teaspoon coarse sea salt or kosher salt, or to taste

10 tablespoons extra-virgin olive oil

10 garlic cloves, peeled and sliced

½ teaspoon peperoncino flakes

1 cup tomatoes *al filetto*—fresh or canned plum tomatoes seeded and sliced in thin strips

4 tablespoons chopped fresh Italian parsley

1 pound vermicelli

Recommended Equipment
A clam- or oyster-shucking knife, or other knife with a sturdy, short, sharp blade

A heavy-bottomed skillet or sauté pan, 14-inch diameter or larger

A large pot, 8-quart capacity or larger, with a cover, for cooking the pasta

Put the clams in a single layer on a tray or platter, and freeze them for about ½ hour. Working over a bowl to catch every drop of clam liquor, open the clams with the shucking knife, cut the meat free from both half-shells, and let the meat and liquor fall into the bowl.

Strain the collected clams through a sieve set over a small bowl or measuring cup. Let the sediment in the liquor settle, then pour off the clean liquor on top—½ cup or so—and save for the sauce. Chop the clams roughly into large pieces.

Before starting the sauce, begin heating the pasta-cooking water—at least 6 quarts water and 1 tablespoon salt.

Pour ½ cup of the olive oil into the big skillet, and set over medium-high heat. Scatter in the sliced garlic, heat to sizzling, and sprinkle over it the peperoncino. Cook another minute, add the sliced tomatoes and the reserved clam liquor, stir, and bring to the boil. Cook for 2 to 3 minutes and stir in the clams. Return to the boil, and cook at a bubbling simmer for 3 or 4 minutes—if the clams release a frothy scum, scoop it off the surface and discard. When the sauce has achieved a nice density, lower the heat, and season with salt to taste. Stir in the parsley and the remaining 2 tablespoons of olive oil.

With the pasta water at a rolling boil, drop in the vermicelli when the clams are cooking in the sauce. Cook briefly, and lift the pasta from the pot while still quite *al dente*, let it drain briefly, and drop it onto the simmering sauce. Toss the vermicelli in the sauce for a couple of minutes, until the pasta is cooked through and dressed with the sauce and there's no soupiness in the pan. Serve immediately.

Ditalini with Potatoes and Provola

PASTA, PATATE, E PROVOLA

The 200-year-old L'Europeo, one of the best restaurants in Naples, serves the most delicious rendition of a favorite Neapolitan dish—*pasta, patate, e provola*. You can probably translate this yourself: pasta, potatoes, and provola cheese—the kind of cheese we usually call "provolone." All varieties of provola (there are many) are pulled-curd cheeses, like mozzarella, but after they are formed into pear shapes they are hung to dry, and sometimes smoked.

Neapolitans have strong opinions on what makes a good dish of *pasta, patate, e provola*. As prepared by my Neapolitan friend Bruno di Rosa's mother, Rita, it is considered a soup and eaten with a spoon. At L'Europeo it was definitely a pasta, dense and cheesy and full of flavor—with all the comforts of baked macaroni and cheese.

Serves 6

6 tablespoons extra-virgin olive oil

1 cup chopped bacon, in ¼-inch pieces

1 onion, chopped (about 1 cup)

4 cups russet potatoes, peeled and cut in ½-inch cubes

½ teaspoon sea salt or kosher salt, plus more for the pasta pot

1 pound ditalini

1 cup seeded and diced fresh tomato

8 ounces smoked provola or mozzarella, in ½-inch cubes

½ cup freshly grated Parmigiano-Reggiano

Recommended Equipment
A heavy-bottomed skillet or sauté pan, 12-inch diameter or larger

Put 4 tablespoons of the olive oil and the chopped bacon in the big skillet and set over medium-high heat. Stir and cook for 3 or 4 minutes, to render bacon fat. Stir in the chopped onion, and cook until it is sizzling and wilting, about 3 minutes. Spill in the cubed potatoes, toss well in the fat, then spread them in the pan. Season with the salt, and cook, tossing and turning the potatoes frequently, for another 3 or 4 minutes, until the cubes are lightly crisped all over.

Pour in 4 cups water, stir everything around, and scrape up any crust on the skillet bottom. Bring the water to a gently bubbling boil and cook, stirring frequently, for about 20 minutes, until the potatoes are cooked. The soup (or sauce, depending on your point of view) should reduce so it barely covers the potato cubes.

Meanwhile, bring 6 quarts of salted water to the boil in a pasta pot. After the potatoes have cooked for about 10 minutes, drop the ditalini into the pot and cook *al dente*. Drain the ditalini, and stir into the thickened potato soup/sauce. Stir in the remaining 2 tablespoons olive oil, and simmer the *pasta e patate* together for another 3 minutes or so, to an even denser consistency.

Stir in the diced tomatoes, cook for a minute, and adjust salt to taste. Turn off the heat, scatter the cubed provola all over, and stir into the *pasta e patate* continuously as it melts into threads. Finally, stir in the grated cheese. Serve immediately, in warm bowls.

Stuffed Escarole

SCAROLELLE IMBOTTITE

Escarole is a great vegetable that is used much in Neapolitan cuisine, in soups and salads or just braised with garlic and oil. In this recipe, blanched escarole leaves are wrapped around a savory stuffing (as cabbage often is) and baked. Serve these rolls as an elegant antipasto, or as a vegetarian main course.

Makes 8 rolls

2 medium heads escarole, 1 pound each

¼ cup pine nuts, toasted

½ cup bread crumbs, toasted

½ cup grated pecorino

9 tablespoons extra-virgin olive oil

1 tablespoon sliced garlic

¼ cup oil-cured black olives, pitted and roughly chopped

2 tablespoons golden raisins, plumped in warm water, drained, and roughly chopped

3 tablespoons small capers, drained

½ teaspoon coarse sea salt or kosher salt

Recommended Equipment

An 8-quart pot for blanching the escarole

A medium skillet

A 9-by-13-inch baking dish or shallow casserole

Bring 6 quarts or more water to the boil in the large pot. Remove any damaged outer leaves from the escarole heads, but otherwise keep them whole and attached at the base. To clean them, spread the leaves open and dunk the heads, leaves first, into a sink or basin filled with cold water, to rinse away any dirt or debris.

To blanch the escarole, push the heads, leaves first, into the boiling water, submerging them completely. Return the water to the boil, and cook for 2 to 3 minutes, to soften the leaves. Place the heads, still attached, in a colander to drain and cool.

Toss together the toasted pine nuts, bread crumbs, and ¼ cup of the grated pecorino in a bowl. Remove about a third of the mixture and set aside for topping the rolls; leave the larger amount in the bowl for the filling.

Pour 5 tablespoons of the olive oil into the skillet and set over medium heat. Stir the sliced garlic in the oil, and cook for a minute or so, until sizzling. Stir in the olives, toast them for a minute, then toss in the raisins and capers and cook for just a minute more. Scrape all the savories and oil from the skillet into the bread-crumb filling mixture and toss together.

Heat the oven to 375° and put a rack in the center. Pour 2 tablespoons of the olive oil into the baking dish.

Lay the blanched heads of escarole on a large cutting board. Divide each head in half, slicing lengthwise through the core and base; now slice each half in two lengthwise. You should have eight clusters of escarole leaves, each cluster still attached at the base. Spread each cluster open like a fan and flatten the leaves, so they resemble a single large leaf, which will enclose the filling—just like a cabbage leaf.

When all the clusters are open, cut off and discard the tough bases holding the leaves together. Move leaves from one cluster to another so the escarole fans are of equal size and shape.

Divide all the filling equally among the fans (2 to 3 tablespoons each), laying it in small oblong mounds near the base of the leaves. Roll up the escarole just enough to cover the filling, fold in the sides of the leaf fans, then continue rolling to form fairly compact oval rolls.

Arrange the rolls in the oiled pan, leaving space between them. Sprinkle the salt all over the rolls, then the reserved mixture of bread crumbs and pine nuts and the remaining grated cheese. Finally, drizzle the remaining 2 tablespoons of olive oil all over the rolls.

Cover the baking dish with a sheet of aluminum foil, arched so it doesn't touch the rolls, and press it against the sides. Bake for about 30 minutes, remove the foil, and bake another 5 or 10 minutes, until the escarole rolls are lightly caramelized and the toppings are crisp and golden brown. Serve hot.

Sausages with Potatoes and Hot Peppers

SALSICCE CON PATATE E PEPERONCINO

This zesty dish is suitable for all sorts of occasions. As a first course, it will turn an ordinary meal into a festive occasion. It's also a great main course for a family dinner, with a salad and pasta. Heap the sausages and potatoes on a big platter, and let people help themselves.

Serves 6

2 pounds red potatoes or new potatoes (4 medium-sized is best)

½ cup extra-virgin olive oil

6 plump garlic cloves, crushed and peeled

½ teaspoon peperoncino flakes, or to taste

1 cup Tuscan-style peperoncini (small whole peppers) in vinegar, drained, seeded, and thinly sliced (12-ounce jar)

¾ teaspoon coarse sea salt or kosher salt, or to taste

1½ pounds sweet Italian sausages, preferably thin

Recommended Equipment
A heavy-bottomed skillet or sauté pan, 13-inch diameter or larger, with a cover

Scrub and dry the potatoes, but don't peel them. Slice them lengthwise into sticks and wedges, about ½ inch wide (French-fry size).

Pour the olive oil into the skillet and set over medium-high heat. Scatter the garlic and peperoncino flakes in the oil. Stir and toss the garlic for a minute or so, until lightly colored, then, with a slotted spoon or skimmer, scoop all the cloves from the pan and reserve. Strew the sliced pickled peperoncini in the oil and toast them, stirring, for about a minute, just to get them sizzling, then scoop them out—letting all the oil drain back into the pan.

Scatter the cut potatoes in the skillet, and toss them in the flavored oil. Season with ½ teaspoon of salt, and cook for 6 minutes or so, over moderate heat. Toss and turn them frequently, until lightly crisped on all sides.

Push the potatoes to the side of the skillet, and lay all the sausages in the pan. Cook for 5 or 6 minutes, rotating and shifting the sausages until they're sizzling and lightly browned on all sides; turn the potatoes as needed so they don't burn.

Cover the pan, lower the heat, and keep the potatoes and sausages sizzling and caramelizing slowly for about 20 minutes, turning and moving them in the skillet now and then. Remove the cover, and scatter the reserved garlic and peperoncini all over. Taste a potato, and season with more salt if you like. Cook uncovered for another 10 minutes or so, over low to moderate heat, until all the potatoes and sausages are caramelized and crisp on the outside, and tender and fully cooked inside.

Serve hot (and spicy).

Savory Potato Cake

GATTÒ DI PATATE

This rich and fluffy potato dish takes its name from the French word *gâteau*, but to me it is quite Italian, layered with cheese, like a *pasticiatta* or lasagna. It is a great dish for large gatherings: all the goodness of mashed potatoes with an Italian twist.

Serves 12

4 to 4½ pounds baking potatoes

8 ounces (2 sticks or 16 tablespoons) butter, or more as needed

½ cup hot milk

3 large eggs

2 egg yolks

2 teaspoons coarse sea salt or kosher salt

1¼ cups freshly grated Grana Padano or Parmigiano-Reggiano

½ cup bread crumbs

1 pound fresh *fiore di latte* mozzarella, in ½-inch cubes

Recommended Equipment
A wide, heavy-bottomed saucepan or high-sided sauté pan, 5-quart capacity or larger

A potato ricer

A baking dish or shallow casserole, 9 by 13 inches or similar size

Cook the potatoes, whole and in their skins, in a large pot with plenty of water to cover, until they are cooked through and easily pierced but still intact. Drain the potatoes, and peel them while hot.

Put 6 ounces of the butter (1½ sticks) in the heavy pan, and set it over low heat. Rice the potatoes directly into the pan as the butter melts. Stir the mound of riced potatoes vigorously to blend them with the butter, then stir in the hot milk. Beat the eggs and yolks together, and blend into the potatoes along with the salt. Finally, sprinkle 1 cup of the grated cheese on top of the potatoes, and incorporate thoroughly.

Heat the oven to 375°. With some of the remaining butter, grease the insides of the baking dish well, then coat the bottom and sides with ¼ cup of the bread crumbs. Spread half of the whipped potatoes in the dish in a smooth layer, distribute the cubed mozzarella evenly on top, then cover the cheese with the rest of the potatoes, spread smooth.

Toss the remaining bread crumbs and grated cheese together, and sprinkle on top of the potatoes. Melt the last 2 tablespoons of butter (or get some more), and drizzle it all over. Cover the dish with a sheet of aluminum foil, pressed against the sides to seal the *gattò*, and place it in the oven.

Bake for 30 minutes, remove the foil, and bake another 20 minutes, or until the top is crisp and nicely colored. Cut portion-sized squares in the hot *gattò* and lift out with a spatula, keeping the layers of potato and cheese intact.

Icy Espresso Frappe

FRAPPÈ DI CAFFÈ

Like Torino and Trieste, Naples is a great *caffè* town. And in their warm climate, Neapolitans have perfected the art of iced coffee, as exemplified by this blender-whipped refreshment. It is a dessert and espresso break all in one—just the kind of treat to enjoy while engaging in the sport of people-watching at a *caffè* in Naples.

Serves 4

2 cups hot, strong, freshly brewed espresso

6 tablespoons sugar, or more to taste

3 cups finely crushed ice or ice cubes

½ cup whipping cream

Recommended Equipment
A blender *and* a food processor, if needed

4 tall glasses, chilled, and 4 long spoons

While the espresso is hot, stir in 5 tablespoons sugar (or to taste). Let the coffee cool to room temperature.

If you don't have crushed ice, pulverize the ice cubes in a food processor (my preference) or a blender, into fine bits. Return the crushed ice to the freezer.

Whip the cream, with a tablespoon of sugar if you like, until smooth and holding soft peaks. Keep it chilled.

When espresso is thoroughly cool, pour it into the empty blender jar. Churn on high speed for at least 2 minutes, until it becomes light in color and frothy.

Pour an equal amount of the espresso frappe into each chilled glass, quickly add a share of crushed ice, and top with a mound of whipped cream. Serve right away, with a long spoon.

Fried Cream

CREMA FRITTA

The "cream" in this popular dish is actually a simple stovetop custard that is firm enough, when chilled, to cut into small blocks, coat with bread crumbs, and fry. Crispy on the outside, creamy on the inside, it is served in many regions of Italy. In some places, *crema fritta* is considered a savory, as in Emilia, where it is part of the *fritto misto*. But in Naples, I had *crema fritta* as a *dolce*, and I hope you enjoy this wonderful sweet.

Makes about 20 pieces, serving 6 or more

For the custard
4 cups milk

1 cup plus 2 tablespoons all-purpose flour

½ cup sugar

¼ teaspoon salt

4 large egg yolks

For frying and serving
½ cup all-purpose flour, or more if needed

1½ cups bread crumbs, or more if needed

3 large eggs

Pinch of salt

1 to 2 cups vegetable oil, or as needed

3 tablespoons sugar

1 teaspoon cinnamon

Recommended Equipment
A sturdy wire whisk

Pour the milk in the heavy pan. Whisk together the flour, sugar, and salt, to break up any lumps, then whisk the dry mixture gradually into the milk. Break up the egg yolks a bit in a bowl, then whisk (and scrape) every bit of yolk into the milk.

Set the pan over medium heat, and bring the milk near to a simmer, whisking constantly. Lower the heat a bit, and cook the custard, still whisking, as it starts to thicken and gradually comes to a slow bubbling boil. Cook for at least 15 minutes, to make sure the flour has cooked, always whisking (ask someone to take a turn!). When the custard is quite thick and creamy—it won't get stiff—take the pan off the heat.

Turn the hot custard into the baking dish, and spread it in an evenly thick layer covering the bottom. Let it cool at room temperature, then cover with plastic wrap and chill thoroughly in the refrigerator, for several hours or a day or so.

When you're ready to fry the "cream," spread the flour in a small plate, the bread crumbs in a large plate, and whisk the eggs with the pinch of salt in a wide, shallow bowl. Pour vegetable oil into the skillet to a depth of ¼ inch, and start heating it, slowly. Stir together the sugar and cinnamon in a small bowl.

Unwrap the chilled custard, dip a sharp knife in warm water, and slice the sheet into squares, rectangles, or diamonds, 1½ to 2 inches on a side. (Since larger pieces are more fragile, cut a couple of test portions and lift them from the pan with a spatula. Cut smaller pieces if necessary.)

Working in batches that you can fry without crowding, coat the custard blocks in flour, then eggs, then bread crumbs—handle gently; use a spatula or fork to turn and lift them. Lay the pieces in

A wide, heavy-bottomed saucepan, 3-quart capacity or larger

A 9-inch square baking dish or cake pan, or similar-sized container with a flat bottom, to chill the custard sheet

A heavy skillet, 10 inches or wider, for frying

the hot oil, and fry for 1½ to 2 minutes on each side, until nicely browned (if the crumbs darken quickly, lower the heat). Set the fried creams on paper towels to drain.

Let the creams cool briefly, then sprinkle with cinnamon-sugar—to taste. Serve while they're still warm.

Neapolitan Desserts

With pizza and spaghetti reigning in Naples, for a long time I did not realize how important and integral the desserts were to the Neapolitan way of life, and how much I enjoy Neapolitan desserts. There are *pasticcerie* all over Naples, retailing and serving their delicious desserts with what some consider the best coffee in Italy. Some of my favorites are the limoncello-soaked baba (page 269), *Crostata di Pere Mastatuone* (page 266), and *crema fritta* at Scaturchio.

Poached Pear Tart

CROSTATA DI PERE MASTANTUONE

This tart is a specialty of Calvizzano, a town near Naples, made with the *mastantuono* pear, which grows there. You will have to visit Calvizanno to taste the *mastantuono*—a small round yellow-green pear—but several of our American varieties, such as small Seckel pears or medium-sized Anjou or Bosc, are perfect for this great tart. In this recipe, the fruit is first cooked and saturated in a natural syrup, then baked in a pastry crust. Make sure to use pears that are still firm.

This tart is delicious with a dollop of whipped cream, or served warm with some vanilla ice cream. I also like it with sour cream.

Makes a 10-inch tart, serving 8 or more

For the tart dough
2¼ cups all-purpose flour

¼ teaspoon salt

4 tablespoons sugar

8 ounces (2 sticks) very cold butter, cut in ½-inch pieces

4 egg yolks

2 tablespoons ice water, or more as needed

For the filling
2⅓ cups sugar

Grated zest and juice of 1 lemon

2 tablespoons soft butter

2 to 2½ pounds firm, nearly ripe pears (Seckel, Anjou, or Bosc)

½ cup apricot jam

1 egg yolk beaten with 1 tablespoon water for glazing the pastry

To make the tart dough: Put the flour, salt, and sugar into the bowl of a food processor fitted with the metal blade. Process for a few seconds to mix the dry ingredients. Drop the cut-up butter on top of the flour, and pulse the machine in a dozen or more short bursts, until the mixture is crumbly, with only small bits of butter visible. Pour the egg yolks over the crumbs, and pulse in bursts, about 5 seconds total, to moisten the dough. Scrape down the sides of the bowl, sprinkle 2 tablespoons of ice water on the dough, and pulse again for a few seconds.

The dough should begin to clump together but not form a solid mass. Scrape it all out onto a board or into a large bowl; gather and press the clumps into a firm ball that holds together. If it crumbles apart, sprinkle more ice water over the dough and knead gently. When the dough sticks together, flatten it into a disk, wrap well in plastic, and refrigerate for 6 hours or up to a day before rolling. Freeze the dough for longer keeping.

To make the filling: Put the sugar, the lemon zest and juice, and the butter in the heavy pan. Spread the sugar around the pan bottom. Cut the pears in half, and neatly pare away the cores and stems. Lay the halves in one layer on top of the sugar in the pan, cut side down.

Set the pan over medium heat, and let the sugar and butter melt and form a syrup with the juices released by the fruit. As it heats, spoon the syrup over the skins of the pear halves. When the syrup starts to boil, adjust the heat to maintain a bubbling simmer, and

Recommended Equipment
A heavy-bottomed sauté pan or shallow saucepan, wide enough to hold all the pear halves in one layer

A 10-inch metal tart mold with fluted sides and removable bottom

cook, still cut side down, for about 10 minutes. Carefully turn the pears over, and simmer them for 15 minutes on the skin side. Turn them to cook once again on the cut side for another 10 minutes or more, until they are cooked through—easily pierced with the tines of a fork, and very soft to the touch. (If you are using small Seckel pears, turn them sooner and expect shorter total cooking time.)

Remove the pan from the heat, and let the pears cool completely in the syrup. Make sure they are cut side down, so they become saturated. (Steep them in the syrup overnight, refrigerated, if you like.)

When you are ready to roll out the pastry and assemble the tart, lift the pear halves and drain all the syrup back into the pan. Set the pears on paper towels to dry the cut sides. Place the pan with all the residual syrup over medium-high heat, bring to a boil, and cook it rapidly, until it reduces and just begins to caramelize. Lower the heat, and when the syrup turns deep gold, pour it into a heat-proof cup.

Heat the oven to 350°, with a rack set in the center. Place a baking stone on the rack if you have one.

To form the tart shell: Cut off a third of the sweet dough in a single piece for lattice top. Keep it chilled.

Place the larger piece of dough between two large sheets of parchment, and roll it out to an even 12-inch round. Peel off the top sheet of parchment, invert the dough circle over the tart pan, and peel off the remaining sheet.

Press the dough gently down into the pan so it covers the bottom and lines the sides. Trim the edges of the dough round so it is even with the pan rim. With your fingers, form an even wall all the way around. Use scraps of dough to fill cracks or thin spots on the bottom or sides.

Now roll the smaller piece of dough between the parchment sheets to an 11-inch round. Remove the top parchment sheet, and cut the dough in 1-inch-wide strips with a pastry cutter or sharp knife. Leave the strips in place on the parchment sheet (and, if your kitchen is warm, refrigerate them) until you are ready to form the lattice.

Spread the apricot jam to cover the bottom of the tart crust. Place the pear halves in the crust, skin side up, in one layer. Drizzle the golden pear syrup all over the fruit.

Form the lattice top, first laying half the strips over the pears, parallel and spaced about an inch apart. Lay the other half of the strips at an angle, covering the whole tart in an even pattern. Press and pinch the ends of the strips neatly into the rim of dough in the pan. Finally, brush the lattice strips with the egg-yolk glaze.

Bake the tart—on the stone if you have one—for about 40 minutes, or until the lattice is deep golden brown and the exposed pear tops are lightly caramelized. Cool the tart on a wire rack. When the crust has cooled a bit and contracted, slip off the fluted side ring. Serve warm or at room temperature, cut in wedges—with your favorite kind of cream.

Babas Infused with Limoncello

BABÀ AL LIMONCELLO

Babà al rhum is a favorite dessert in Naples, found in most *pasticcerie*, filled with whipped cream, or *crema pasticciera* (custard cream), or cannoli cream— or just oozing with syrup.

In this recipe, I give you a limoncello syrup to soak the babas, and you can fill them with ice cream or whipped cream, the ricotta filling for cannoli (page 307), Espresso Zabaglione (page 156), or the cream for Limoncello Tiramisù (page 120).

If you don't have baba molds, you can bake the cakes in small (not mini-) muffin pans. You could also use two small Bundt pans.

Makes 12 to 16 small babas

For the dough
1 package (2 teaspoons) dry yeast

2¼ cups all-purpose flour

Pinch of salt

2 tablespoons sugar

4 large eggs, lightly beaten

¼ pound (1 stick) butter, softened, plus more for the bowl and molds

For the syrup
1 cup freshly squeezed lemon juice

3 cups sugar

1 cup limoncello

Recommended Equipment
A food processor fitted with the metal blade

Baba molds or mini cake molds

To make the dough, dissolve the yeast in 2 tablespoons warm water in a small bowl and let it sit for several minutes to start to bubble. Put the flour, salt, and sugar in the bowl of the food processor, and run the machine for a few seconds to blend the dry ingredients.

Mix the beaten eggs with the dissolved yeast. With the food processor running, pour all the liquid into the flour, and process for 20 seconds or so. A stiff dough will gather on the blade and clean the sides of the bowl. Now drop in the soft butter, and process for another 20 to 30 seconds, until it is fully incorporated. Turn the soft dough out, knead by hand briefly to form a smooth round, and drop it into a lightly buttered bowl. Cover it with plastic wrap, and let the dough rise for 30 minutes or so—it does not need to double.

Butter the baba molds. Deflate the dough, and cut it into twelve equal pieces (about 2 ounces each). Roll each piece into a round, and place dough in the molds to fill them two-thirds full. Let the babas expand to fill the molds, about 30 minutes or more.

Meanwhile, heat the oven to 400°, arranging two racks if necessary. Bake the babas for 15 to 20 minutes, or until they are dark gold on top; shift the pans on the racks for even baking. Turn them out of the pans, and cool.

To make the syrup, bring 3 cups water, the lemon juice, and the sugar to a full boil in a wide pot; add the limoncello, and boil for 10 minutes. Turn off the heat, and immediately push as many babas as will fit into the hot syrup, weighting with a plate or pot cover to keep them submerged. When they have soaked up enough syrup to expand, in about 10 minutes, remove them from the pot, and drain on a wire rack set over a dish. If you have more babas to soak, heat the syrup to the boil again, then submerge another batch.

Serve the soaked babas within a short time, or set them, sitting in a shallow layer of syrup, in a pan to stay moist. For serving, slice them in half lengthwise, and spoon in your filling. If you like, drizzle some warm syrup over the top.

The Market in Naples

The Porta Nolana market in Naples is like a swarm of bees; on any given market day it hums with the sounds of people excited by the pleasures of shopping for food.

At the fish stands, one can find displayed like a fountain tiers of different types of seafood: calamari (squid), *calamaretti* (pencil squid), *polipo* (octopus, still moving its tentacles), *moscardini* (miniature octopus), *seppie* (cuttlefish), *branzini* (sea bass), *orate* (gilded bass, still tense and U-shaped, a sure sign of freshness), *sgombri* (mackerel), *gronghi* (eels), *alici* (fresh anchovies), *triglie* (red mullet), *bianchetti* (unborn baby eels). The display looks like a species poster. Then there is the diversity of the shellfish display, which can include *lupini, telline* (wedge-shell clams), *vongole veraci* (carpet-shell clams), *fasolari* (cockles), *cannolicchi* (razor clams), *sconcigli* (sea conch), and *cozze* (mussels). Unless these mollusks are alive, and there is an occasional spit of water from the *vongole veraci,* there is no sale, the locals know.

This market has a heartbeat. The vendors of fish and other goods all belt out the promise of their wares periodically, beckoning a sale, their voices floating in the air like Sunday church bells chiming above the stalls.

Orange and Red Onion Salad

INSALATA DI ARANCE E CIPOLLE

In Sicily, citrus fruits (*agrumi*) are enjoyed as a savory as well as a sweet, usually served between courses or at the end of a meal. A salad—called *pirettu*—is made from thick-skinned citrons (*cedri*). The green rind is peeled off, the center pulp is discarded, and the pith is sliced and dressed with salt, pepper, oil, and a pinch of sugar.

Since fresh citrons are hard to find in America, here's another citrus salad popular in Sicily, especially in the winter months, when oranges are at their best. Customarily it is made with blood oranges—*sanguine* or *tarocchi*—and that's the way I like it best, though any small, juicy oranges will be delicious.

Serve this in the Sicilian style, laying the rounds of orange and rings of red onion artfully on a platter with the dressing drizzled over, rather than tossing everything together. It is great as an appetizer, a refreshing end-of-the-meal salad, or an accompaniment to boiled or grilled meats.

Serves 6

8 or more small blood oranges or other oranges

1 medium red onion

½ teaspoon coarse sea salt or kosher salt, or to taste

Coarsely ground black pepper to taste

2 tablespoons best-quality extra-virgin olive oil, or to taste

1 tablespoon chopped fresh Italian parsley

With a sharp thin-bladed knife, shave off the peel and pith of each orange completely, exposing the flesh of the fruit. Slice the oranges into rounds about ⅓ inch thick (you'll have about 4 cups of slices in all). Handle them gently so they remain intact.

Peel the onion, and slice it into very thin rounds (about 1½ cups in all).

Lay out the orange rounds on a serving platter prettily (I pile up all the broken pieces in the center, making a colorful mound). Separate the onion rings, and scatter all over the oranges.

Sprinkle the salt over the top. Grind lots of coarse pepper over the top. Drizzle 2 tablespoons of your best olive oil all over the top. Shower the parsley over all. And serve!

Fried Chickpea Polenta

PANELLE

Frigitterie, found all over Palermo, means things fried, and the selections are endless. Breaded eggplant, broccoli, artichokes—all of the vegetables in season are coated with a flour paste (*pastella*) and find their way into a fryer. In Palermo, one of the undisputed specialties is *panella*, made of chickpea flour and cooked like polenta, chilled, and then cut into thick slices that are fried in olive oil. Fried *panelle* are eaten as is, or multiple slices are piled in a sesame bun and enjoyed as a big sandwich.

Panelle can make a great accompaniment to fish or meat, but everybody loves them passed around as an hors d'oeuvre. Convenient to prepare in advance, they can be cooked up in a big batch, left to cool in the sheet pan, then refrigerated for up to 3 days. You can cut out a few *panelle* and fry them for a snack or side dish whenever you want. If you're serving bite-sized *panelle* for a cocktail party, I suggest you fry all the pieces ahead of time and keep them warm in the oven until your guests arrive.

Makes a large sheet of *panelle*, serving 8 or more

4 cups water

1 teaspoon coarse sea salt or kosher salt

½ cup extra-virgin olive oil, plus more for the baking sheet and for frying

½ pound chickpea (garbanzo) flour

Recommended Equipment
A heavy-bottomed 3-quart saucepan or deep sauté pan, about 10-inch diameter

A stiff wire whisk

A rimmed baking sheet, 9 by 13 inches (a quarter-sheet), or a shallow baking pan of the same size, bottom and sides lightly brushed with olive oil

A stiff metal spatula

Pour 4 cups water, the salt, and the olive oil into the saucepan, and gradually whisk in the chickpea flour until smooth. Set over medium heat, and whisk constantly as the batter slowly heats. It will thicken and eventually steam but does not need to boil. Cook and keep whisking, scraping the bottom and sides of the pan frequently, until the mixture is quite stiff and starts to pull away from the sides as you stir it, 15 to 20 minutes.

Turn the batter into the oiled pan, and spread it quickly with the spatula, before it cools and sets, so it fills the pan in an even layer. Wet the spatula with water, and smooth the top of the batter. Let cool for an hour or longer, until completely firm.

Cut pieces with a sharp knife, in whatever size or shape you like and in the amount you need. I cut 1½-inch squares for appetizers and Sicilian-style sandwiches; 2-by-3-inch bars—at least two per person—to accompany a main course. Lift the cut pieces from the pan with a spatula (seal the remainder with plastic wrap and refrigerate for longer keeping).

To fry the *panelle*, pour enough extra-virgin olive oil into the heavy skillet to cover the bottom with ⅛ inch of oil, and set over medium heat. When the oil is hot, lay in the *panelle*, leaving plenty of space between them. Fry about 3 minutes, until the underside is crisp and golden, then flip them over and brown the second side, about 2 minutes more. Set the *panelle* on paper towels to drain and cool for a minute, but serve while they are still warm (though they taste good at room temperature too!).

Grilled Tuna with Oregano (see recipe page 300)
and Fried Chickpea Polenta

Smothered Eggplant and Summer Vegetables

CAPONATA

Caponata is a dense condiment of chunky fried eggplant and other vegetables and seasonings, jam-packed with flavor—sweet, sour, and salty all at once. Sicilians make caponata in many variations and enjoy it in countless ways. Here's a version I love. Use it as a condiment on grilled meats and steamed fish, as a sauce for pasta, or as topping for bruschetta.

Makes 8 cups, serving 6 or more

4 or 5 small firm eggplants
(2 pounds total)

2½ teaspoons coarse sea salt or
kosher salt, or to taste

½ cup red-wine vinegar

2 tablespoons sugar

2 medium onions (1 pound)

2 or 3 celery ribs

1 pound fresh plum tomatoes

1 cup Cerignola or other large
green brine-cured olives

1 cup vegetable oil

6 tablespoons extra-virgin olive oil

⅓ cup small capers, drained

10 large fresh basil leaves

Recommended Equipment
A small pan for reducing the
vinegar and sugar

A heavy-bottomed skillet or sauté
pan, at least 12-inch diameter

Trim the eggplants, and slice them (skin on) into chunks about 2 inches long and 1 inch thick. Toss the chunks with 2 teaspoons of salt, and drain in a colander for 30 minutes to an hour. Rinse, and pat them dry with paper towels.

Meanwhile, pour the red-wine vinegar and ½ cup water into the small pan, stir in the sugar, and bring to a boil. Cook until reduced by half and syrupy, then remove from the heat.

Slice the onions into 1½-inch pieces—you should have about 4 cups. Trim the celery stalks (and peel them if they're tough and stringy), then chop in 1-inch chunks. Slice the plum tomatoes lengthwise into 1-inch-thick wedges; scrape out the seeds and put the wedges in a sieve to drain off the juices. Roughly chop the pitted olives into ½-inch pieces.

To fry the eggplant, pour the cup of vegetable oil into the skillet, and set over medium heat. Spread all the eggplant chunks in the hot oil, and fry for 10 to 15 minutes, tossing and stirring frequently, until the eggplant is soft and cooked through and nicely browned on all sides. Turn off the heat, lift the chunks out of the oil with a slotted spoon, and spread them on paper towels to drain. Discard the frying oil, and wipe out the skillet.

Pour ¼ cup of the olive oil in the skillet, and set it over medium heat. Stir in the onion and celery chunks, season with ¼ teaspoon salt, and cook, tossing often, until they've wilted and lightly colored, 8 minutes or so. Toss in the olives and the capers, heat quickly until sizzling, then scatter in the tomato wedges and fold them in with the other vegetables. Season with another ¼ teaspoon salt, and cook until the tomatoes are hot and softened but still holding their shape, about 5 minutes.

Spread the eggplant chunks on top of the onions and tomatoes, still over medium heat, and turn them in gently with a big spoon or spatula. When everything is sizzling, pour the vinegar syrup all over and stir it in. Cook a bit longer, then drizzle the remaining 2 tablespoons of olive oil over it and stir in.

Cook the vegetables together for about 10 minutes, then turn off the heat. Tear the basil leaves into shreds, and stir them into the caponata. Taste, and adjust the seasonings; let cool to room temperature and serve.

Dishes from Trattoria Ferdinando in Palermo

Food in Palermo is as wonderful in restaurants as it is in private homes. Trattoria Ferdinando III, a family restaurant run by three brothers, has some of the best pasta and fish in Palermo. *Bavette al Pesce Spada,* page 289, is another of their specialties: perfectly cooked cubes of swordfish are suspended in the sweetest tomato sauce, which coats the fettuccinelike pasta. *Pasta alla Norma,* page 286, is a traditional favorite, pasta dressed with fried eggplant and ricotta salata (dried salted ricotta). To make *Pesce alla Matalotta,* page 290, either a whole fish or a fillet—any fresh fish will do—is cooked with tomatoes, celery, and aromatic herbs for a perfectly balanced dish that is easy to make at home. At Ferdinando's, we also had some delightful simply grilled veal rollatini (page 296) and *scaloppine alla Marsala* (page 292), both simple dishes made with local products that were perfectly delicious.

Ziti with Tomatoes, Eggplant, and Salted Ricotta

PASTA ALLA NORMA

Sicilians are passionate about both food and opera, so it is no surprise that one of the island's most celebrated dishes is *pasta alla Norma*. What better way to honor the composer Vincenzo Bellini, a native son of Catania (on Sicily's eastern coast), than to name a delicious pasta for *Norma*, one of the great operatic masterworks of all time?

I love both the opera and the dish, and, I can assure you, aside from their name, they're quite different. Those of you familiar with opera know that the title role of *Norma* is so difficult that only the greatest sopranos ever sing it. On the other hand, this recipe is simple and easily made.

Serves 6

2 or 3 small firm eggplants
(1 pound total)

1½ tablespoons coarse sea salt
or kosher salt, or to taste

1 cup vegetable oil

⅓ cup extra-virgin olive oil, plus
more for a final flourish

4 garlic cloves, crushed and peeled

¼ teaspoon peperoncino flakes

4 cups (or a 35-ounce can)
canned Italian plum tomatoes,
preferably San Marzano,
crushed by hand

1 pound ziti

6 large fresh basil leaves

2 cups ricotta salata (see
Sources, page 340), freshly
shredded on a hand grater

Trim the eggplants, and slice them (skin on) into 1½-inch chunks. Toss them with 1 teaspoon of salt, and drain in a colander for 30 minutes to an hour. Rinse, and pat them dry with paper towels.

To fry the eggplant, pour the cup of vegetable oil in the skillet, and set over medium heat. Spread all the eggplant chunks in the hot oil, and leave them in place for a few minutes to start browning. Fry for about 10 minutes, tossing and stirring occasionally, until the eggplant is soft and cooked through and nicely browned on all sides.

Lift the chunks out of the oil with a slotted spoon, and spread them on a platter lined with paper towels. Put the eggplant in a warm spot (such as a briefly heated oven) while you make the sauce and pasta. Discard the frying oil, and wipe out the skillet.

Pour 6 quarts of water, with 1 tablespoon salt, into the big pot, and bring to a boil.

Pour the olive oil into the skillet, toss in the garlic cloves, and set over medium-high heat. Sprinkle the peperoncino in, and cook until the garlic is lightly colored, then pour in the crushed tomatoes. Slosh a cup of water in the tomato container to rinse it clean, and stir that in along with another ½ teaspoon salt. Bring the tomatoes to a boil, then lower the heat and cook the sauce at a bubbling simmer for 12 minutes or so, until slightly thickened.

Meanwhile, when the pasta water comes to a rolling boil, stir in the ziti. Cook until almost *al dente*, then lift them out with a spider, drain for a moment, and drop into the simmering tomato sauce.

Recommended Equipment

A heavy-bottomed skillet or sauté pan, 12 inches or wider, for frying the eggplant and then cooking the sauce and pasta

A large pot, 8-quart capacity, with a cover, for cooking the pasta

Toss together for a minute or two, until the ziti are cooked and coated with sauce. Turn off the heat.

Tear the basil leaves into shreds, and scatter over the pasta along with a cup of the shredded ricotta salata. Drizzle a couple of tablespoons of olive oil all over, and toss well. Now spread the eggplant chunks on top of the pasta, and sprinkle over it the remaining ricotta salata.

Serve immediately, spooning both pasta and a portion of eggplant chunks into individual warm pasta bowls.

Gemelli with Smothered Cauliflower and Saffron

PASTA CON CAVOLFIORE E ZAFFERANO

Cauliflower is delicious cooked with anchovy. At Trattoria Ferdinando III
they add distinctively Sicilian touches like raisins, pine nuts, and saffron to
make a marvelous cauliflower dressing for pasta.

Serves 6

1½ tablespoons coarse sea salt
or kosher salt, or to taste

1 large cauliflower, 2½ to 3 pounds

⅛ teaspoon saffron
(about 7 threads)

⅓ cup extra-virgin olive oil, plus
more for finishing

1 onion, finely chopped (1 cup)

3 small anchovy fillets, finely
chopped (1 tablespoon)

¼ cup golden raisins

¼ cup pine nuts

1 pound gemelli (dry pasta)

8 large fresh basil leaves

½ cup grated pecorino, plus
more for the table

Recommended Equipment
A large pot, 8-quart capacity,
with a cover, for cooking the
cauliflower and the gemelli pasta

A heavy-bottomed skillet or
sauté pan, 14-inch diameter
or larger

Fill the large pot with 6 quarts of water, add 1½ tablespoons of
coarse salt, and heat to a boil. Trim the cauliflower, and cut all the
florets and tender stems into 1-inch pieces. Rinse the pieces, and
blanch them in the boiling water until slightly *al dente*, about 5 minutes. Lift the cauliflower from the pot with a spider, drain briefly,
and drop the pieces into a bowl.

Ladle 1 cup of the hot water into a spouted measuring cup, and
drop in the saffron to soak. (Cover the big pot and keep over low
heat, so it is ready to cook the gemelli.)

Pour the ⅓ cup of olive oil in the big skillet, place over
medium-high heat, and stir in the onion. Cook until the onion is
wilted and lightly colored, about 5 minutes, then stir in the
chopped anchovy. When the anchovy sizzles and melts in the oil,
pour in the saffron-infused water, the blanched cauliflower, the
raisins, and the pine nuts. Toss everything together, cover the pan,
and cook for a couple of minutes in the steam.

Meanwhile, return the big pot of water to a rolling boil, and
drop in the gemelli at the same time as the cauliflower goes into
the skillet. Cook them simultaneously. Boil the gemelli for about
10 minutes, until almost *al dente*. Uncover the skillet, lower the
heat, and cook the cauliflower dressing slowly, evaporating all
the moisture, so the vegetables are caramelized and flavorful
when the pasta is ready. Taste, and adjust seasoning.

Lift the gemelli from the cooking pot, and drop them, still wet,
into the skillet. Toss pasta and cauliflower together for a minute or
two. If the dish seems dry, ladle in a bit more pasta water and toss
until amalgamated. Turn off the heat, tear the basil leaves in small
shreds, and toss in. Sprinkle over it the pecorino, drizzle with olive
oil, and toss well. Serve right away, passing more grated cheese at
the table.

Dry Fettuccine with Swordfish

BAVETTE AL PESCE SPADA

This is traditionally made with swordfish, but you can substitute tuna, bass, or other firm-fleshed fish in the recipe. You don't need to buy expensive swordfish or tuna steaks—end pieces or chunks sold for skewered grilling are perfect for the sauce. *Bavette* is a long, flat dry pasta, like a narrow fettuccine. If you can't find it, use good-quality dry fettuccine.

Serves 6 as a first course or 4 as a main course

1 teaspoon coarse sea salt or kosher salt, or to taste, plus more for the pasta pot

1½ pounds swordfish (1 chunk or several pieces)

½ cup extra-virgin olive oil

1 onion, chopped (1 cup)

½ teaspoon peperoncino flakes, or to taste

2 cups canned Italian plum tomatoes, preferably San Marzano, crushed by hand

2 teaspoons fresh mint leaves, sliced in thin shreds

1 pound *bavette* (dry narrow fettuccine)

Recommended Equipment

A large pot for cooking the pasta

A heavy-bottomed skillet or sauté pan, 14-inch diameter, with a cover

Heat pasta-cooking water—at least 6 quarts, with 1 tablespoon of salt—in the large pot as you cook the fish and sauce.

Cut the swordfish into small cubes, 1 inch or less, and season lightly with salt. Pour 6 tablespoons of the olive oil into the big skillet, and set over medium-high heat. When the oil is hot, scatter the fish cubes in the pan. Toss and turn them for a minute or a little longer, just until they are opaque. Remove the fish chunks to a plate, and sprinkle a few pinches of salt on top.

Stir the chopped onion in the skillet, sprinkle over it ¼ teaspoon salt and the peperoncino, and cook for 3 minutes or so, until wilted and sizzling. Pour the tomatoes into the pan, stir, rinse the tomato container with ½ cup hot water, and stir that in too. Raise the heat, and bring the tomatoes to a boil quickly. Stir in the rest of the salt and the shredded mint, and adjust the heat to maintain a gentle boil.

Cook the sauce for 5 minutes, then slide in the swordfish chunks and any juices on the plate. Tumble them in the sauce to heat and cook for just a minute, then turn off the heat.

Meanwhile, cook the *bavette* until quite *al dente*. Return the sauce to a simmer (if it's off the heat) when the pasta is ready. Lift the *bavette* from the pot with tongs, drain briefly, and drop into the skillet. Toss pasta and sauce together for a minute or so, incorporating the remaining 2 tablespoons olive oil. Adjust the seasonings, and serve, heaping the *bavette* into warm bowls, and spooning the saucy chunks of swordfish (which fall to the bottom of the skillet) on top.

Grouper Matalotta Style

PESCE ALLA MATALOTTA

In Sicily, the most popular fish to cook *alla matalotta* is whatever was just caught fresh! The aromatics and technique remain the same, and the outcome is always delicious. (Interestingly, it is one of the few Sicilian fish preparations that call for celery.) My top fish recommendation for this recipe is grouper; it has flesh that cooks and stays intact in the sauce. Halibut, striped bass, and black bass are other good choices. A whole black bass cooked *alla matalotta* is delicious—just mind the bones.

Serve with grilled bread, couscous (page 304), or *panelle* (page 281). You can make this ahead of time and reheat to serve—just take the pot off the heat a bit before the fish and sauce are thoroughly cooked.

Serves 6

2 pounds skinless grouper fillet

1 teaspoon coarse sea salt or kosher salt, or to taste

½ cup extra-virgin olive oil, plus more for finishing

All-purpose flour for dredging (½ cup or so)

1 onion, thinly sliced (1 cup)

4 garlic cloves, crushed and peeled

½ cup finely chopped celery heart and leaves

½ teaspoon peperoncino flakes, or to taste

1 cup Sicilian or other large green brine-cured olives, pitted and cut in half

2 tablespoons small capers, drained

Slice the grouper fillet into six chunks, roughly equal in size, and season with ¼ teaspoon of the salt.

Pour the ½ cup olive oil into the big saucepan, and set it over medium-high heat. Dredge the fish chunks in flour, shake off any excess, and lay them in the hot oil. Cook for about 1½ minutes, until opaque on the underside; turn the pieces and lightly color the second side. Remove the grouper chunks with a spatula to a platter.

Scatter the onion slices in the pan, stir, and scrape any bits left in the pan. Toss in the garlic cloves and the chopped celery, stir well, and season with the peperoncino and another ¼ teaspoon salt. Stir for a couple of minutes as the vegetables sizzle, strew olives and capers in the pan, and stir until they're sizzling too.

Pour in the crushed tomatoes and 3 cups of hot water. Turn up the heat, and stir up all the vegetables as the liquid comes to a boil. Adjust the heat to keep it bubbling, stir in the shredded basil and ½ teaspoon salt, and partially cover the pan.

Simmer the sauce for 10 minutes or so, then lay the grouper chunks in the pan in one layer, and pour in any fish juices that accumulated in the platter. The chunks should be nearly covered by the sauce; add more hot water if necessary. Heat rapidly back to the boil, then simmer gently, partially covered. Shake the pan occasionally to distribute the sauce and slosh it over the fish.

2 cups canned Italian plum tomatoes, preferably San Marzano, crushed by hand

3 cups hot water, or as needed

6 large fresh basil leaves, shredded

3 tablespoons chopped fresh Italian parsley

Recommended Equipment
A heavy-bottomed saucepan or sauté pan, 13 inches or wider, with a cover

When the grouper is tender and the sauce is slightly thickened and flavorful, 20 to 25 minutes, turn off the heat. Taste, and adjust the seasoning. Just before serving, drizzle over it a tablespoon or two of olive oil, and sprinkle the parsley all over the top.

Pork Scaloppine with Mushrooms and Marsala

SCALOPPINE DI MAIALE AL MARSALA

We have all seen countless dishes called *al Marsala* on the menus of Italian-American restaurants. Too often, I have found, they disappoint me.

The pork scaloppine I enjoyed at the Ferdinando brothers' trattoria reminded me that this simple preparation depends so much on the quality of the wine that is splashed into the skillet. And I was not surprised to learn that the superb sauce coating the meat was made with a carefully chosen Marsala, dry and aromatic. After all, the town of Marsala lies just a few hours west of Palermo, and from that western tip of the island comes all authentic Marsala, in a wide range of vintages, colors, and degrees of sweetness.

The finest Marsalas, aged a minimum of 10 years, are ranked with the great fortified wines of the world—sipping one of these is a pleasure you shouldn't miss. But for good cooking, I recommend a moderately priced Superiore (aged 2 years) or Superiore Riserva (aged 4 years). I always prefer dry (*secco*) Marsala, even for desserts like Espresso Zabaglione (page 156); for these scaloppine, *secco* is a must.

Makes 12 scaloppine, serving 6

2¼ pounds (or a little more) boneless center-cut pork loin

2 teaspoons coarse sea salt or kosher salt, or to taste

Freshly ground black pepper to taste

½ cup all-purpose flour or more

6 tablespoons extra-virgin olive oil, or more if needed

5 tablespoons butter, or more if needed

2 tablespoons finely chopped shallots

3 fresh sage leaves

Trim the pork loin, leaving only a thin layer of fat, and cut it crosswise into twelve equal slices. Using a meat mallet (or other heavy implement), flatten and spread the slices into scaloppine about ¼ inch thick. Season lightly on both sides with salt and freshly ground pepper. Dredge the scaloppine in the flour, coating both sides, and shake off the excess.

Meanwhile, put 4 tablespoons of the olive oil and 2 tablespoons of the butter in the skillet, set over medium-high heat. When the butter begins to bubble, lay four or more scaloppine in the skillet—as many as can lie flat without crowding—and let them sizzle in place until the underside is opaque and tinged with brown, about 3 minutes. Flip them over and color the second side for a couple of minutes; then lift out the slices, let the fat drain off, and put them on a platter. Add a bit more olive oil and/or butter to the skillet if it seems dry, and fry the rest of the scaloppine in the same way.

When all of the pork is browned, pour off the frying oil but leave any crusty caramelization in the skillet. Put in the remaining 2 tablespoons of olive oil and 3 tablespoons of butter, and return to medium-high heat. When the butter is foaming, drop in the shal-

2 cups sliced fresh mushrooms (a single variety such as porcini, shiitake, cremini, white mushrooms, or a mixture)

1 cup dry Marsala

1 cup light stock (chicken, turkey, or vegetable broth), or more if needed

2 tablespoons chopped fresh Italian parsley

Recommended Equipment
A meat mallet

A heavy-bottomed skillet or sauté pan, 14 inches in diameter

lots and sage leaves, and cook, stirring, for a minute. Scatter the sliced mushrooms in the pan, season with ½ teaspoon salt, and stir continuously as the mushrooms sizzle and start to release their juices. Cook, tossing and stirring, until the moisture has evaporated and the mushroom slices are shrunken, soft, and caramelized, 6 minutes or more.

Pour in the Marsala, raise the heat, and stir until it boils. Let the wine bubble and reduce for a minute or two, then stir in the stock. Bring to a boil, and cook at a gentle bubbling pace until the sauce is slightly viscous but loose, about 5 minutes. Season to taste with salt and freshly ground pepper.

One by one, slide the scaloppine into the simmering sauce, and pour in any juices accumulated on the platter. Shake the pan, spoon sauce over the scaloppine, and flip them over once or twice, until they are heated through and glistening with sauce on both sides. If the sauce is too dense to coat all the meat, loosen it with a bit of stock. Turn off the heat, sprinkle the parsley all over, and serve.

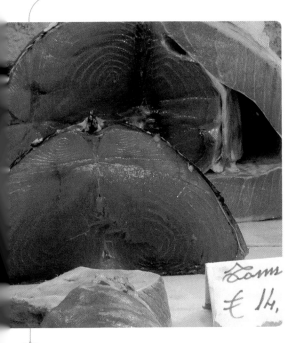

Dinner at Manfredi Barbera's

During one of my visits to Palermo, I was invited to the home of Manfredi Barbera, an oil merchant who loves to cook, and he made us a contemporary yet traditional Sicilian meal. There were eight of us for dinner, all thoroughbred Sicilians except for me. The menu was simple but *azzeccata*—right on the mark. We started with deliciously crispy *panelle.* Then there were meaty calamari that had been perfectly steamed in a colander over lemon-and-bay-leaf-infused water, served warm with a dressing of olive oil, orange rind, parsley, and just a few drops of lemon juice. What followed was strips of bright-rose tuna dipped in olive oil and bread crumbs, then baked with some capers scattered on top. It was delightfully sweet and tender, and served with a platter of *pollo alla cacciatora* but with meaty chunks of eggplant rather than, as in the traditional version, peppers and mushrooms. Many of these recipes follow.

Manfredi's Steamed Calamari

CALAMARI ALLA MANFREDI

This is the warm salad we enjoyed at Manfredi Barbera's as one of the appetizers. It is also delicious at room temperature—and in the heat of summer, it makes a marvelous main course or an accompaniment (*contorno*) to grilled fish or chicken.

Serves 6 as an appetizer or 3 or 4 as a main course

2½ pounds medium-large calamari (uncleaned), or 2 pounds cleaned, uncut calamari

1 lemon

2 fresh bay leaves

¾ teaspoon coarse sea salt or kosher salt, or to taste

5 tablespoons best-quality extra-virgin olive oil, or more if needed

2 tablespoons freshly squeezed lemon juice (from lemon used above)

¼ teaspoon peperoncino flakes, or to taste

1 teaspoon finely grated orange zest

2 tablespoons chopped fresh Italian parsley

Recommended Equipment
A large steamer, or improvise with a colander set inside a large deep pot with a lid that fits snugly inside

Clean the calamari one at time, if necessary, by pulling the tentacles slowly until all the innards come out of the body. Cut off the tentacles below the eyes, and discard the rest of the head and the innards; pop out and discard the small hard beak where the tentacles join. Cut off the pointy tip of each body, and peel off the skin; discard both. Rinse the trimmed tentacles and the body, holding it open under running water to flush the cavity. Slice the cleaned body crosswise, in rings ⅓ inch thick. Drain all the cleaned tentacles and rings in the steamer basket colander.

Meanwhile, pour enough water into the steamer or deep pot so that when you set the basket in position it doesn't touch the water.

Shave off the lemon peel (zest layer only) with a vegetable peeler, in short strips. Squeeze the juice of the lemon and reserve. Drop the zest into the water with the bay leaves, cover the pot, and simmer the water for about ½ hour, to infuse it with the aromas of lemon and bay.

Keep the water simmering, and set the steamer basket with all the calamari in it inside the pot. Put on the cover, making sure it fits snugly inside, and steam the calamari gently. After 2 minutes, lift the cover, tumble the calamari over a couple of times in the colander, and sprinkle over it a couple pinches of salt. Cover and steam another 2 minutes, tumble, and salt again. Repeat after 2 more minutes—you should have used ¼ teaspoon salt in all. Steam for a total of 8 to 10 minutes.

When the calamari is tender but slightly resilient to the bite, remove the colander, season the pieces with another ¼ teaspoon salt, mix well, then let them drain and cool for 5 minutes.

Turn the calamari into a bowl while still quite warm. Toss with the olive oil and lemon juice, sprinkle over the remaining salt, the peperoncino, grated orange zest, and parsley, and toss well again. Taste, and adjust the seasonings.

Serve warm or at room temperature.

Grilled Veal Rollatini

BRACCIULITTINI ARRUSTUTI

You don't need to go to Ferdinando's in Palermo to enjoy these savory rollatini. They're easy to assemble and cook in just a few minutes on the grill. For a lovely main course in summer, serve with a tossed green salad or a tomato-and-basil salad.

Makes 12 rollatini, serving 6

3 or more plump garlic cloves, thinly sliced (2 tablespoons slices)

½ cup extra-virgin olive oil

12 veal scallops, 2 to 3 ounces each (about 2 pounds total)

1 cup bread crumbs

⅔ cup freshly grated pecorino

½ teaspoon dried oregano

4 tablespoons chopped fresh Italian parsley

1 teaspoon coarse sea salt or kosher salt

Recommended Equipment
A meat mallet with toothed face

Toothpicks

A gas or charcoal grill, with a *clean* grill rack

Drop the garlic slices into the olive oil, and let it infuse for 30 minutes to an hour.

Pound the veal scallops into thin scaloppine: First, place each slice between sheets of wax paper and tenderize it, preferably with the toothed face of a meat mallet—don't tear through the meat. Flatten and spread the meat into a thin oval, roughly 8 inches long and 4 inches wide and ¼ inch thick. The pieces will vary in size.

To make the rollatini filling, toss together the bread crumbs, pecorino, oregano, chopped parsley, and ½ teaspoon salt in a bowl. Drizzle over it 4 tablespoons of the garlic-infused oil (discarding the slices), and keep tossing the crumbs until they're evenly moistened.

Lay out the scaloppine and lightly salt the top surface. Sprinkle a tablespoon or a bit more of the bread crumbs over each scaloppine, covering the top almost to the edges. Starting at one of the narrow ends, roll up each of the scaloppine the long way, enclosing the crumbs. Stick a toothpick into the flap end of the meat all the way, and all the way through the roll, to hold it together.

Brush the rolls with some of the remaining oil, set them on a platter, and sprinkle the remaining bread crumbs on top. Let the rollatini sit (so the flavors permeate the meat) for 20 minutes.

Meanwhile, light your grill and heat the rack over a medium flame or bed of charcoal or wood coals (my favorite for flavor). Set the rollatini on the grill, and rotate them every 1½ to 2 minutes, to keep them evenly moist as they cook. Occasionally brush or drizzle over them more garlic-infused oil. When they're grill-marked all around, after 7 minutes or so, check doneness by slicing into a roll. If the center is not warm, continue grilling slowly, lowering the flame or spreading out the coals as needed.

Remove to a warm platter, brush the rollatini again with oil, and let them sit for a couple of minutes before serving.

Raw and Cooked Salad

INSALATA CRUDA E COTTA

This recipe is much like the wonderful salad I had at Manfredi's house. In Palermo, as I mentioned earlier, the *insalata cruda e cotta* that you can buy at the markets will vary with the season. In America, we can enjoy that same variety, so do not feel confined by these ingredients: use other greens, such as escarole, mesclun, and frisée, together with cooked vegetables such as roasted squash, boiled leeks, boiled beets—anything else you have on hand or enjoy.

Serves 6 or more

1 pound sweet onions, such as Vidalia or Walla Walla

½ cup extra-virgin olive oil, or as needed

½ teaspoon coarse sea salt or kosher salt, or to taste

¾ pound Red Bliss potatoes (3 to 6 potatoes, depending on size)

½ pound fresh green beans

1 or 2 ripe fresh tomatoes (about ½ pound)

1 or 2 heads of Bibb lettuce (about ¾ pound)

½ cup black olives, pitted

3 tablespoons small capers, drained

Freshly ground black pepper to taste

3 tablespoons red wine vinegar

Recommended Equipment
A large bowl for dressing, tossing, and serving

For the *verdura cotta* (cooked vegetables): Peel and trim the onions, and slice into rounds about ¾ inch thick. Brush with olive oil, and sprinkle salt lightly on both sides. Lay the onions on a baking sheet, and roast in a preheated 375° oven for 20 minutes or longer, turning once, until slightly softened and nicely caramelized on the flat sides and edges. Cool, then separate the rounds into thick onion rings.

Meanwhile, drop the potatoes, whole with skin on, into a pot with plenty of water. Bring to a gentle boil, and cook just until a sharp knife blade slides through the potatoes—don't let them get mushy. Extract the potatoes, and cut them into wedges about 1½ inches thick.

Trim the ends of the green beans, and when the potatoes are out of the boiling water, drop the beans in and cook until *al dente*, 4 minutes or so. Scoop them from the pot with a spider, and drop the beans into very icy water, to set the color. Once they are chilled, drain and dry the beans, and cut them in 2-inch lengths.

For the *verdura cruda* (raw vegetables): Rinse, dry, and core the tomatoes. Slice them into wedges about the same size as the potatoes. Separate, rinse, and spin-dry the lettuce leaves.

Put everything in the bowl except the lettuce: onions, potatoes, beans, olives, capers, and tomatoes. Sprinkle over all the remaining salt and freshly ground pepper, drizzle over it the rest of the olive oil and the red wine vinegar, and tumble the vegetables to coat them with dressing.

Scatter the lettuce on top, tearing the larger leaves in two, then toss the greens with the vegetables, gently but continuously, for about a minute, to distribute the dressing evenly. Taste, and adjust the seasonings if you like, and toss again. Serve immediately—always including some of the heavier goodies that drop to the bottom of the bowl and hide under the lettuce.

Dried Oregano

Dried oregano is more pronounced in taste than fresh, and it is an essential ingredient in dishes from Puglia and in many of my recipes from Sicily. I recommend buying dried oregano on the branch, if you can find it, rather than crushed leaves in jars. In my market, bouquets of dried oregano stalks, usually from Sicily, are packed in cellophane. To use in recipes, pull out one branch and, over a piece of parchment or wax paper, rub it lightly between your palms. Gather up the fallen leaves and measure. Keep rubbing until you have the amount called for.

Grilled Tuna with Oregano

TONNO RIGANATU

Of the treasures taken from the sea that surrounds Sicily, tuna is among the most prized. Sicilian cooks prepare tuna with care and respect, which usually means simply, as exemplified by these grilled tuna steaks. Aromatic wild oregano is found all over Sicily, and bouquets of the dried herb hang in almost every Sicilian home. When the tuna steaks come off the grill, they get a drizzle of virgin olive oil and a shake of the oregano bouquet—simply perfect.

Serves 6

3 or more plump garlic cloves, thinly sliced (2 tablespoons slices)

1 teaspoon coarse sea salt or kosher salt, plus more for finishing

½ teaspoon freshly ground black pepper

6 tablespoons extra-virgin olive oil

6 tuna steaks, cut 1½ inches thick, about 8 ounces each

1½ teaspoons dried oregano

Recommended Equipment
A gas or charcoal grill, with a *clean* grill rack

For the marinade, stir the sliced garlic, salt, and pepper into the olive oil, and let sit for 30 minutes to an hour.

Spoon off and reserve 2 tablespoons of the infused oil. Place the tuna steaks on a large platter, and pour the remaining marinade over, turning the steaks so both sides are coated. Marinate the tuna for 2 to 3 hours, flipping them over two or three times.

Light your grill, and heat the rack over a medium flame or bed of charcoal. Drain the marinade from each piece of tuna, and lay it on the grill. Sear for about 2 minutes, and flip the steaks with a spatula.

Grill the second side for 2 minutes, turn the steaks again, and check for doneness by slicing into a steak—the flesh should not be fully cooked. Remove to a platter where the fish will continue to cook off the grill.

Stir the oregano into the remaining 2 tablespoons of garlic-infused oil, and immediately brush on top of the tuna. Sprinkle over it some coarse salt. Let the tuna rest for a minute before serving.

Chicken Cacciatora with Eggplant

POLLO ALLA CACCIATORA CON MELANZANE

Manfredi's version of chicken cacciatora was chock-full of delicious Sicilian eggplant. Indeed, the vegetable chunks shared the spotlight with the meat and made it more bountiful and satisfying. Undoubtedly, I realized, this dish must reflect the resourcefulness of cooks in Sicily in generations past. With many mouths to feed, and a limited supply of chickens (or money to buy them), they could extend the dish with the sweet tomatoes and meaty eggplants that grow so prolifically in every small garden patch.

I hope you'll be creative with this recipe too: if your chicken is smaller than the one called for here, or if you want to serve more people, fry up more eggplant and cook up more tomatoes for sauce. From one small chicken, you'll have prepared a feast, all in one pot. Serve this with *panelle* (page 281) or polenta (page 109), or dress a bowl of pasta with the sauce and eggplant. Rest assured, no one will leave your table hungry.

Serves 6

2 or 3 small firm eggplants (1 pound total)

2 teaspoons coarse sea salt or kosher salt, or to taste

3½-pound chicken (preferably organic), trimmed and cut in pieces

1 cup vegetable oil

1 or 2 tablespoons all-purpose flour

2 tablespoons extra-virgin olive oil

½ cup finely chopped bacon (2 thick-cut strips)

6 garlic cloves, crushed and peeled

½ teaspoon peperoncino flakes, or to taste

Trim the eggplants, and slice them (skin on) into chunks 2 inches long and 1 inch thick. Toss them with 1 teaspoon of salt, and drain in a colander for 30 minutes to an hour. Rinse, and pat them dry with paper towels. Rinse the chicken pieces, pat them dry as well, and season all over with ½ teaspoon salt, so they're ready for frying after the eggplant.

Pour the vegetable oil in the skillet, and set over medium-high heat. Sprinkle flour over the eggplant chunks, dusting them on all sides. Spread them in the hot oil in one layer, leave them in place until sizzling, then turn and toss until nicely browned on all sides, about 4 minutes. Lift out the eggplant chunks with a slotted spoon, leaving the oil in the pan, and spread them on paper towels to drain.

With the skillet again over medium-high heat, lay in all the chicken pieces in one layer in the hot oil. Let them sizzle in place for a minute or two, coloring the underside, then turn to brown another side. Fry the chicken, turning frequently, until each piece is golden all over, 6 minutes or longer. As the pieces are done, lift them, let the oil drain off, and set on a platter.

Meanwhile, start the sauce in the deeper pan (or wait until you've finished frying the eggplant and chicken, if you prefer).

1 cup dry white wine

3 cups (or a 28-ounce can) canned Italian plum tomatoes, preferably San Marzano, crushed by hand

2 tablespoons chopped fresh Italian parsley

Recommended Equipment
A heavy-bottomed skillet for frying the eggplant and chicken, 12-inch diameter

A heavy-bottomed saucepan or sauté pan, with sides 3 or 4 inches high and 12 inches in diameter or wider, with a cover

Pour in the 2 tablespoons olive oil, and set the pan over medium-high heat. Stir in the chopped bacon, and cook until the fat starts to render, then scatter in the garlic cloves and peperoncino flakes. Cook, stirring and tossing, until the bacon and garlic are lightly colored.

Pour in the wine, stir well, and raise the heat. Boil for a minute or so, until the wine is reduced by half. Pour in the crushed tomatoes, and stir well. Slosh a cup of water in the tomato container to rinse it clean, and stir in along with another ½ teaspoon salt. Bring to a boil, and adjust the heat to keep the sauce perking steadily.

One at a time, submerge all the browned chicken pieces in tomato sauce, and pour in any juices collected on the platter. Return the sauce to a bubbling simmer, and set the cover slightly ajar. Simmer the chicken for about 20 minutes, then drop the eggplant chunks on top of the sauce. Don't push or mush the eggplant down, but shift the chicken aside so the eggplant chunks fall into the sauce and are completely covered.

Heat until simmering again, and cook 10 minutes or so, until the chicken and eggplant are cooked through and tender. Leave the pot uncovered if you want the sauce to reduce and thicken. Near the end of cooking, taste the sauce and adjust the seasoning.

Remove the pan from the heat, and let the dish rest for 20 minutes before serving. Or let it cool in the pan and reheat slowly, gently turning the pieces in the sauce. Just before serving, sprinkle the chopped parsley over the chicken and sauce.

Seafood Brodetto with Couscous

BRODETTO DI PESCE CON COUS COUS

Anna Cornino Santoro's memorable couscous with scorpion-fish *brodetto* inspired me to create this version when I got home. I use grouper, a delicious fish, widely available and easy to work with (and certainly with fewer bones than scorpion fish!). Making couscous by hand, as Anna does, is not feasible for most of us, I realize. Fortunately, good-quality packaged couscous is in every supermarket these days. Almost all commercial couscous is precooked, so it takes barely 5 minutes to make a flavorful, fluffy base for the *brodetto*.

Serves 6

For the brodetto
2 pounds skinless grouper fillet

1 teaspoon coarse sea salt or kosher salt, or to taste

½ cup extra-virgin olive oil, plus more for finishing

Flour for dredging (½ cup or so)

1 tablespoon chopped garlic

1 large onion, finely chopped (2 cups)

½ teaspoon peperoncino flakes, or to taste

¼ teaspoon cinnamon, or to taste

2 tablespoons tomato paste

2 cups canned Italian plum tomatoes, preferably San Marzano, crushed by hand

For the couscous
3 cups water

⅓ cup extra-virgin olive oil

Slice the grouper fillet into chunks 3 to 4 inches wide, and season with ¼ teaspoon salt.

Pour the olive oil into the big saucepan, and set it over medium heat. Dredge the fish pieces in flour, shake off any excess, and lay them in the hot oil. Cook for about 2 minutes, until crisp and opaque on the underside; turn the pieces, and brown them for another minute or two on the other side. Remove to a platter.

Drop the chopped garlic into the pan, stir until sizzling, then add the onion and stir well, scraping up any caramelized bits on the bottom. Sprinkle in the peperoncino, the cinnamon, and another ¼ teaspoon salt, and cook, stirring, as the onion wilts and lightly colors. Push the onion aside to clear a small space on the pan bottom. Drop in the tomato paste, stir it in the clear hot spot for a minute to toast, then incorporate into the onions.

Pour in the crushed tomatoes and 2 cups of hot water (use some of the water to rinse the tomato container), raise the heat, stir well, and bring the liquids to a boil. Stir in ½ teaspoon salt, and adjust the heat to keep the *brodetto* bubbling gently.

After 10 minutes, nestle the grouper chunks into the simmering *brodetto*, and pour in any fish juices accumulated in the platter. The chunks should be nearly covered by the sauce; add more hot water if necessary. Heat rapidly until the sauce is bubbling again, then simmer gently, partially covered. Shake the pan occasionally to distribute the *brodetto* and slosh it over the fish.

When the grouper is tender and flakes easily, in about 10 to 15 minutes, turn off the heat. Drizzle a tablespoon or two of olive oil all over the top.

1 teaspoon coarse sea salt or
kosher salt

2 bay leaves, preferably fresh

2½ cups quick-cooking couscous

Recommended Equipment
A heavy-bottomed saucepan
or sauté pan with high sides,
13 inches or wider, with a cover

A heavy 3-quart saucepan with
a cover, for the couscous

Meanwhile, prepare the couscous: Put 3 cups water, the olive oil, salt, and bay leaves in the smaller saucepan, cover, and bring to a rolling boil. Pour in the couscous, and stir until the water begins to boil again, then turn off the heat and cover the pan tightly. Let the couscous sit to soften and completely absorb the water, about 10 minutes. Fluff it with a fork, breaking up any lumps, and remove the bay leaves.

To serve, do as Anna does: Heap the couscous in a warm deep serving-platter bowl. Lay the chunks of grouper on top, spoon half of the *brodetto* over the fish and couscous, and pour the rest into a bowl for passing at the table. Serve immediately.

Anna Cornino's Sicilian Kitchen

A short trip out of Palermo to the west, I found the kitchen of Anna Cornino Santoro in Custonaci. She is the couscous specialist par excellence, and we had it with a *brodetto* of scorpion fish. The flavor of her couscous was nutty and complex, cooked just enough to be mellow and to absorb the sauce, but resilient to the bite. The *brodetto* was sweet and flavorful, with a residual taste of cinnamon. She also whipped up a quick plate of pasta dressed with Sicilian pesto: garlic, oil, basil, almonds, and fresh ripe cherry tomatoes set in a processor and made into a paste (traditionally made with mortar and pestle). Spaghetti was cooked, drained, and tossed with the tomato-almond pesto, then a handful of fried *ciccirielli* (little fishes) were mounted on top. A traditional dish, it was new to me, and I just loved the *Spaghetti di Anna*, page 306. This way of adorning pasta dishes with fried goodies is common in Sicily. See also the *Pasta alla Norma*, page 306, in which fried eggplant is put on top of pasta dressed with tomato and basil.

Anna's Spaghetti and Pesto Trapanese

SPAGHETTI AL PESTO TRAPANESE ALLA ANNA

The beauty and delight of this dish is that it is so fresh and clean—and it is a cinch to make. It's important to make the pesto with the best ingredients, then just toss in the hot cooked spaghetti to coat it, and enjoy.

Serves 4 to 6

¾ pound (about 2½ cups) cherry tomatoes, very ripe and sweet

12 large fresh basil leaves

1 plump garlic clove, crushed and peeled

⅓ cup whole almonds, lightly toasted

¼ teaspoon peperoncino flakes, or to taste

½ teaspoon coarse sea salt or kosher salt, or to taste, plus more for cooking the pasta

½ cup extra-virgin olive oil

1 pound spaghetti

½ cup freshly grated Grana Padano or Parmigiano-Reggiano

Recommended Equipment
A blender (my preference) or a food processor

A pot for cooking the spaghetti

Rinse the cherry tomatoes, and pat them dry. Rinse the basil leaves, and pat dry.

Drop the tomatoes into the blender jar or food-processor bowl, followed by the garlic clove, the almonds, basil leaves, peperoncino, and ½ teaspoon salt. Blend for a minute or more to a fine purée; scrape down the bowl, and blend again if any large bits or pieces have survived.

With the machine still running, pour in the olive oil in a steady stream, emulsifying the purée into a thick pesto. Taste, and adjust seasoning. (If you're going to dress the pasta within a couple of hours, leave the pesto at room temperature. Refrigerate for longer storage, up to 2 days, but let it return to room temperature before cooking the pasta.)

To cook the spaghetti, heat 6 quarts of water with 1 tablespoon salt to the boil in the large pot. Scrape all the pesto into a big warm bowl.

Cook the spaghetti *al dente*, lift it from the cooking pot, drain briefly, and drop onto the pesto. Toss quickly to coat the spaghetti, sprinkle the cheese all over, and toss again. Serve immediately in warm bowls.

Cannoli Napoleon

CANNOLO A STRATI

Pasticcerie, pastry shops, also referred to as *Catlisch* (a name inherited from the Swiss), are a grand tradition in Palermo. The city was greatly influenced by the French and Swiss in their pastry-making. When I am in Sicily, cannoli and desserts made with citrus are my favorites. In Palermo, I always enjoy desserts and a great cup of espresso at my dear friend's pastry place, Pepino Stancanpiana's Catlisch.

My Sicilian chef at Felidia, Fortunato Nicotra, makes an elegant version of this, Sicily's favorite *dolce*, with deep-fried disks of cannoli pastry stacked high with layers of ricotta cream in between. I like to fry squares of pastry in a skillet—no deep-fryer needed—and build a crispy, creamy cannoli napoleon.

In Sicily, cannoli filling is made with sheep's-milk ricotta, which has a distinctive flavor that can't be matched by ordinary processed ricotta. Fresh cow's-milk ricotta, which is widely available now, is what I use. Be sure to drain it well, sweeten lightly, mix with chopped bitter chocolate, candied orange, and toasted almonds for real Sicilian cannoli and add a touch of Grand Marnier for additional flavor.

Makes 6 to 8 cannoli napoleons

For the pastry dough
1½ cups all-purpose flour, plus more for rolling

2 tablespoons sugar

¼ teaspoon salt

2 tablespoons olive oil

1 teaspoon white vinegar

½ cup dry red wine, or as needed

For the cannoli cream
1 pound (2 cups) *fresh* ricotta

⅔ cup powdered sugar, plus more for decoration

1 tablespoon Grand Marnier (optional, but very good!)

Make the pastry dough in the food processor a day or two in advance—or at least 4 hours—for the best texture. Put the flour, granulated sugar, and salt in the bowl, and process just to mix. Mix the olive oil, vinegar, and wine together, and, with the machine running, pour all but 1 tablespoon in and process for 20 seconds or so, until a dough gathers on the blade. If it feels hard and dry, sprinkle in the remaining liquid and process briefly. It should be moist and malleable—incorporate more wine if needed. Turn the dough out of the bowl, scraping any bits from the sides and blade, and knead by hand into a soft, smooth ball. Flatten to a disk, wrap very tightly in plastic, and refrigerate for up to 2 days.

Put the fresh ricotta in a fine-meshed sieve, and set inside a bowl to drain for at least 12 hours or a whole day in advance. Cover the ricotta with plastic wrap and refrigerate.

To make the cannoli cream, whip the ricotta with the whisk attachment of an electric mixer until smooth. Whip in the ⅔ cup powdered sugar and the Grand Marnier. Chop the chocolate (or

1 ounce unsweetened chocolate, or 3 tablespoons bittersweet chips

2 tablespoons candied orange rind

2 tablespoons whole toasted almonds

1 cup vegetable oil, or as needed

Optional garnish: honey or finely grated chocolate

Recommended Equipment
A food processor to mix the pastry dough

An electric mixer for whipping the ricotta cream

A wide, heavy skillet and tongs for frying the pastry

chips) into coarse bits—big enough to bite into and to be visible. Coarsely chop the candied peel and almonds to the same size. Fold the chopped pieces into the cream; refrigerate until you assemble the cannoli.

Cut the pastry dough in half. On a lightly floured surface, roll out one piece of dough to a rectangle 14 inches by 11 inches (or as close as possible). With a sharp knife and ruler, trim the edges and divide the rectangle into a dozen squares, about 3½ inches on a side. (If you can get only nine squares of that size or slightly larger, that's fine!) Set the squares aside, on a lightly floured tray, to rest for 15 minutes before frying. Meanwhile, roll out and divide the remaining half of the dough the same way.

To fry the pastry, pour oil into the skillet to a depth of ¼ inch and set over medium heat. With the point of a small sharp knife, pierce each pastry square about ten times, all over its surface, as though you were making pinpricks through the dough. (These tiny holes will prevent the pastry from ballooning when fried.)

Heat the oil until the edge of a square sizzles gently when dipped into it, then lay in as many squares as you can, 2 inches apart. Raise the heat to keep the oil temperature up (but lower it as soon as the sizzling gets too fast). Fry the squares for about 3 minutes on the first side, pushing them under the oil occasionally to heat the top surface. As the tops begin to bubble, press with tongs to prevent big bubbles from ballooning—small bubbles are OK. When the bottom is golden brown, flip the squares over and fry until evenly colored and crisp on both sides, about 2 minutes.

As soon as they're done, lift the squares with tongs, let excess oil drip off, and lay them to drain on folded paper towels; flip them over to blot the oil from both sides. Fry all the squares this way, adding oil as needed and heating it between batches.

Assemble your cannoli napoleons shortly before serving, with three nice squares for each. Set one square on the plate, drop about 1½ tablespoons of cannoli cream in the center, lay another square on top—sides aligned—and press gently to spread the cream. Drop on another layer of cream, cover with the third square, and press. Finally, shower the top of each Napoleon with powdered sugar (and embellish with drizzles of honey or a sprinkle of finely grated chocolate), and serve.

Tanya's Tour

SICILY

PALERMO'S "OPERA OF PUPPETS": A Folk Art for Eight Hundred Years
Location: The Pasqualino Marionette Museum is on the second floor
at Via Butera 1, in central Palermo. The Cuticchio Puppet Theater is
located on the Via Bara all'Olivella.

The old center of Palermo was once crowded with the workshops of fine artisans, whose crafts are now remembered only in street names like Via dei Candelia, street of candlemakers, and Via dei Bambinai, street of doll-makers. One charming tradition that still flourishes, though, is found in Palermo's several groups of marionette-makers and puppeteers.

Marionette theater has been a distinctive part of Sicilian folk culture since the late Middle Ages, entertaining audiences through the centuries with comic folktales and grand dramatizations of medieval epics. Even in the Internet age, every self-respecting Sicilian city still has its own marionette theater, or *opera dei pupi*—literally, opera of puppets.

The Pasqualino International Museum of Marionettes (founded by a prominent family of puppeteers) provides a fascinating introduction to this make-believe world, with a collection of thousands of handcrafted marionettes, antique and contemporary, from around the globe. Whether diminutive or fully human-sized, they're all elaborately dressed and decorated with amazing detail.

The Cuticchio family, another dynasty of Palermitan puppeteers, presents contemporary versions of classic *opera dei pupi* at its Cuticchio Puppet Theater. The dramas date from the twelfth century, but tickets are available online.

PALAZZO ABBATELLIS: Two Enchanting Women

Location: Via Alloro 4. Via Alloro is parallel to Via Vittorio Emanuele and lies halfway between the Botanical Garden and Via Vittorio Emanuele.

The Palazzo Abbatellis, one of the finest art galleries in the city, is my favorite place to spend a rainy day in Palermo. With a collection of works spanning five centuries, there's no scarcity of treasures, yet time and again I find myself returning to two enchanting women.

Antonello da Messina's Virgin, painted in oil in the mid-fifteenth century, is an extraordinary portrait of Mary, depicted as if she could be the Sicilian beauty next door. To me, she has both sensual beauty and profound spiritual depth. She is hauntingly sad, yet at the same time deeply at peace with herself and the sad fate of her son.

Although the Abbatellis is primarily dedicated to paintings, I find myself fascinated by a particular sculpture, Laurana's bust of Eleanor of Aragon. Cut from marble nearly six centuries ago, Eleanor transcends the solidity and opacity of the stone. The chiffon garb she wears is so light that it appears to billow in a breeze. And as the eye wanders slowly across her face, the veins of the marble become the delicate veins beneath Eleanor's translucent skin. I want to reach out and touch her.

Three Villas in Palermo—Lives of the Rich and Royal

PALAZZO MIRTO

Location: Via Merlo, south of Via Vittorio Emanuele

In 1982, the home of Maria Concetta Lanza Filangeri, the last heir of a noble family, was bequeathed to Sicily's Ministry of Cultural Assets. Thus the historic Palazzo Mirto, built in the seventeenth century on the foundations of earlier structures, became one of the few noble homes of Palermo ever fully opened to the public, an especially rare opportunity because it has been kept almost entirely intact, with the Filangeris' original possessions.

I love to wander through one sumptuous room after another, with chandeliers dripping crystal, floors of inlaid stone, frescoed ceilings, tapestries, smoky mirrors, and painted silk walls. The decorative pieces are everywhere—small bronzes, precious clocks, Sicilian ceramics—displaying the great taste and wealth of a ruling family with roots going back to the Norman conquest of Sicily in the eleventh century.

My favorite room is the Chinese Salon, which must have been considered quite exotic for Palermo when completed at the end of the eighteenth century. Like the Chinese Villa, the royal residence (see below), and many other palaces and villas throughout Europe, the salon in Palazzo Mirto shows how the fashion for things Eastern took hold as the continent's aristocratic elite toured the Orient with ever greater frequency (and lots of cash).

THE CHINESE VILLA

Location: Inside the large Favorita Royal Park; walk into the park through the main entrance, off of Piazza Niscemi

To me the Chinese Villa is a gorgeous example of the Chinese revival style. It is quite stunning in its creativity, and I admire the way in which architectural elements in different styles are mixed, such as the Gothic arches of the ground-floor porticoes and the rather classical columned terraces. Yet even as the eye jumps along the very busy structure—as if examining a small jewel box—the diverse elements surprisingly stick together. It reminds me of the villas built along the Newport coast.

The villa was built for Ferdinando I, the Bourbon monarch who ordinarily ruled his several realms from Naples, until he had to vacate the mainland in the face of Napoleon's occupying forces. In 1816, when the French retreated, Ferdinand returned to Naples and declared Sicily and Naples united in his "Kingdom of the Two Sicilies," with Naples as the capital. (This declaration soon led to a revolution by angry Sicilians.)

The villa is located in the Favorita Royal Park, originally the royal hunting grounds, and (since you can't see the interior of the palace) it's a pleasure to walk through the gardens and park to get spectacular views of the ornate villa set against the backdrop of Mount Pellegrino. If you are visiting Palermo in the hotter months, the Chinese Villa makes a great place to stop on the way to the city's famous Mondello Beach.

VILLA MALFITANO

Location: Via Dante

Villa Malfitano is strikingly different from Palazzo Mirto, enclosed in its own English-style garden. The palazzo was originally constructed for the Whitaker family, leading British merchants in the early days of the Marsala industry. Built in the Liberty style, the architectural elements support flowering vines that surround the villa with gorgeous blossoms. Inside, the Summer Room is decorated with painted plants so realistic that you feel as though you were standing in an outdoor gazebo. The Whitakers also adorned the interiors with the most spectacular collection of Flemish tapestries in Sicily.

Another fine collection is of seventeenth- and eighteenth-century coral, including the *Triumph of Apollo*, a true masterpiece of the craft, all delicately carved out of salmon-pinkish coral.

THE ROYAL LODGE AT FICUZZA PARK: Grandeur in Godfather Country
Location: 40 kilometers from Palermo—about 1 hour by car

In her recipes, my mother gives you a taste of Sicilian country cooking *alla* Anna Cornino Santoro. But for a taste of the grandeur of Sicily, country-style, make a day trip south of Palermo to the township of Corleone to visit the Royal Hunting Lodge, Ficuzza. (Yes, this is the town that Don Corleone, the fictional Godfather, came from. And the home of Bernardo Provenzano, the real-life "boss of all bosses" of the Sicilian Mafia, who successfully hid in the neighboring countryside around Corleone for forty-three years while running the mob, before his arrest in 2006.)

King Ferdinando I, who enjoyed his power more openly than the dons, had the Royal Hunting Lodge in Ficuzza Park built in the same period as his Chinese Villa in Favorita Park, during his forced absence from Naples, and he divided his time between the two mansions. At Ficuzza, though, his retreat was designed in the English style, with simple and elegant exterior lines.

Today the lodge serves as the headquarters of the park rangers. Tour guides also lead visitors through the royal residence, including the cellars (and maybe some of Ficuzza's rumored secret passages). Of particular interest are the elliptical family chapel and the royal bedroom, walls covered in mythological frescoes, and vaulted ceiling appropriately depicting Diana, goddess of the hunt, with forest animals all around.

Behind the lodge, trails welcome visitors to walk the real forest. Lovers of nature (or opponents of hunting) can also visit the renowned wildlife hospital in town, where injured birds and mammals—from eagles to porcupines—are treated and rehabilitated for return to the wild.

PUGLIA

Chapter 10

Long Fusilli with Roasted Tomatoes
FUSILLI LUNGHI CON POMODORINI AL FORNO

Cavatelli with Arugula and Tomatoes
CAVATELLI ALLA RUCOLA E POMODORINI

Bucatini with Toasted Bread Crumbs
PASTA CU RA MUDDICA

Onion-Tomato Focaccia
FOCACCIA D'ALTAMURA

Tagliatelle with Chickpeas
CECI E TRIA

Baked Onions from Acquaviva
CIPOLLOTTO DI ACQUAVIVA

Celery Chutney
MOSTARDA DI SEDANO

Mussels with Farro, Cannellini, and Chickpeas
FARRO CON FAGIOLI, CECI, E COZZE

Farro with Tuna and Tomatoes
FARRO AL TONNO E POMODORO

Almond Tart from Andria
CROSTATA DI MANDORLE

Caramelized Almond Wafers
OSTIE RIPIENE

Puglia is the heel of Italy. As you see it on the map, it looks like an appendage of Italy. In the north there is the area called Gargano-Daunia, known as "Il Tavoliere," the bread basket of Italy. It is where most of the Italian *grano duro* (durum wheat) is produced. Traveling south, you come to Andria, where 40 to 50 percent of all Italian oil comes from. And way down toward the tip of the heel is the Salento, where wine, legumes, vegetables, and fruits flourish. From Lecce down to the tip, Santa Maria di Leuca, lie miles of fava, lentil, and chickpea fields and chicory gardens. There one can find beautiful isolated Baroque churches, which in the setting sun look as if they were made of gold.

I travel periodically to Puglia because I always enjoy eating the perfect burrata cheese in Andria and the best bread in all of Italy in Altamura, two cities in Puglia that are approximately thirty kilometers apart. It is worth a special journey to seek out the best burratas in Caseificio Asseliti in Andria, made by Domenico Asseliti and his two sons, Giandomenico (twenty-one) and Riccardo (twenty-three). Signora Graziella Asseliti mans the front of the shop, selling their still-warm mozzarella and burrata.

Making burrata is an extension of the process of making mozzarella. The mozzarella paste is stretched into rectangles three by five inches, and air is blown into the rectangle to make a sac. The sacs are then filled with *stracciatella,* shredded pieces of mozzarella left to soak in rich cream overnight. After the sac is filled with the *stracciatella,* with some of the cream clinging to the strands, it is then tied with a blade of grass. It ends up looking like a chubby pear.

Traditionally, a burrata is cut in half and served in a deep plate. The ideal burrata has a textural interplay between the chewier outside and silky, creamy inside, which oozes out as the outer layer remains resilient. It is as though you are tasting three different textures and flavors all at once—the sweetness of the cream, the shredded mozzarella with a tinge of acidity, and the more complex and cheesy outer layer. If you ask anyone in Puglia what is the best way to enjoy burrata, "as is" will be the response, along with crusty Pugliese bread with a drizzle of a Pugliese extra-virgin olive oil.

Burrata is available now in the United States at specialty-food stores. At our restaurants, Becco and Felidia, we serve it on top of grilled bread, nestled in braised broccoli rabe. Grilled bread topped with half a burrata and a spoonful of caviar is a combination that Chef Fortunato Nicotra of Felidia serves—a special treat.

Pasta

The landscape in Puglia is fascinating. Driving through, one can enter stretches of roads that are tunnels of overhanging olive trees. Then, like a window, the road opens to fields of golden, swaying grain. This is the land of *grano duro,* durum wheat, also known as semolina, a varietal with high gluten content. Only *grano duro* makes fine dry pasta. The wheat grown in Puglia is used by pasta-makers all over Italy and around the world. Not surprisingly, the Pugliese themselves make superb dry pasta, notably the diminutive shapes that are characteristic of the region. Some of the best cavatelli, orrechiette, and *strascinate* I have ever tasted are made by local manufacturers in Puglia, whose traditional methods and machines preserve all the flavor of the wheat. (A few of these artisan-made Pugliese pastas are available here; see Sources, page 340.)

My greatest admiration, however, is for those many women all over Puglia who still make these special small shapes at home, by hand—the original pasta machine. I've marveled at the speed and skill with which they drag each bit of dough on a board—*strascinate* means "dragged"—so it curls precisely and in the same instant picks up the textures of the wood. With this finely roughened surface and many curves and hollows, this is perfect pasta—the kind that captures a flavorful dressing and won't let it go.

Long Fusilli with Roasted Tomatoes

FUSILLI LUNGHI CON POMODORINI AL FORNO

This dish is finished in an unusual manner that at first surprised me. But it is so practical, and the results are so delectable, that it is one of my treasured discoveries from Puglia. The dressing is essentially completed in advance—fresh plum tomatoes roasted with seasoned bread crumbs. When you are ready to eat, just slide these intensely savory tomatoes on top of the fusilli in a big bowl and toss; the steaming pasta, just out of the pot, does the final cooking all by itself.

Serves 6

½ cup dry bread crumbs, coarsely crushed

2 tablespoons small capers, drained and chopped

2 tablespoons chopped fresh basil, packed tight to measure (about 6 large leaves)

½ teaspoon coarse sea salt or kosher salt, plus more for the pasta pot

½ teaspoon peperoncino flakes

1 teaspoon dried oregano

1⅓ cups freshly grated Canestrato Pugliese (see box, page 319) or Pecorino Romano

10 tablespoons extra-virgin olive oil, or more as needed

1½ pounds ripe plum tomatoes

2 plump garlic cloves, sliced

1 pound long fusilli (sometimes packaged as *fusilli lunghi*)

Set a rack in the middle of the oven, and heat to 375°. (If using a convection oven, which roasts the tomatoes well, set the thermostat to 350°.)

Put the bread crumbs in a medium-sized bowl, and mix in the chopped capers, 1 tablespoon of chopped basil, ½ teaspoon salt, the peperoncino, oregano, and ⅓ cup of grated cheese. Drizzle 4 tablespoons of the olive oil over the crumbs, tossing to moisten and mix thoroughly.

Rinse and dry the tomatoes, and slice them in half lengthwise. Oil the baking sheet lightly with a bit of the olive oil. Working over the bowl of bread crumbs, cover the cut side of each tomato half with a layer of the crumb mixture—a tablespoon, more or less, depending on the size of the tomatoes. Compress the crumbs lightly so they stay on, and set the tomato (crumbs up) on the baking sheet. Use up all the crumbs, topping all the tomatoes equally. Separate the tomatoes as much as possible on the sheet, so all sides are exposed to the heat, drizzle a little more olive oil over each, and put the sheet in the oven.

Now pour 4 more tablespoons olive oil in a small bowl, drop in the garlic slices, and let steep—you'll use the infused oil for dressing the pasta.

Roast the tomatoes for 30 minutes, or until the crumbs are nicely browned and the halves are slightly shriveled. Remove the sheet from the oven, and let the tomatoes cool for 15 minutes or so, then slice each one lengthwise, right through the crumbs, making two narrow wedges. If the tomatoes are fat, slice the roasted halves into three or four wedges that will be easy to toss with the

Canestrato Pugliese: A Rare Treat for Cheese Lovers

In Puglia, as in all the southern regions, a bowl of pasta is rarely served without a shower of local aged pecorino over the top. As a lover of sheep's-milk cheeses of almost every kind, I am especially happy when this shower falls from a block of Canestrato Pugliese, the region's most prized and flavorful pecorino.

Produced in small quantity, Canestrato Pugliese is not as well known as Pecorino Romano *genuino* and Pecorino Toscano. But, like them, it is recognized as a culinary treasure of Italy, and has been granted the coveted status of Denominazione di Origine Controllata (DOC), which means its name, character, and quality are protected by law. Canestrato Pugliese is made only with milk from sheep grazing on Puglia's lushest pastures, and hardripened to exacting specifications in reed baskets (*canestri*)—which accounts both for the name and the distinctive pattern on the rind. Most important to me, it tastes marvelous, rich and complex, with nuances that somehow express the flavor of the land and the grasses from which it comes.

In recent years, during which so many of Italy's superb regional cheeses have become available in the States, Canestrato Pugliese has remained a treat to be enjoyed only when visiting Puglia. At last, though, I am happy to report, it is being imported on a regular basis. Thanks to the Internet (see Sources, page 340), you can now have a basket-patterned round of this rare and delightful cheese delivered to your door!

For all the pastas in this chapter—and wherever a hard, aged pecorino is listed—Canestrato Pugliese will provide a truly special final flourish.

Recommended Equipment

A large, rimmed baking sheet, such as a half–sheet pan (12 by 18 inches)

A large pot, 8-quart capacity or larger, with a cover, for cooking the pasta

A very large bowl, ceramic or glass to retain heat, for mixing the cooked pasta and dressings and serving

pasta. With a wide spatula, loosen the cut tomatoes and slide them together on the sheet, so you can transfer them to the pasta bowl easily and quickly.

Meanwhile, heat 6 quarts of water, with 1 tablespoon salt, to the boil in the large pot. Drop in the long fusilli, and cook until the strands are *al dente*, as you like to eat them. In this dish, the pasta does not cook longer with the dressing in a hot skillet: instead, the heat of the pasta cooks the dressing when they're tossed in the bowl.

Have the big bowl near the stove, and heat it with some boiling water from the pasta-cooking pot before the fusilli are done (remember to pour out the heating water). When the pasta is perfectly cooked, lift it out with tongs, drain off the moisture for a moment, and drop it into the warm bowl.

Immediately scatter the garlic-infused olive oil (and the garlic slices) all over the pasta, and toss well. Slide all the wedges of roast tomato off the sheet and on top of the hot fusilli. Toss well to disperse the tomatoes and seasoned crumbs and dress all the pasta. Sprinkle the remaining chopped basil over it, and toss in. Finally, toss in the grated cheese and serve right away, in warm bowls.

Cavatelli with Arugula and Tomatoes

CAVATELLI ALLA RUCOLA E POMODORINI

In Puglia, cavatelli or *strascinate* would be the star of this delightful dish, dressed with ripe cherry tomatoes quickly softened in the skillet, and a heap of tangy arugula, tossed into the pot to cook with the pasta. Artisan-made pasta from Puglia is my preference, but any good-quality cavatelli or orecchiette would be a fine substitute. In summer, when ripe sweet tomatoes and tender arugula are plentiful, this dish will always be delicious.

Serves 6

3 cups (about 1 pound) ripe cherry tomatoes or ripe plum tomatoes, rinsed

1 teaspoon coarse sea salt or kosher salt, or to taste, plus more for the pasta pot

¼ cup extra-virgin olive oil, plus more for finishing

4 plump garlic cloves, sliced

¼ teaspoon peperoncino flakes, or to taste

1 pound cavatelli, *strascinate,* or orecchiette, preferably from Puglia (see Sources, page 340)

1 pound fresh, tender arugula, rinsed and drained

½ cup freshly grated Canestrato Pugliese (see box, page 319) or Pecorino Romano

Recommended Equipment
A large pot, 8-quart capacity or larger, with a cover, for cooking the pasta

A heavy-bottomed skillet or sauté pan, 14-inch diameter

Cut the cherry tomatoes in half, or, if using plum tomatoes, cut them into ½-inch chunks, to have 3 cups of cut-up fresh tomato.

Start heating 6 quarts of water with 1 tablespoon of salt in a large pot.

In the big skillet, heat the ¼ cup olive oil, sliced garlic, and peperoncino over medium-high heat, stirring, until the garlic is sizzling and starting to color. Pour in the cut tomatoes, season with a teaspoon salt, and bring to a bubbling simmer. Cook, stirring frequently, about 3 or 4 minutes, just until the tomatoes have softened a bit and the juices are slightly thickened. Turn off the heat.

When the pasta water is boiling, stir in the cavatelli or other pasta. Return to the boil, and cook for 7 to 8 minutes (or 6 minutes less than time indicated on the package), then drop all the arugula into the pot. Stir well, cover, and bring the water back to the boil rapidly. Cook pasta and arugula together for 5 minutes, or until the pasta is nearly *al dente.*

Meanwhile, bring the cut tomatoes in the skillet back to a simmer. Lift out the pasta and cooked greens with a spider, drain for a moment, then drop into the skillet. Cook over high heat, tossing continuously, until the pan juices have thickened and nicely coat the pasta. Turn off the heat, sprinkle the grated cheese over the pasta, and toss. Drizzle on more olive oil, toss, and serve immediately in warm bowls.

Bucatini with Toasted Bread Crumbs

PASTA CU RA MUDDICA

This is one of those elemental yet marvelous pastas made from almost nothing but a cook's inventiveness. If you lived in Puglia and all you had in the pantry was oil, garlic, a handful of pasta, a hunk of bread, and a sheaf of dried oregano, this is what you would make for your family. And they would be happy.

Don't wait for an empty refrigerator to make this. Just have some good country bread—a couple of days old is best—and some bucatini. The contrasting textures of those thick, hollow strands, perfect for slurping, and the hand-torn crumbs of bread, crisp and crackling, is just great. (And if you happen to have some Canestrato Pugliese, grate some on top. It will take you straight to Puglia.)

Serves 6

6-inch chunk of country-style bread, day-old preferred

About 1½ tablespoons coarse sea salt or kosher salt

1 pound bucatini (also called perciatelli)

½ cup extra-virgin olive oil, or more if needed

3 tablespoons sliced garlic

1 teaspoon dried oregano

3 tablespoons chopped fresh Italian parsley

½ cup freshly grated Canestrato Pugliese or other pecorino (optional)

Recommended Equipment
A large pot, 8-quart capacity, to cook the pasta

A heavy-bottomed skillet or sauté pan, 12-inch diameter

Cut off the crust of the bread chunk, and with your fingers tear the interior of the bread into irregular shreds, ¼ inch or a bit larger—big enough to crunch nicely when toasted. For a pound of pasta, shred 2 full cups of the rough crumbs.

Heat at least 6 quarts of water, with 1 tablespoon salt, to a rolling boil in the big pot, and add the bucatini. Bring it back to the boil, and cook, partially covered, until *al dente*.

As soon as the pasta is in the pot, pour ½ cup olive oil into the big skillet, set over medium-high heat, and scatter in the garlic slices. Cook for a couple of minutes, until the garlic is sizzling and fragrant but still pale. Drop in the torn bread crumbs, and stir and tumble them over to coat with oil. Keep tossing as they start to toast and color, sprinkle the oregano over the pot, and continue stirring and tossing. Lower the heat to avoid burning, and as soon as the crumbs and garlic slices are deep gold and crisp, turn off the heat.

Meanwhile, keep checking the pasta for doneness. As soon as it is cooked *al dente*, lift out the bucatini with tongs and a spider, let the water drain off for just a second or two, then drop it into the skillet.

Turn the heat up a bit, and immediately toss the pasta with the bread crumbs and garlic. Sprinkle on ½ teaspoon salt, and keep tossing. If the crumbs absorbed all the oil and the pasta seems dry, drizzle over them 2 or more tablespoons extra-virgin olive oil, and toss well. Taste, and season with more salt if needed. Finally, sprinkle on the parsley (and grated Canestrato Pugliese, if you have it, or other pecorino), toss, and serve right away.

Onion-Tomato Focaccia

FOCACCIA D'ALTAMURA

It is hard to reproduce an authentic version of a typical Pugliese bread without the special starter and the wood-burning oven for baking. But, as you will find with the following recipe, this memorable focaccia is one that you can bake successfully at home.

The topping of marinated onions and cherry tomatoes is simple and delicious. With this dough as a base, however, you can be creative and make a focaccia with mushrooms, leeks, sausages, and cheese in any combination. Keep in mind, though, that a simple topping, with a few distinct and harmonious flavors, is always more successful than a topping that tries to incorporate too many things. Be sure to season your topping ingredients and, where appropriate, cook and cool them before assembling the focaccia, so they don't just dry out in the oven.

Makes a large round focaccia, serving 10 or more

2 packets active dry yeast

2¼ cups warm water or as needed

5½ cups all-purpose flour, plus more for handling the dough

2 teaspoons salt

1 tablespoon extra-virgin olive oil for the bread bowl

For the topping
1 large onion, peeled, halved, and thinly sliced (about 2 cups slices)

2 cups ripe cherry or grape tomatoes, cut in half

½ cup extra-virgin olive oil, or as needed

1 teaspoon coarse sea salt or kosher salt, or as needed

To make the dough, dissolve the yeast in ¼ cup warm water and let it sit for several minutes, until it begins to bubble. Put the flour and salt in the food-processor bowl.

Stir together the active yeast and 2 cups lukewarm water in a spouted measuring cup. With the processor running continuously, blend the flour and salt briefly, then pour in all the liquid through the feed tube and process for about 30 seconds. A soft, moist dough should gather on the blade, with some sticking to the sides of the bowl. If it's very sticky and hasn't come off the sides at all, incorporate more flour, a tablespoon or two at a time, to stiffen the dough and bring it together. If the dough is dry, process in more water in small amounts.

Turn out the dough onto a lightly floured surface, scraping the bowl and blade clean. Knead by hand for a minute, using as little flour as possible, until the dough forms a smooth round, still soft and a bit sticky. Coat a big bowl with the tablespoon of olive oil, drop in the dough, and turn it to oil it all over. Seal the bowl with plastic wrap, and let it rise in a warm place until doubled, about an hour.

While the dough is rising, toss together the sliced onion, cherry-tomato halves, 4 tablespoons of the olive oil, and ½ teaspoon salt in a small bowl, and let them marinate.

Coat the baking dish or pan, bottom and sides, with 2 tablespoons or more olive oil. Deflate the risen dough, and lay it in the

½ teaspoon dried oregano

Recommended Equipment
A food processor fitted with the metal blade

A shallow round baking dish or pizza pan, 14-to-16-inch diameter

A baking stone or pizza stone

pan. Gently press and stretch it into an evenly flat round that fills the pan. If the dough is resistant, let it relax for a few minutes.

Lift the marinated onion and tomatoes out of the bowl with a slotted spoon, draining off the juices. Scatter the vegetables all over the focaccia, and lightly press in with your fingertips, creating dimples in the soft dough. Finally, drizzle the marinating oil over the top.

Let the focaccia rise, uncovered, for about 20 minutes. Set a baking stone, if you have one, on a center oven rack and heat to 425°. Just before baking, gently dimple the dough again with your fingertips, and sprinkle another ½ teaspoon coarse salt all over.

Bake the focaccia for about 20 minutes, rotate the pan back to front for even cooking, and bake another 10 to 15 minutes, or even longer, until the bread is golden brown and the onion and tomatoes are nicely caramelized.

Remove the pan and top with remaining olive oil and crumbled oregano. Let the focaccia cool for at least 15 minutes before slicing. Serve it warm or at room temperature.

The Breads of Puglia

Made with flour from the region's prized durum wheat, and still baked in traditional wood-burning ovens, the breads of Puglia are renowned as some of the best in all Italy. They are robust in texture, yet light with many air pockets. The interior is golden yellow; the crust, a thick golden brown, is resilient but cracks like glass when eaten. The flavor is sweet and nutty.

In Andria, at the Panificio Di Noia, one can taste the art of bread-making perfected by more than four generations, according to Vito Di Noia, twenty-eight years of age. He has worked with his father and grandfather at the shop, and not much has changed since they were young, except for the introduction of the large electric mixer. His description of making the bread is rather simple: it is the flour, the water, the starter (passed down from generation to generation), and the ovens that make the family's bread so good.

Vito shapes his bread into a braid by using one long piece of dough, folding it into a twist. In Altamura, however, thirty kilometers away, the traditional shape looks like a slivered roasted chestnut. There you'll find La Fornaccia—*"Forno a legna di Carlucci Tommaso"*—at Via Liguria 1, a small bakery with bundles of firewood on the sidewalk in front of it. Down two big stone steps, there is a simple glass counter on which are spread the most inviting round focaccias, pudgy and encrusted with caramelized olives, onions, and tomatoes (see page 323). The bread is soft, and yet the crust is firm and crunchy, redolent of olive oil. Angela sells the goods while her husband, Tommaso, and son, Giuseppe, make the bread.

Indeed, the breads from both these places are some of the best I have ever eaten.

Tagliatelle with Chickpeas

CECI E TRIA

Antichi Sapori, a family-run restaurant in Montegrosso, a few kilometers south of Andria, is where I had some of the best local products and traditional dishes. Pietro Zito, the chef and owner, is tied to the land and works with local seasonal products. One of several memorable dishes I enjoyed there was *ceci e tria*, this dense soup of chickpeas with the textural interplay of cooked and fried pasta. It's a flavorful simple dish, very rustic and yet mellow.

Serves 6

For the ceci
1 pound dried *ceci* (chickpeas)

1 medium onion, peeled and cut in half

1 large carrot, peeled, cut in half, and sliced lengthwise

1 large celery stalk, cut in half

1½ cups cherry tomatoes, rinsed

2 bay leaves, preferably fresh

1½ teaspoons coarse sea salt or kosher salt, plus more if needed

⅓ cup extra-virgin olive oil, plus more for finishing

3 plump garlic cloves, smashed and peeled

½ teaspoon peperoncino flakes

2 tablespoons chopped fresh Italian parsley

For the tagliatelle
½ cup all-purpose flour, plus more for handling the dough

½ cup semolina flour

Rinse the chickpeas, and put them in a large bowl with cold water covering them by at least 4 inches; let soak in a cool place for 12 hours or more.

Drain and rinse the *ceci*, place them in the big saucepan with 10 cups fresh cold water, and drop in the cut vegetables, cherry tomatoes, and bay leaves. Bring the water to a boil, stirring occasionally, then partially cover the pan and adjust the heat to maintain a low but steady simmer. Cook until the chickpeas are tender but not mushy, 2 hours or more, stirring now and then—add water if necessary to keep the chickpeas and vegetables submerged as they cook.

Meanwhile, make the pasta dough and tagliatelle by hand. Stir the flours together in a medium-sized mixing bowl. Break up the egg with a fork. In a cup or small bowl, stir in the olive oil and 1 tablespoon cold water, and pour over the flour—scrape in *all* the liquid. Toss and mix with the fork until all the flour is moistened and starts to clump together. Gather the clumps with your hands or a plastic scraper, and knead them, right in the bowl, into one lump of dough.

Turn the dough out onto the work surface, and continue kneading by hand for a couple of minutes. If it's stiff or crumbly, sprinkle over it more cold water, a teaspoonful at a time, and knead in. If it's wet or sticky, dust the work surface with a small amount of flour and knead in. When the dough is smooth, soft, and stretchy, press it into a disk, wrap well in plastic, and let it rest at room temperature for 30 minutes. (Mix the dough in the food processor if you prefer.)

1 large egg

2 tablespoons extra-virgin olive oil

Recommended Equipment
A 7- or 8-quart heavy-bottomed saucepan with a cover

A rolling pin and wooden board for rolling the pasta

A 6-inch-diameter sauté pan or saucepan for frying the tagliatelle

To roll the dough, lightly flour the rolling pin and wooden board (or other work surface). Cut the dough in half, and roll each piece to a thin rectangular sheet about 17 inches long and 8 inches wide, dusting with flour as needed.

Set one sheet with the long side in front of you, and fold it over several times, to make a long, narrow rectangle. With a sharp knife, slice crosswise through the folded dough, at ½-inch intervals. Immediately separate and unfurl the cut pieces, opening them into ribbons 7 inches long and ½ inch wide. Dust the tagliatelle with flour, and set them on a floured towel or tray. Repeat with the second rolled sheet. (If you prefer, roll the sheets with a pasta machine; pass them through the ½-inch-wide cutting attachment; and cut the strands into tagliatelle.) Keep the pasta covered so it doesn't dry out while the chickpeas stew.

When the chickpeas are tender, scoop out the pieces of onion, carrot, and celery and the bay leaves with a slotted spoon and discard. The *ceci* should be covered with a bit of cooking liquid; add water if needed. Return to a bubbling simmer, and stir in the salt.

Pour the ⅓ cup olive oil into the small saucepan, drop in the garlic cloves and peperoncino, and set over medium-high heat. Let the garlic sizzle and caramelize, stirring occasionally, for a couple of minutes.

Put the tagliatelle in a colander, shake to remove excess flour, pick up a third of the strands, and drop them into the small saucepan, on top of the garlic. Quickly spread the tagliatelle so they're covered in hot oil. Let them heat and start sizzling without stirring. Immediately drop the rest of the tagliatelle on top of the simmering chickpeas, and stir in well. Raise the heat a bit, and bring back to the boil, stirring the pasta frequently.

While the beans and tagliatelle boil gently in the big pot, shake the small pan occasionally so the hot oil flows over the frying tagliatelle. Turn them over with tongs if the oil doesn't cover the ribbons on top. Fry the tagliatelle until evenly golden brown and crisp, 4 minutes or so, then lift them out with tongs, draining off the oil, and lay on a warm plate.

Now pour and scrape all the oil, caramelized garlic, and peperoncino from the small pan into the chickpea pot—the bean liquid will sizzle—and stir well. Cook for another couple of minutes, or until the boiling tagliatelle are soft and fully cooked. Adjust the salt to taste, and turn off the heat.

Stir in another 2 or 3 tablespoons olive oil (fresh and uncooked), scatter the fried tagliatelle on top of the chickpeas, sprinkle the parsley all over, and serve right away. Be sure to scoop some of the crisp tagliatelle into every portion.

Baked Onions from Acquaviva

CIPOLLOTTO DI ACQUAVIVA

Cipollotto di Acquaviva, small sweet onions baked with a sprinkle of bread crumbs, is another one of those simple gems from the Antichi Sapori restaurant. Acquaviva is a nearby town famed for the sweetness of its onions. Chef Pietro Zito prepared them for me this way, and they were as sweet as apples.

To make these at home, buy any of the sweet onions in the market—such as Vidalia, Walla Walla, or Maui—preferably small, flattish ones, about 2 ounces each. Serve three or four baked onion halves as an appetizer. You can also season and roast the onions on a slow grill, covered—they make a great accompaniment to grilled fish and meat. And very small onions baked Acquaviva style are a wonderful bite-sized hors d'oeuvre.

Serves 6

½ cup extra-virgin olive oil, or as needed

1½ pounds small sweet onions, preferably flat, about 3 inches wide and 1 inch high

½ cup dried bread crumbs

½ teaspoon coarse sea salt or kosher salt

1 tablespoon chopped fresh thyme leaves

Recommended Equipment
A large, rimmed baking sheet, such as a half–sheet pan (12 by 18 inches)

Preheat the oven to 400° with a rack in the center. Coat the baking sheet with a light film of olive oil.

Peel the onions thoroughly. Trim a thin slice off the stem and root of each onion, so both ends are flat. Slice each onion in half—through its wide equator—and set the halves on the baking sheet, resting on the large cut side. Drizzle a bit of olive oil on the onion halves.

Toss the bread crumbs with the salt and chopped thyme leaves. Drizzle a tablespoon of olive oil on the crumbs, and toss until evenly moistened.

Sprinkle some of the crumbs on the flat tops of the onions—about a teaspoon on each. Finally, drizzle the remaining olive oil over all. Cover the sheet pan with aluminum foil, arching it so it does not touch the onions and crimping it against the rim of the pan.

Bake for about 20 minutes, then remove the foil and bake for another 20 minutes, or until the crumb topping is golden and crisped and the onions are soft and slightly caramelized. Remove from the oven, and let the onions sit on the sheet for a few minutes. While they're still warm, arrange the onions on a platter and serve.

Celery Chutney

MOSTARDA DI SEDANO

Sheep's-milk ricotta served with *mostarda di sedano* was a discovery and delight at Antichi Sapori. Crunchy small diamonds of glasslike celery pieces cooked with sugar and lemon were served as an accompaniment to fresh sheep's-milk ricotta rounds—simple but extraordinary.

Mostarde have been part of the Italian culinary repertoire for centuries, originally as a way of preserving vegetables and fruits—such as squash, apples, and pears—for the winter months. Cooked in sweet syrup with hot mustard added, *mostarde* were enjoyed as a crisp and fresh-tasting condiment when there was no fresh produce. The epicenter of the Italian *mostarda* culture is in and around Modena, but every region has some form of it.

I am familiar with all kinds of *mostarde*, but celery? This I had never seen before. I love celery anyway, and in this preparation I absolutely adore it. I serve this with good ripe cheese as well as with fresh sheep's-milk ricotta. It is a fine condiment for boiled meats, or grilled or poached poultry. And, suspended in its sweet syrup, it is also delicious on ice cream! It keeps in the refrigerator for months, so make a batch and enjoy it in all these ways.

Makes about 2 cups

2 pounds firm celery stalks, medium-sized

1 cup sugar

¼ teaspoon fine sea salt

½ cup freshly squeezed lemon juice (from about 4 lemons)

Recommended Equipment
A heavy 3- or 4-quart saucepan with a cover

Rinse, dry, and trim the celery stalks. Shave off any tough and stringy outer peel with a vegetable peeler. Slice the stalks crosswise in half; slice all these chunks lengthwise into very thin sticks, about ⅛ inch thick. Cut the sticks crosswise into ⅛-inch cubes and bits (the size of pickle relish). You should have 6 to 7 cups of fine celery pieces.

Put the cup of sugar and the salt in the saucepan, pour the lemon juice on top, and then all the celery. Set the pot over medium-low heat, and stir as the sugar dissolves and the celery heats and starts releasing its juices. Bring the syrup to a gentle simmer, stirring frequently.

Cover the pot, and adjust the heat to maintain a gentle bubbling around the edges of the pan. Cook for about 15 minutes, stirring now and then. Uncover the pot, and cook at the simmer, stirring occasionally, until almost all of the liquid has been absorbed or evaporated, about 35 minutes or more.

Remove the pan from the heat, and let the *mostarda* cool completely before using. Store in a sealed container in the refrigerator.

Mussels with Farro, Cannellini, and Chickpeas

FARRO CON FAGIOLI, CECI, E COZZE

As much as Puglia is about the land, it is also flanked by water: the Adriatic on one side and the Ionian Sea on the gulf side. Hence, one finds a big tradition of seafood as one travels down to the tip of the heel.

In the quaint seaside city of Trani, along the Adriatic shoreline, is a delightful restaurant called Le Lampare. There I was introduced to *farro con legumi e cozze*, a beautiful stew of *ceci* and cannellini beans cooked with farro, one of my favorite grains, tossed before serving with savory mussels and their juices.

Serves 6

1 cup dried chickpeas

1 cup dried cannellini beans

½ cup chopped carrot

½ cup chopped celery

1 cup chopped onion

1½ cups cherry tomatoes, cut in half

½ cup extra-virgin olive oil, plus more for finishing

1 cup farro (see Sources, page 340) or pearled barley

1½ teaspoons coarse sea salt or kosher salt, plus more if needed

½ teaspoon peperoncino flakes

4 garlic cloves, crushed, peeled, and sliced

2 pounds mussels

4 tablespoons chopped fresh Italian parsley

Rinse the chickpeas, and place in a bowl with cold water covering them by 4 inches. Do the same with the cannellini, in a separate bowl. Soak both for 12 to 24 hours.

Drain and rinse the chickpeas, and put them in the big saucepan with about 7 cups of fresh cold water. Set the pot over medium-high heat, and drop in the chopped carrot, celery, and onion, the halved cherry tomatoes, and 4 tablespoons of the olive oil. Bring the water to a boil, partially cover the pan, and adjust the heat to maintain a steady, bubbling simmer. Stir occasionally.

After the chickpeas have cooked for an hour, drain and rinse the cannellini and stir them into the pot. There should be at least an inch of liquid covering the beans; add more water if necessary. Return to the boil, partially cover, and simmer for 45 minutes, stirring now and then.

Rinse the farro grains in a sieve, and stir in with the beans, along with the 1½ teaspoons salt and ¼ teaspoon of the peperoncino. There should be about ¼ inch of liquid covering the beans and grain; add more water if necessary. Return to the boil, partially cover, and simmer for about 30 minutes or longer, until the beans and the farro are tender—add water if needed to keep the beans and grains barely covered with liquid as they finish cooking. When they are done, most of the surface water should have been absorbed or evaporated, but the stew should be slightly soupy.

While the farro cooks, prepare the mussels. Pour the remaining 4 tablespoons olive oil in the sauté pan, and scatter in the garlic

Recommended Equipment
A heavy-bottomed saucepan with a cover, 5-quart capacity

A heavy sauté pan or shallow saucepan (3- or 4-inch sides), 12-inch diameter, with a tight-fitting cover, for cooking the mussels

cloves and remaining ¼ teaspoon peperoncino. Cook for 3 minutes or so over medium-high heat, until the garlic is lightly colored, then add all the rinsed mussels at once. Tumble them around the pan quickly, to coat with oil, and put on the cover. Cook over high heat for about 2 minutes, shaking the covered pan a couple of times, just until the mussels are open, and take the pan off the stove.

Shuck the mussels right over the pan, letting the juices and meat drop in. Discard the shells (and any mussels that did not open). If you like, leave a dozen or so mussels in the shell for a garnish.

When the farro and beans are cooked, pour the shucked mussels and their juices into the pot and stir well—the consistency should be rather brothy. Heat to the boil, and cook for just a minute, to make sure everything is nice and hot. Taste, and adjust salt. Stir in the chopped parsley, and spoon portions into warm pasta bowls; garnish with unshucked mussels if you saved them. Drizzle good olive oil over each, and serve immediately.

To prepare in advance: Cook the beans and farro until tender, following recipe, and remove from the heat. Let them sit in the saucepan up to 3 hours (they will absorb liquid and thicken). Shortly before serving, cook and shuck the mussels. Stir the mussel juices into the beans and farro, and heat slowly to a simmer. Stir in the mussels, and finish as above.

Farro

For the real taste of Trani, I urge you to try farro, if you are not familiar with it. An ancient form of wheat (also called emmer), farro cooks like pearl barley or rice, with no soaking. It has a wonderful nutty flavor and is quite nutritious. Since it is now is sold in many specialty markets and easily ordered online (see Sources, page 340), I hope it becomes a staple in your pantry.

Farro with Tuna and Tomatoes

FARRO AL TONNO E POMODORO

Here's another of my delicious discoveries at Le Lampare, in Trani. Farro is again paired with seafood, the simply cooked grain tossed and dressed, like pasta, with a lively sauce of cured tuna, tomatoes, and capers.

We can't match the tuna used at Le Lampare—theirs was expertly house-cured from the flavorful and expensive *ventresca* (belly flap) of the fish—but with this recipe you can make a version that is truly delicious in its own right, using good-quality Italian canned tuna (packed in olive oil, of course). It is a great summer dish, as a main course or an appetizer.

Serves 6 as a first course, 4 as a main course

1 pound farro (or 500 grams, as packaged in Italy)

2 bay leaves, preferably fresh

About 1 tablespoon coarse sea salt or kosher salt

10 tablespoons extra-virgin olive oil, or more if needed

6 plump garlic cloves, peeled and sliced

½ teaspoon peperoncino flakes

3 cups (or a 28-ounce can) canned Italian plum tomatoes, preferably San Marzano, crushed by hand

4 tablespoons small capers, drained

Two 6-ounce cans tuna in olive oil

2 tablespoons chopped fresh Italian parsley

Recommended Equipment

A heavy 3- or 4-quart saucepan

A heavy-bottomed 12-inch skillet

Rinse the farro well, and drain in a sieve. Put it in the pot with 6 cups of water, the bay leaves, ½ teaspoon salt, and 2 tablespoons olive oil. Bring to the boil, stirring occasionally, then set the cover slightly ajar and adjust the heat to maintain a steady, bubbling simmer. Cook about ½ hour, stirring from time to time, until the farro grains are cooked through but still *al dente*, then turn off the heat. Most of the liquid should have been absorbed; if there's water still visible, pour it off. Discard the bay leaves. Keep the farro in the covered pot to stay warm while you make the sauce.

Pour ⅓ cup of the olive oil into the big skillet, and set over medium-high heat. Scatter the sliced garlic and peperoncino in the pan, and cook for a couple of minutes, to caramelize. Stir in the crushed tomatoes, 2 teaspoons salt, and the capers, and heat to a moderate boil, letting the tomatoes bubble away, uncovered.

Meanwhile, drain the canned tuna and break it up into thick flakes, ½ inch or a bit larger. After the tomatoes have cooked about 5 minutes, drop the tuna in the skillet, and stir it into the tomatoes slowly, so the flakes of fish stay together. Cook at the same bubbling boil for another 5 minutes, until the tomatoes are cooked and slightly reduced.

Lower the heat a bit, and stir in the remaining olive oil (about 3 tablespoons). Now spill the cooked farro on top of the sauce, and toss and stir, still over moderate heat, until the grains are very hot and thoroughly mixed with the tomatoes and tuna. Turn off the heat, toss in the chopped parsley, and serve.

Almond Tart from Andria

CROSTATA DI MANDORLE

Filled with nuts and meringue, this lattice-topped tart is quite lovely, quite easy, and typically Italian. In Andria, Carlo Tottolo gets almonds from the area of Toritto, some of the best in all of Italy.

Makes a 9-inch tart, serving 8 or more

For the tart dough
2 cups all-purpose flour

¼ teaspoon salt

3 tablespoons sugar

12 tablespoons (1½ sticks) very cold butter, cut in ½-inch pieces

3 egg yolks

2 tablespoons ice water, or more as needed

For the filling
4 large egg whites

Large pinch of salt

¾ cup sugar

1 tablespoon grated lemon zest

1½ cups sliced almonds, lightly toasted

Recommended Equipment
A food processor for making the tart dough

A 9-inch metal tart mold with fluted sides and removable bottom

An electric mixer with whisk attachment

Make the tart dough at least 6 hours before rolling it (preferably longer). Put the flour, salt, and sugar into the bowl of the food processor. Process for a few seconds to mix the dry ingredients. Drop the cut-up butter on top of the flour, and pulse the machine in a dozen or more short bursts, until the mixture is crumbly with only small bits of butter visible.

Pour the egg yolks over the crumbs, and pulse in bursts for about 5 seconds total, to moisten the dough. Scrape down the sides of the bowl, sprinkle the 2 tablespoons of ice water on the dough, and pulse again for a few seconds. The dough should begin to clump together but won't form a solid mass.

Scrape it all out onto a board; gather and press the clumps into a firm ball. If it's dry and crumbles apart, sprinkle more ice water over the dough and knead gently. When the dough sticks together, flatten it into a disk, wrap well in plastic, and refrigerate for 6 hours or up to a day before rolling; freeze the dough for longer keeping.

When you're ready to roll the dough and fill the tart, preheat your oven to 350°, with a rack set in the center. Place a baking stone on the rack if you have one.

Cut off a third of the dough in a single piece for the lattice top; keep it chilled.

Place the larger piece of dough between two sheets of parchment, and roll it out to an even round, 11 inches in diameter. Peel off the top sheet of parchment, invert the circle over the tart pan, and peel off the remaining sheet. Press the dough gently down into the pan so it covers the bottom and lines the sides. Trim the edges of the dough round so it is even with the pan rim. With your fingers, form an even wall all the way around. Use scraps of dough to fill cracks or thin spots on the bottom or sides. Put the lined tart pan in the refrigerator.

Now roll the smaller piece of dough between the parchment sheets to a 10-inch round. Remove the top parchment sheet, and cut the dough in 1-inch-wide strips with a pastry cutter or sharp knife. Leave the strips in place on the parchment sheet, and refrigerate them while you make the filling.

Put the egg whites with the pinch of salt in the bowl of the electric mixer, and start whisking at medium speed. When the whites are frothy, pour in the sugar gradually, and raise the speed as the whites expand and thicken. When all the sugar has been incorporated, drop in the lemon zest, and continue whipping until the whites are very light, smooth, and glossy. Sprinkle the sliced almonds on top, a handful at a time, and fold in gently with a spatula so they are evenly dispersed.

Take the pastry-lined tart pan and lattice strips from the refrigerator. Scrape the filling into the pastry shell, and spread it evenly.

To form the lattice top, lay half the strips right over the filling, parallel and spaced about an inch apart. Lay the other strips diagonally across the first set, covering the entire top of the tart in an even pattern—cutting the strips or piecing them together to make different lengths. When they're all arranged, press and pinch the ends of the strips securely into the top rim of dough in the pan.

Bake the tart—on a stone, if you have one—for about 45 minutes, or until the filling has risen and dried and appears firm and lightly browned in the lattice. The dough strips and rim should be golden brown.

Cool the tart on a wire rack. When the crust has contracted a bit, slip off the fluted side ring. When it is completely cool, transfer the tart to a serving plate, if you wish, by sliding a long wide spatula (or two spatulas) under the pastry bottom and lifting the tart off the metal disk. Cut it in wedges, and serve.

Desserts from Puglia

Not too far from Andria is Toritto, known for its large and delicious almonds, which are used in many desserts in Puglia. Carlo Tottolo runs a *caffè* and pastry shop in walking distance from the burrata *caseificio* in Andria, and shared with me his traditional recipes for *Crostata di Mandorle* and *Ostie Ripiene,* page 336.

Caramelized Almond Wafers

OSTIE RIPIENE

Legend has it that this dessert was born in 1600, in the monastery of Monte Sant' Angelo, where there is a sanctuary dedicated to the Archangel Michael. As the story goes, while the nuns in the monastery were preparing the dough for the *ostie*—the Communion wafer or host—some of the almonds fell in the hot honey. Not having anything close by to pick them out, they used the hosts they were making, and so the dessert was born.

In this simple dessert, two wafers are filled like a sandwich with almonds caramelized in honey. It is a treat for the faithful on the special holiday of St. Michael the Archangel on September 29—even nonbelievers will love them.

Makes about 30 small cookies

½ pound whole unblanched almonds

Rice paper wafer sheets (from candy-and-cake-decorating supply stores; see Sources, page 340)

⅔ cup honey

¼ cup sugar

¼ teaspoon cinnamon

Recommended Equipment
A heavy skillet or sauté pan, 12-inch diameter

Spread the almonds on a sheet pan, and toast them in a 300° oven for 15 minutes, or until they are light gold and fragrant.

Cut sixty wafers from the rice paper with sharp scissors. For square cookies, fold the sheet over at about 2-inch intervals, cut along the folds to make strips, and cut the strips into squares. For round wafers, cut 2-inch circles from each strip.

Pour the honey and the sugar into the skillet, and set over medium heat. Stir in the cinnamon as the honey melts, and continue stirring as the sugar dissolves and the mixture starts to bubble. Cook at a moderate boil for 5 to 10 minutes, until the mixture has caramelized to a deep golden brown and thickened noticeably.

Stir in the almonds, heat to bubbling again, and cook for 2 or 3 minutes, until the nuts are hot and thoroughly coated with the caramelized honey. Don't let the syrup or almonds get too dark. Turn off the heat, but leave the filling in the pan.

Lay out twelve wafers in a line on a cool counter, scoop up some of the hot honey and almonds with a wooden spoon, and drop a small mound on six of the wafers—a rounded teaspoon or more. While the honey is still soft, top each with a second wafer. With a flat board, press down lightly on all at once, flattening and spreading the nut filling. Fill all the wafer sandwiches this way. Whenever the caramel gets too thick to drop, return the pan to low heat and warm the honey until it loosens.

When the filled wafers are completely cool and the filling is crunchy, enjoy. Store in an airtight container for a week or so.

Tanya's Tour

PUGLIA

CASTEL DEL MONTE: The Emperor's Octagon
Location: Not far from Andria, in the province of Bari

This extraordinary building is one of the many landmarks left all over southern Italy by Frederick II, one of the most unusual monarchs of the Middle Ages, a man known in his own time as Stupor Mundi—Wonder of the World.

Frederick was Holy Roman Emperor and King of Sicily and Jerusalem, but he must have loved Puglia in a special way, as he built ninety-six castles and forty-two cathedrals in the region, and died in one of them in 1250. To me, no place is as imbued with the power and mystery of this man as the Castel del Monte. The structure itself has been studied and measured for its mathematical precision and symbolic significance, both of importance to Frederick. Some theorize that the eight-sided structure symbolizes the Resurrection; others say it represents an intermediate point between earth and sky. Still others point out that it is set geographically between Chartres Cathedral and the Pyramid of Cheops in Giza. When I am there, on the walls of the solitary hilltop castle overlooking the Pugliese landscape, I feel as if I am standing exactly where Frederick must have stood.

TRANI: Somehow I See Venice
Location: On the coast of Puglia, about 51 kilometers north of Bari

Trani is a small port town that clings to the Adriatic Sea—and where my mother found the wonderful seafood restaurant Le Lampare. During the reign of Frederick, however, Trani was the most important maritime mercantile center in the southern Adriatic. On the edge of the Jewish ghetto, near where fishermen come and go with their daily catch, is the Church of the Knights of Templar, built in the twelfth century, for the Crusaders who embarked from Trani for the Holy Land. Frederick's castle in Trani is a large, imposing structure not far from the church.

The cathedral, with its boldly serene Romanesque interior, dominates the cityscape, its already imposing height made even greater by having one side that literally drops into the ocean, especially when viewed from a boat on the water. The colors of the stone can appear to be bleached white at certain times in the day, and rosy pink as the sun slowly sets over the sea. The delicate, almost lacy bell tower, supported only by an arch on the ground floor, appears to float over air. It immediately makes me think of St. Mark's bell tower in Venice.

SAFARI ZOO: Simply Unforgettable
Location: Near Fasano, about 59 kilometers south of Bari

I remember this as one of the most exciting visits I had in Puglia, especially since I'd brought the kids along. I had a rental car and drove through a part of the zoo, almost as if on safari. We drove with the windows open, and often the animals would try to peer in, as a rather large dromedary species of camel attempted to do in my case. In the lion section—windows closed, of course—there was an enormous feeling of excitement as we drove through, nothing separating us from the lions but our rather small Italian rental car. However, my favorite was the monkeys. The minute we came through the gate, they attacked, pouncing all over the exterior of the car, removing the side mirror (good that I had a rented car). They are a blast—the trip is almost worth it just for the monkeys. Alas, today you aren't allowed to bring your own car, and you have to take the monorail that runs through the zoo. The plus side is that you will see more animals, including a reptile house and an animal theme park with rides and attractions.

ALBEROBELLO: Tranquillity Amid the Trulli
Location: About 83 kilometers north of Brindisi, a bit inland from the coast

The distinctive dwellings known as *trulli*—with conical roofs and white walls of earth and stone—can be found throughout Puglia, but in Alberobello they make up almost the entire city. The origin of these structures is unknown, though the discovery of prehistoric artifacts in the vicinity of *trulli* has convinced many that they must be quite ancient. A walk through Alberobello, past the sun-bleached structures, always evokes in me a tremendous inner peace (partly, perhaps, because of the beating hot sun and usual absence of automobiles). In contrast to the stark white exteriors, the spaces inside *trulli* are filled with bright fabric curtains that delineate separate rooms—only the bathrooms are enclosed with walls—and add color to the homes. Though *trulli* are quite small, often two or three conical segments are built together, creating an expansive open living quarter. It's usually not hard to see the interiors of *trulli*, as friendly locals may invite you in to take a look, or you can sneak a peek through an open window or door as you walk through town. Of course, you can also stop at the Hotel dei Trulli to get a better sense of what it is like to be inside a *trullo*.

MARTINA FRANCA: A Gem on a Hill
Location: 20 kilometers southwest of Fasano, in the province of Taranto

Often structures seem to pop out of nowhere when you are traveling the country-side in Puglia, and that is how I always feel approaching Martina Franca, a lone, walled city on top of a hill (not common in this flat region). Martina Franca is a true gem, dotted with towers and city gates from different epochs, some of them Baroque and elaborate in style, others starkly simple, like the *trulli*. The Palazzo Ducale is a lovely, well-balanced structure that crowns the piazza in which it sits. You can see Bernini's only sure work in Puglia and some wonderful frescoes. I also admire the Basilica di San Martino, and think of it as "slender Baroque": what Baroque architecture looks like on a diet. The height of the church and many vertical elements diminish the heavy, saturated feeling one often experiences when looking at Baroque structures. Here the elements are well tied together, and the façade is cohesive and pleasant to admire. The interior is just as pleasing, rich with colored marble, Baroque statuary, and elaborate decoration, but never heavy or inelegant.

Sources

SOURCES FOR FINE ITALIAN FOODS

Thanks to Internet technology, it is easier than ever for American cooks to find authentic Italian ingredients. Search engines and all-purpose shopping Web sites can hunt for any ingredient in my recipes and purchase them, either through big marketplaces like Amazon or eBay or from the scores of smaller merchants that select and sell good products. Of course, not all products are available at all times of the year—and Web vendors, like ordinary markets, sometimes change their products or close their doors. Therefore, I recommend that you visit several of the following sites to see what they have in stock. All of them carry quality products, imported from Italy.

- *A. G. Ferrari Foods* (www.agferrari.com): Large selection of Italian foods in many categories, organized by type and region.

- *Amazon.com Gourmet Food* (www.amazon.com): A convenient place to search for products in every category. Also a good way to find the names of small producers and vendors.

- *Corti Brothers* (www.cortibros.biz): A good source for Italian groceries in many categories.

- *D'Artagnan* (www.dartagnan.com): Well-known vendor of fine poultry and game, meats, and other specialty products.

- *GourmetStore.net* (www.gourmetstore.net): A good source for imported Italian pasta and other specialties.

- *Gustiamo.com "Italy's Best Foods"* (www.gustiamo.com): Fine oils, grains, pastas, and other specialty products, organized by category and region.

- *iGourmet.com* (www.igourmet.com): A good source for imported Italian cheeses.

- *ItalianConnectionUSA* (www.italianconnectionusa.com): Imported Italian products, including pastas and packaged goods, organized by region of origin.

- *Kitchenkapers.com* (www.kitchenkapers.com): A good source for kitchen tools and equipment, including pasta machines.

- *Seeds from Italy* (www.growitalian.com): Traditional Italian vegetable, herb, and flower seeds.

- *Zabar's* (www.zabars.com): A huge selection of high-quality products from this very reliable New York institution.

SOME SPECIAL STORES IN NEW YORK CITY

The Internet is fantastic, but whenever possible I still prefer to visit real Italian markets to see, smell, feel, and taste the products. In almost every city in the United States, you can find a reputable merchant for imported specialties and homemade items like mozzarella, ricotta, Italian sausages, and *salumi* (salt-cured meat products). Here are two markets where I enjoy shopping, in New York City—my hometown.

- *Salumeria Biellese:* 376–378 Eighth Avenue, New York, N.Y. 10001; (212) 736-7376; www.salumeriabiellese.com: This delicatessen makes a variety of wonderful *salumi* but what I go there for is the *guanciale* (cured pork cheek) for pasta *all'amatriciana*, page 228.

- *DiPalo Fine Foods:* 200 Grand Street, New York, N.Y. 10013; (212) 226-1033 (no Web site): This renowned *latticini* (dairy store) specializes in fresh cheeses such as burrata and mozzarella di bufala but also has a great selection of Grana Padano and Parmigiano-Reggiano, of different ages, from selected producers. Proprietor Lou DiPalo is extremely knowledgeable and will happily explain the nuances and delights of his different cheeses.

SOURCES FOR SPECIFIC RECIPE ITEMS

- Boar tenderloin: Available from D'Artagnan (www.dartagnan.com)

- Canestrato Pugliese cheese: Available from iGourmet (www.igourmet.com)

- Farro grain: Available from Amazon (www.amazon.com) or Gustiamo (www.gustiamo.com)

- Gramigna pasta: Available from Corti Brothers (www.cortibros.biz)

- Guanciale (cured pork cheek): Available from Biellese Salumeria (www.salumeriabiellese.com) and Niman Ranch (www.nimanranch.com)

- Pugliese pasta, such as cavatelli, *strascinate*, and orecchiette: Available from A. G. Ferrari Foods (www.agferrari.com) and ItalianConnectionUSA (www.italianconnectionusa.com)

- Ricotta affumicata and ricotta salata: Available from iGourmet (www.igourmet.com)

- *Torchio* pasta press: Available from Pasta Biz (www.pastabiz.com)

- Truffle butter: Available from Amazon (www.amazon.com) and D'Artagnan (www.dartagnan.com)

- Wafer sheets: Available from Pastry Chef Central (www.pastrychef.com)

The PBS Television Series of *Lidia's Italy*

NAPLES AND GAETA (Chapter 8)

Spaghetti and White Clams—A Classic Plus More
Vermicelli with Clam Sauce
Bucatini Mock Amatriciana

Neapolitan Macaroni and Cheese
Ditalini with Potatoes and Provola
Sausages with Potatoes and Hot Peppers

Tutto Pasta
Dry Fettuccine with Squash and Cauliflower
Maltagliati with Onion-Tomato Sauce
Spaghetti with Quick Garlic-Tomato Sauce

Rolling with Nonna Lisa
Nonna Lisa's Tiella with Filling of Escarole, Olives, and Capers
Icy Espresso Frappe
Fried Cream

Savory and Sweet Napoli
Little Turnovers Stuffed with Escarole and Sausage
Babas Infused with Limoncello

MAREMMA (Chapter 6)

The Essence of Maremma
Alma's Cooked Water Soup
Beefsteak Maremma Style

The Galloping Figs
Beef Braised with Black Peppercorns
Poached Fresh Figs

Autumn in Maremma
Pappardelle with Long-Cooked Rabbit Sugo
Roasted Chestnuts with Red Wine

Maremma Chard Pillows
Tortelli Filled with Chicken Liver, Spinach, and Ricotta
Sage Pudding

Porcini Wrap
Crespelle Stuffed with Mushrooms
Gramigna with Spinach, Chickpeas, and Bacon
Braised Swiss Chard and Cannellini Beans

What a Boar
Filet of Wild Boar with Prune and Apple Sauce
Chickpea Soup with Porcini Mushrooms

ROME (Chapter 7)
When in Rome Eat Pasta
Bucatini with Onion, Bacon, and Tomato
Spaghetti with Crushed Black Pepper and Pecorino Cheese

Two Essentials of Roman Cuisine
Chicken with Artichokes
Baked Fennel with Prosciutto

Kneading with an Old Friend
Fresh Pasta for Fettuccine
Fettuccine with Tomato and Chicken Liver Sauce
Fennel and Orange Salad

Sausage Alla Romana
Sausages with Fennel and Olives
Ricotta Cake with Almonds

Sea and Land, Roman Way
Monkfish in Brodetto with Artichokes
Skillet Fennel with Capers

Vegetarian Rome
Roasted Potatoes and Artichokes
Braised Artichokes with Pecorino
Artichokes Braised in Tomato Sauce

SICILY (Chapter 9)
The Raw and the Cooked
Raw and Cooked Salad
Pork Scaloppine with Mushrooms and Marsala

A Sicilian and His Calamari
Manfredi's Steamed Calamari
Anna's Spaghetti and Pesto Trapanese

Anna the Couscous Lady
Seafood Brodetto with Couscous
Orange and Red Onion Salad

Eggplant and Tuna Alla Siciliana
Smothered Eggplant and Summer Vegetables
Ziti with Tomatoes, Eggplant, and Salted Ricotta

Sicilian Street Food
Grouper Matalotta Style
Fried Chickpea Polenta

Stack Those Cannoli
Dry Fettuccine with Swordfish
Cannoli Napoleon

FRIULI (Chapter 3)
The Lamb of the Land
Crispy Swiss Chard Cakes with Montasio
Roasted Lamb Shoulder

Braciole—A Cinnamon Roll
Frico with Potatoes and Montasio Cheese
Frico with Apples and Montasio Cheese
Sautéed Spiced Beef Cutlets

Gnocchi Savory and Sweet
Potato Gnocchi Friuli Style
Apple Torte with Bread Crumb and Hazelnut Crust

Tender Pork Chops, Loose Polenta
Velvety Cornmeal-Spinach Soup
Braised Pork Chops with Savoy Cabbage

Risotto—Fresh and Green
Risotto with Spinach
Tangy Skillet Turnips and Potatoes

Istrian Seafood Mix
Istrian Mixed Seafood Stew
Asparagus and Rice Soup
Quince Soup

Index

Page numbers in *italics* refer to illustrations.

A Note About the Authors

Lidia Matticchio Bastianich was born in Pula, Istria, a peninsula that belonged to Italy at the time and is now part of Croatia. She came to the United States in 1958 and opened her first restaurant, Buonavia, in Queens, in 1971. A tremendous success, it inspired her to launch Felidia in 1981 in Manhattan, followed by Becco and Esca del Posto (also in New York) and Lidia's in Kansas City and Pittsburgh.

Lidia Bastianich is the author of four previous books, *La Cucina di Lidia, Lidia's Italian Table, Lidia's Italian-American Kitchen,* and *Lidia's Family Table.* She has also been the host of several public-television series, *Lidia's Italian Table, Lidia's Italian-American Kitchen,* and *Lidia's Family Table,* and she gives lectures on Italian cuisine across the country. Ms. Bastianich lives on Long Island.

Tanya Bastianich Manuali's visits to Italy as a child sparked her passion for the country's art and culture. She dedicated herself to the study of Italian Renaissance art during her college years at Georgetown and earned a master's degree from Syracuse University and a doctorate from Oxford University. Living and studying in many regions of Italy for seven years, she taught art history to American students in Florence, and also met her husband, Corrado Manuali, a law student from Rome. In recent years, Tanya cocreated, with Shelly Burgess, Experienze Italiane, a custom tour company devoted to the discovery of Italian food, wine, and art. She has also led the development of her mother's Web site, lidiasitaly.com, and related publications and merchandise lines. Tanya and Corrado live in New York City with their children, Lorenzo and Julia.

A Note on the Type

This book was set in Janson, a typeface long thought to have been made by the Dutchman Anton Janson, who was a practicing typefounder in Leipzig during the years 1668–1687. However, it has been conclusively demonstrated that these types are actually the work of Nicholas Kis (1650–1702), a Hungarian, who most probably learned his trade from the master Dutch typefounder Dirk Voskens. The type is an excellent example of the influential and sturdy Dutch types that prevailed in England up to the time William Caslon (1692–1766) developed his own incomparable designs from them.

Design by Carole Goodman
Map by David Lindroth
Composition and separations by
North Market Street Graphics, Lancaster, Pennsylvania
Printing and binding by R. R. Donnelley & Sons, Willard, Ohio